I0802408

Cultures and Critical Perspectives in Literature by Women of Color

TEACHING at the CROSSROADS

Laurie Grobman

Aunt Lute Books | San Francisco

First Edition
Aunt Lute Books
P.O. Box 410687
San Francisco, CA 94141

Cover Design: Laurie Smith and Shay Brawn
Text Design: Jacqueline Teele
Typesetting: Kathleen Wilkinson

Senior Editor: Joan Pinkvoss
Managing Editor: Shay Brawn
Production: Gina Gemello, Shahara Godfrey, Marielle Gomez, Tasha Marks, Tamara Martínez, Laura Reizman, Golda Sargento

This book was funded in part by grants from the California Arts Council and the National Endowment for the Arts.

Earlier versions of some parts of this book appeared in the following publications: Chapters 4 and 5: "Re-Educating the American Ethnic Woman/Re-Educating Ourselves: (An)Other Bildungsroman Tradition." *Representations of Education in Literature.* Ed. Paul G. Nixon. Lewiston: Edwin Mellen, 2000. 109-31; Chapters 2 and 5: "Toward a Multicultural Pedagogy: Literary and Non-Literary Traditions." *MELUS: The Journal of the Society for the Study of the Multi-Ethnic Literatures of the United States* 26.1 (2001): 221-40; Chapters 2 and 4: "(Re)-Interpreting *Storyteller* in the Classroom: Teaching at the Crossroads." *College Literature* 27.3 (2000): 88-110.

Library of Congress Cataloging-in-Publication Data

Grobman, Laurie, 1962-
Teaching at the crossroads : cultures and critical perspectives in literature by women of color / by Laurie Grobman.—1st ed.
p.cm.
Includes bibliographical reference and index.
ISBN 1-879960-63-X
1. American literature—Minority authors—History and criticism. 2. American literature—Women authors—History and criticism. 3. American literature—Minority authors—Study and teaching. 4. American literature—Women authors—Study and teaching. 5. Minority women in literature. 6. Ethnic groups in literature. 7. Minorities in literature. 8. Race in literature. I.Title.

PS153.M56 G76 2001
810.9'9287'8693—dc21 2001053765

Printed in the United States of America
10 9 8 7 6 5 4 3 2 1

For Jim, Alex, and Andrew

Acknowledgments

This project has been long in the making, so there are many people who have helped me through it. First, I'd like to thank Professor Betsy Fifer from Lehigh University who saw promise and wisdom in my ideas. I am grateful to Gene Slaski, Mike Riley, and Maryellen Weimer at Penn State University, Berks-Lehigh Valley College, who generously supported release time for me to spend considerable time researching and revising the manuscript. I'd also like to thank Ken Fifer, Liberal Arts Division Head, and Carl Lovitt, Associate Dean for Academic Affairs, Penn State University, Berks-Lehigh Valley College, for their generous funding which allowed me to complete this book. I thank my mentor, colleague, and—most importantly—friend Candace Spigelman, who found ways to help me think through the overall structure and encouraged me to push on at my lowest moments.

The editors at Aunt Lute Books have been especially wonderful. I want to thank Joan Pinkvoss for her confidence in my work and for taking a risk with a newer kind of book for Aunt Lute. Gina Gemello's copyediting was so graceful that I wish she could copyedit everything I write! I am especially grateful to Shay Brawn, whose vision, suggestions, insights, and overall enthusiasm for my work have been so inspiring.

Finally, I want to thank my family. My mom, Debora Grobman, helps and encourages me to strike that delicate balance of motherhood and career. I am grateful to my dad, Bob Grobman, for his unwavering confidence in me. I want to acknowledge my children, Alex and Andrew Blickle, who I hope will grow up in a world with love and peace. Most of all, I want to thank my husband, Jim Blickle, for his unconditional support and for the way he took it for granted that my book would be published.

Table of Contents

1 INTRODUCTION

Literature by Women of Color in the Classroom: Beyond the Perils

I have never seen so much power in the ability to move and transform others as from that of the writing of women of color.
—*Gloria Anzaldúa, "Speaking in Tongues: A Letter to Third World Women Writers"*

[Multicultural education] should be allowed as a means to broaden acceptance by addressing issues that divide and create narrow-minded thinking.... Society needs to stop thinking of immigrants becoming American, but as each culture's introduction as enriching our own.

—*Student*

Everyone who is in America is here by choice, not by force. Those people who believe that different cultures in the United States should be appreciated and accepted are sometimes wrong. People who go around speaking different languages and have a flag of their native country on their car don't belong in America. They should speak English and have an American flag. If not, why did these people leave their precious countries and come to America in the first place. Sometimes "multicultural literature" actually degrades the United States and praises a different country.

—*Student*

We're studying the part in Toni Morrison's *Beloved* when Baby Suggs and her family celebrate with the black community the arrival of Sethe and her children into freedom. With both sincerity and confusion, one student asks how such poor people were able to get so much food for the celebration. While most of the class considers the question seriously, one student in the back row chuckles to the young woman next to him, "Maybe they stole it."

The Promise and Perils of Multicultural Women's Literary Study

We begin with the paradox of multiculturalism in literary studies: its potential and its peril. While some students respond positively to studying issues of cultural diversity in English studies, many others do not. Sometimes the best instructors can hope for from students in teaching multicultural materials is apathy, for the alternatives are frequently worse. Often, students do not feel free and comfortable to voice their beliefs, fearful of what may happen when the claims of their cultures come into contact—and conflict—with the claims of others'. As Richard Miller observes, students are adept at "hyperconformity" (398): avoiding "conflicts about or contact between fundamental beliefs and prejudices" (399). Still even worse, scholar-teachers who write about homogenous classes frequently note the level of resistance and anger multicultural literature evokes in white students.[1] Discussions of issues of power—especially when compounded by race and gender—frequently result in what Candace Spigelman accurately describes as "that almost palpable silence" (48-49) signaling students' "profound discomfort" (49).

Mary Louise Pratt's metaphor of multicultural classrooms as "contact zones" accurately defines the tensions inherent in the multicultural classroom, capturing both the promise and peril of multiculturalism in English studies ("Arts" 34). Defining the "contact zone" as a social space "where cultures meet, clash, and grapple with each other, often in contexts of highly asymmetrical relations of power" (34), Pratt interrogates the model of the classroom as community, arguing that the community model precludes resistance and critique. By reconceiving the classroom as a space that enacts conflict and contact, Pratt theorizes a classroom in which conflicting belief systems are made visible for extended scrutiny. Because the diverse perspectives students (and instructors) bring to class are aired and exposed, differences do not get ignored, marginalized, or silenced, and the classroom potentially leads students to reconsider hegemonic structures and systems that oppress the "other." But airing and exposing these differences can also lead to troubling consequences, and contact zone ideals often go unfulfilled.

The frequent problems and dangers of the contact zone are particularly likely to emerge when writing by women of color is introduced to students—especially white students, who may never have been exposed to multicultural literature (or possibly to "other" cultures) before. The complexities of multicultural women's literature and the multiple systems of oppression it reflects pose significant challenges to instructors. As such, writing by women of color has dramatically influenced literary pedagogical work, compelling us to reimagine what we do in the classroom with *all* literature, and, equally important, how we do it.[2] Indeed, teachers of multicultural women's imaginative literature find themselves on new pedagogical ground.

Despite differences in interpretations and critical methods, teaching canonical texts has not presented such uncertainties for instructors, mainly because the values and ideologies underlying such texts are, presumably, shared. Texts written by white males, in their universality and timelessness, could speak to all, instructor and students alike—or so it was thought. New Critical approaches to criticism and pedagogy asked students to seek out the ways in which the formal qualities of a literary work revealed the work's meaning (assumed to be knowable) through creating and resolving tension.[3] Literature instructors expected students to read carefully and closely in order to grasp the text's formal qualities of plot, character, tone, point of view, syntax, diction, symbol, imagery, and metaphor, qualities that would ultimately lead them to the text's meaning. Students were to read literary texts *literarily*, without the "stain" of politics and history.[4] Within the text's intrinsic meaning, instructors could impart to students a specific, prescribed set of values and ideas because, as Raman Selden asserts, "the quality of a text's form, imagery and style was inseparably bound up with the quality of its moral insights" (3).

As Gerald Graff points out, however, this "once tacit agreement about what the study and teaching of literature is all about" no longer exists ("Why Theory" 24). We now know that those texts did/do not speak to us all, did/do not represent the experiences and belief systems of everyone who was expected to teach and read them. Moreover, we have come to understand the ways in which traditional notions of literariness led to the exclusion of works by all women and by men of color. Our more recent understanding of literary texts as rhetorical arguments that arise out of the cultural constructions that produce them rather than as insular aesthetic expressions has opened the traditional canon—in scholarship and in the classroom—to minority and women writers.

But serious questions remain for teaching these texts in the classroom. From casual conversations in hallways to formal conference presentations and journal articles, more and more scholar-instructors are reflecting on their teaching practices—with both excitement and trepidation—as they incorporate multicultural texts, especially by women, into syllabi that were once comprised of white male literary "masters." Many of us find ourselves in a new critical and pedagogical space, eager to rise to the challenges of texts which may be unfamiliar to us. However, we still lack a comprehensive conceptual framework that connects criticism and pedagogy, particularly for texts by women of color.

In response to these and other questions, a tremendous amount of quality research and scholarship in multicultural studies has appeared in recent years, contributing to our understanding of the complexities surrounding issues of multicultural literary studies and texts, including a number of book-length pedagogical projects.[5] Significantly, many of these projects emphasize the lack of any critical frameworks for teaching multicultural literature and their purpose in constructing one, even as they approach the literature from varied perspectives. John Alberti, for example, writes in his introduction to *The Canon in the Classroom* that the move away from New Critical methods for literary evaluation and interpretation provides an opportunity for a multiculturalism that will be a "truly radical critique," and which he hopes his edited collection will initiate (Introduction xii). John Maitino and David Peck, editors of *Teaching American Ethnic Literatures*, assert the insufficiency of conventional literary criticism for ethnic texts but say the collection of essays in their volume forges a "new" multicultural criticism and pedagogy that incorporates issues related to ethnicity, race, gender, and class (Introduction 4). Abdul JanMohamed and David Lloyd view their edited collection, *The Nature and Context of Minority Discourse*, as part of a larger effort to create and define a "minority discourse," identifying the elements that link various minority cultures with one another, particularly as they share marginalization by the dominant culture (Preface ix). In *The Ethnic Canon: Histories, Institutions, and Interventions*, David Palumbo-Liu calls for a "critical multiculturalism" (Introduction 14) that resists the appropriation of ethnic texts by the liberal establishment by "reinstat[ing] the cultural politics of reading and interpreting ethnic literatures" (18-19). Bonnie TuSmith and Gerald Bergevin, editors of *Colorizing Literary Theory*, urgently attempt to remedy the dearth of multiethnic theory (Introduction 1), while Bruce Goebel and James Hall, editors of *Teaching a "New Canon"?*, reflect on their recognition of the "need for systematic exploration about the relationship between classroom practice and the institutionalization of cultural democratic ideals," leading them to put together a collection of essays to help teachers serve their students and the idea of a "new canon" (xiv).

These major multicultural projects, varying in the perspectives they bring to multicultural literature, successfully address specific gaps in multicultural theory, criticism, and/or pedagogy. But where do we go from here? *Teaching at the Crossroads* takes the next step, connecting new criticism with transformative classroom practice, specifically for teaching literature by women of color. How do we teach these texts in our classrooms without either subsuming them uncritically into "the tradition" as a whole or keeping them at the margins of that tradition by insisting on their "otherness"? How do we overcome the perils to reach the promise?

Beyond the Perils of Multicultural Women's Literary Study

I argue in *Teaching at the Crossroads* that this vast amount of critical and pedagogical work has produced four *separate* strands of critical and pedagogical perspectives vis-à-vis texts by women of color: Western-based, ethnic-specific, mainstream feminist, and ethnic-specific feminist. Western-based and ethnic-specific approaches derive from the primary critical conflict in the general arena of multicultural literary studies: whether to teach multicultural and multicultural women's texts according to traditional categories and paradigms or to invent new ones specific to the cultural contexts of these texts. Mainstream feminist and ethnic-specific feminist approaches to writing by women of color result from the primary conflict concerning difference within feminist literary studies: whether or not mainstream feminist criticism is appropriate for texts by women of color in light of the discipline's longstanding inattention to race, ethnicity, and class. By braiding together these four approaches, I construct the theoretical framework I call *teaching at the crossroads*.

This framework affords teachers a practical, useful entry point into the complexities of teaching texts by women of multicultural backgrounds, drawing from the body of critical scholarship accumulated over the last few decades in a consistent, coherent, and pedagogically accessible manner. Indebted to the intellectual work of critics working in a wide range of disciplines, my work embraces rather than homogenizes or erases diverse perspectives and strategies.

Moreover, this book is, to my knowledge, among the only major scholarly texts on multicultural criticism and pedagogy that focuses specifically on literature by women of color. The important works described earlier have done a tremendous service to the profession, opening the canon both critically and pedagogically to writers of multicultural backgrounds. However, texts by women of color tend to be subsumed in multicultural studies or feminist studies more generally without careful consideration of the complex relationship between feminist issues, ethnic-specific issues, and multicultural studies. For example, in *Teaching a "New Canon"?*, only two out of fifteen chapters specifically deal with feminist issues, but neither addresses ethnic-specific feminism. In their introduction to *Teaching American Ethnic Literatures*, editors Maitino and Peck extrapolate five approaches to ethnic literature from the articles in their collection, identifying one of the five as "the role of gender in ethnic literature and experience" and the "rich body of feminist criticism" developed over the last twenty years (14). Critical and pedagogical work, I suggest, should consider the specific, significant complexities of the multiple oppressions suffered by American women of color.

Teaching at the crossroads provides a nexus for engaging the Western-based, ethnic-specific, mainstream feminist, and ethnic-specific feminist strands so that they interconnect. Gloria Anzaldúa's influential work on women writers of color has been central to my project. In *Borderlands*, Anzaldúa asserts that the *mestiza* exists at the crossroads of cultures (100), and then in later work extends this metaphor to include all women of color. The crossroads model is thus informed by the reality of the lives of women of color, who exist within the intersections of multiple cultural systems. Brenda Greene describes the "multiple spaces" in which women of color live as "spaces which are not constricted by boundaries, spaces which overlap and shift, spaces which are defined and redefined by constructs of race, ethnicity, gender, and/or geographical locations" (98). Texts by women of color cross cultural boundaries to comprise a "nexus where race, class, gender, and history converge" (113), reflecting the complexities of their writers' cultural subjectivities. Because multicultural women's writing comprises a plurality of languages, histories, and experiences, pedagogical approaches should embrace and encompass the dynamics of such multiple identities. Together, these ideas compel us to construct theoretical and pedagogical frameworks that embrace the integrity of these multiple spaces. Teaching at the crossroads ensures the rich interplay of critical and cultural perspectives and experiences, creating a new kind of space from which to conduct our critical and pedagogical work and through which new and richer understandings can emerge.

Teaching and Research at the Crossroads of Theory and Practice

Throughout this book, I try to balance theoretical considerations with practical applications, for I believe that theory is useful and necessary to the extent that it informs our critical and teaching practices. This is especially true for multicultural women's literature, which necessitates a great deal of critical understanding as a prerequisite to effective and responsible teaching. While literary studies has historically subordinated pedagogical practices, concerns, and scholarship to theoretical and pedagogical research, the discipline is undergoing a shift in its priorities. In 1991, James Cahalan and David Downing wrote that the "professional and institutional structure of the literary discipline amply rewards scholarly research through conferences, journals, and books" and does not generally "reward pedagogical practices or answer the educational needs of teachers" (3). There is striking evidence, however, that institutional emphases are changing, attested to by the increasing number of sessions on pedagogy at professional conferences, increasing resources for the development of teaching at colleges and universities, and the launching of the journal *Pedagogy: Critical Approaches to Teaching Literature, Language, Composition, and Culture* in 2000, published by Duke University Press. In my view, we can attribute part of this change to the impact of multicultural studies.

In *Teaching at the Crossroads*, I have attempted to close the gap between theory and practice by embedding theory within the pedagogical model. The crossroads model derives from the conflicts of cultures and subsequent theoretical perspectives within multicultural women's writing, placing them in dialogue. In so doing, the crossroads model integrates theory and teaching to become both "theorized teaching" and the "teaching of theory" (Murray 187).

Teaching at the Crossroads also attempts to make its theoretical/critical components accessible to all instructors, not only those familiar with contemporary critical jargon. Relatedly, the crossroads model resists both the exclusionary trends of high theory, specifically European-derived poststructuralist theories, as well as the counterclaims that these theories are useless for multicultural literature. Deborah McDowell and others have assailed the narrow usages of theory ("Race" 243), and McDowell also points out that poststructuralism is too frequently "regarded as a synonym for theory" in today's literary world ("Transferences" 104). Moreover, Betsy Erkkilä argues that minorities have been challenging notions of "white male systems of knowledge, power, truth, and representation throughout American history" even though the academy has not counted this intellectual work as "theory" (585-86). She keenly observes that the emergence of theories associated with Jacques Derrida, Michel Foucault, and Jacques Lacan occurred simultaneously with demands by women, blacks, and other minorities "for a place and a presence for women and other minority subjects and authors in the academy, the canon, and the curriculum and in American literary, social, and cultural history" (568), implying that the development of high theory may have been deliberately exclusionary.

But the "exclusionary" quality of high theory has more to do with how it says what it says—its function as coin of the literary realm—than with what it actually says, which has often been quite enabling for critics of multicultural literature. As Brenda Marshall rightly observes, when Barbara Christian, an African American feminist, states that African American feminists must attend to the intersections of language, race, class, and gender, "this is a postmodern as well as an African-American feminist assertion" (15). Erkkilä agrees, arguing that by complicating notions of the subject, author, writing, and representation, poststructuralist theories have also "helped to clear the way for alternative modes of subjectivity, authorship, writing, and representation" (571). The point is that there are both convergences and divergences of Euro-derived theory with texts by men and women of color.

The work of "theory" must not be limited to one particular brand of theory. The crossroads model embraces these complementary, rather than competing, perspectives on theory. The issue is not whether we need theory, since no critical or pedagogical work is ever theory-free, but instead, what theory(ies) we need, and when we need them.[6] As William Cain argues, theory "decrees constant experimentation, fosters change, promotes a steady degree of self-consciousness about how one performs one's work" (9). How we perform our work with multicultural women's literature is a serious endeavor that should neither be blind to theory nor be blinded by it.

This book covers a great deal of critical and theoretical terrain, from multicultural to ethnic-specific to mainstream feminist to ethnic feminist critical communities. Given space restraints, I run the risk of oversimplification as I attempt to summarize whole strands of critical theory and many branches of literary tradition. On the one hand, the complexity of these bodies of work is ill-served by the inevitable reductiveness of such summaries. On the other hand, it is precisely this complexity that makes summary so crucial if we are to expect instructors—most of whom are trained exclusively in one or at most two traditions—to venture outside their fields of expertise to teach across multiple traditions, and to do so responsibly, sensibly, and ethically. While I anticipate that some of the readers of *this* text are well-versed in one or more of the critical and literary traditions I discuss, in order to provide the widest possible access to the crossroads model, I think it is necessary to offer such introductory accounts at the risk of repeating what some readers may already know.

I believe this book is most useful for instructors who currently include or want to include multicultural women's literature in their classrooms. I do not try to persuade opponents of the worth of multicultural studies but instead address those who agree with its objectives and want to find specific ways to teach these texts.

Organization

In this book, I present the theoretical rationale, consider the practical and theoretical ramifications on curriculum and pedagogy, and enact models of classroom practice for teaching at the crossroads. Because of the accessibility of their theoretical grounding, these models enable teachers to apply the crossroads approach in their classrooms, not only to teach the four texts used in my study, but a wide range of others. Chapter 2 begins by examining the critical debates within multicultural and multicultural feminist studies that have led to the four dominant approaches to teaching texts by women of color which together comprise teaching at the crossroads: Western-based, ethnic-specific, mainstream feminist, and ethnic-specific feminist. From there, I provide the theoretical rationale for integrating these strands into the crossroads model.

In chapter 3, I examine the implications of teaching at the crossroads for the classroom, taking into account both curricular and pedagogical issues. I suggest that literature by women of color necessitates deliberate reconsideration, even dismantling, of traditional paradigms and categories of curriculum and teaching.

Chapters 4 and 5 provide specific examples of teaching at the crossroads of texts by women writers of color. In chapter 4, I demonstrate how to teach at the crossroads of genre, using Sandra Cisneros' *The House on Mango Street* and Leslie Marmon Silko's *Storyteller*. Chapter 5 suggests a way of teaching at the crossroads of identity, using Toni Morrison's *Beloved* and Maxine Hong Kingston's *China Men* as examples. In these chapters, I offer practical application of the methodology by combining literary criticism with classroom experiences. I have also included an appendix of classroom exercises to enable instructors to go immediately from this book to their own classrooms. Most of these exercises consist of a series of discussion questions, but I have also included some student research ideas as well as more extensive collaborative projects.

I conclude in chapter 6 with another way of conceptualizing the idea of the crossroads: as a pivotal point or place. I consider the sustainability of multiculturalism in literary studies in light of the attacks on multiculturalism from within and outside the academy and on the rifts among scholars of multicultural literature. Finally, I argue that for multiculturalism in literary studies to continue and to succeed, we must not only create comprehensive and informed pedagogical frameworks, but we must do so with an acknowledgment of the ethical implications of multiculturalism in literary studies as well as through careful consideration of the potentially destructive nature of identity politics.

As I end this introductory chapter, I want to clarify four important considerations. The first has to do with defining my terms. No doubt, terms like "multicultural," "people of color," "minority," and "ethnic" are linguistically unsatisfying and even disconcerting. Not only do white people have ethnicities (scholars have recently begun to interrogate the notion of "whiteness" as racialized and ethnic), but most have multicultural backgrounds, when "culture" is defined to include gender, ethnicity, class, sexual orientation, religion, etc. All texts, it would seem, are "multicultural."

However, I believe it is reasonable to use the terms "multicultural" and "multiculturalism" as they have been linked with specific politics, viewpoints, and literary texts.[7] "Multiculturalism" involves a recognition of white privilege and the unequal relations of power determined by race and ethnicity—and compounded by other factors—in American society. In literary studies, specifically, multiculturalism refers to the demand by traditionally marginalized cultures to be heard and represented in the literary, cultural, and social history of the United States. The multicultural movement in literary studies initially referred to the literature of nonwhite racial and ethnic minorities—those texts previously excluded from the traditional canon of American literature. Multiculturalism in literary studies has since been expanded to include class and sexual orientation, but these specific categories are not the focus of my study, except to the extent to which class and sexual orientation are implicated in the multiple exclusions faced by American women of color.

In this book, I use the term "multicultural literature" as an umbrella term to refer to literature by nonwhite ethnic minorities in the United States.[8] But why see that literature as separate from the larger "American" tradition rather than as part of it? Frances Foster asserts that teaching from a multicultural perspective means "to rethink and to re-present American literature" (199). The groundbreaking work of scholars to construct a more inclusive canon, which is still ongoing, would be ill-served by discarding the notion of "multicultural" literature. It is my sincere hope that we will reach the point that "American literature" (and by implication the canon of American literature) will incorporate inclusivity and diversity—based on race, ethnicity, gender, class, and sexual orientation.[9] But Erkkilä reminds us that we have not yet achieved such a goal, as "White studies" remains the "dominant model of American literary and cultural studies" with ethnic and women writers simply "added on to traditional models of American literature and culture" (587). As I demonstrate in chapter 3, I hope my project furthers the process of what Erkkilä refers to as the "reconceptualization of the theory and practice of American literature and studies" (587). I use "multiethnic" literature, "nontraditional" literature, and "noncanonical" literature interchangeably with "multicultural" literature, as is common practice in the discipline.

Relatedly, "multicultural criticism" or "multicultural literary studies" refers to the body of critical and theoretical work in literary studies that focuses on multicultural literature and pedagogy. Admittedly, "multicultural criticism" is also a problematic concept, a nebulous and ill-defined discourse at best. I believe it does exist in its own right, however, practiced by scholars such as Alberti, Bergevin, Goebel, Hall, Jay, Lauter, TuSmith, and many others. It is also making its way into books about literary theory generally, such as Stephen Bonnycastle's *In Search of Authority: An Introductory Guide to Literary Theory*, which includes a chapter called "Postcolonial Criticism and Multiculturalism."

However, because multicultural literary criticism tends to overlook the specific issues raised in interpreting works by women of color, I use the term "literature by women of multicultural backgrounds" or "literature by women of color" to refer specifically to texts by American women writers of color. Multicultural criticism too often ignores and neglects the work of women of multicultural backgrounds in its examination of literature, so I pay careful attention to both the works by women of color as well as a specific theoretical/critical approach to these texts, which I call "ethnic" or "multicultural" feminist criticism. Multicultural feminist criticism is a fairly recent critical paradigm; it is both distinct from and connected to mainstream feminist criticism, and this complex relationship will be discussed at length in chapter 2.

To further complicate matters, multicultural criticism is distinct from what I call ethnic-specific criticism. This term refers to African American, Asian American, Chicano, and Native American criticism, and other subfields of multicultural criticism. Henry Louis Gates, Jr., observes that multicultural literary studies emerged from the growth of ethnic studies programs in the 1960s and 70s ("Ethnic" 289). Because these subfields have often neglected or minimized the specific concerns of women of color, scholars have created further subfields, such as African American feminist criticism, Asian American feminist criticism, Native American feminist criticism, and Chicana feminist criticism. I will discuss these critical communities in chapter 2, highlighting their convergences and divergences from one another and from mainstream feminist criticism.

What about the term "women of color"? Sandra Kumamoto Stanley addresses this very same question in the introduction to her edited collection on women writers of color and literary theory, observing that the category is a "complex, multiple, and problematic site of representation" (2). While Maxine Baca Zinn and Bonnie Thornton Dill generally limit the category to "racial-ethnic" groups such as African American, Asian American, Native American, and Latina women due to historically discriminatory racial laws in the United States ("Difference" 4), other sociologists, women's studies scholars, and literary theorists are more inclusive. I tend to agree with Zinn's and Dill's use of the term "women of color" to refer to "racial-ethnic" women, not because white women are colorless, but because like the term "multicultural," "color" connotes the unequal access to power experienced by nonwhites in American society. As Anzaldúa puts it, "ethnic colored people in this country are *not* on an equal footing with other ethnic American groups" ("Haciendo" xxii).[10] Equally important, Stanley points out that many self-identified women of color view their use of the term as an appropriative and empowering act, despite (or because of) the term's origins in racial discrimination policies in the U.S.

Next, let me address the issue of "literature" itself. It is probably no surprise to anyone reading this book that the conception of literature within English studies has broadened to include "the whole world of 'story,' ranging from the ancient classics to yesterday's soap opera" (Booth, "Ethics" 41). Indeed, the idea of trying to define "literature," to delimit it to a particular type may seem especially contradictory given that the same forces that opened the canon to include multicultural women's writing also broadened notions of literature itself. As we have learned, diverse writers construct diverse types of texts so that any linguistic (or even non-linguistic) act can be a text. Unlike "literature," which is steeped in the elitism of traditional definitions of literary excellence, the term "text" itself connotes neutrality and equity. So, given our understanding that we no longer judge works by their purely "aesthetic value" since definitions of value are contingent rather than fixed, why differentiate at all—in this book or in literature courses across the nation—between imaginative and other kinds of texts? Simply put, imaginative literature possesses a particular power to effect multicultural understanding. Lauter concurs: "it would be shortsighted to slight the emotional power of narratives and of poetic language, or the prestige with which such forms have been invested in our culture" ("Canon Theory" 142). I have chosen to use Sandra Cisneros' *The House on Mango Street*, Leslie Marmon Silko's *Storyteller*, Toni Morrison's *Beloved*, and Maxine Hong Kingston's *China Men* as examples mainly because these books have profoundly influenced me both professionally and personally, because I enjoy reading and teaching them, and because I believe they are powerful examples of imaginative literature's artistry and power.

Moreover, I have deliberately chosen for this study one text each by a Chicana, Native American, African American, and Chinese American woman writer because these groups are the most frequently taught groups of nonwhite ethnic literature in the United States today, what Amy Ling refers to as the "visible minorities" ("I'm Here" 778). Yet I do not intend for these texts to "represent" their writers' respective ethnic groups.

Finally, since I prefer to be thought of as neither a "knave [n]or a fool," let me take a moment to define my own critical identity, the "social location" or "positionality" from which I read, teach, research, and write (Krupat, *Turn* 2). I am a white, Jewish, heterosexual, middle-class, female assistant professor at a small four-year college of a large university in southeastern Pennsylvania. I am not a woman of color in white America, and my experiences as a Jewish middle-class woman do not come close to replicating those faced by racially "marked" women in this nation. I do not present myself to my students as an insider or expert on any cultural context I teach, including texts from the canon (I have never been to Spain, I have never gone hunting, and I have never gone to a bullfight, but I teach Hemingway's *The Sun Also Rises*). But like all teachers, I do my homework—I learn what I think I need to know in order to give my students the tools they need to understand what they are reading. Indeed, like Marjorie-Pryse, I have been willing to "get lost" with my students as I attempt to reinvent not only what and how we define American literature, but also what it means to teach. In the multicultural classroom—a pedagogical space committed to challenging heirarchies and master narratives—teaching must necessarily be a less monovocal and authoritative practice.

2 | Theorizing the Crossroads in Literature By Women of Color

To survive the Borderlands
you must live sin fronteras
be a crossroads.

Gloria Anzaldúa, "To live in the Borderlands means you"

Teaching at the crossroads is a theoretical framework for teaching literature by women of color and is informed by the scholarship in multicultural studies, feminist studies, and ethnic feminist studies. This framework braids together what I identify as the four dominant critical approaches to texts by women of color: Western-based, ethnic-specific, mainstream feminist, and ethnic-specific feminist. This chapter is divided into two main sections: (1) the four critical approaches and their origins, and (2) the theoretical rationale for interweaving them. I begin the first section with a survey of the critical conflicts within the arena of multicultural literary studies that have led to the development of Western-based and ethnic-specific critical approaches to multicultural texts. Next, I turn to the attention to "difference" in mainstream feminist criticism and the subsequent debate over mainstream versus ethnic-specific feminist approaches to texts by women of color. In the second section, I present the theoretical basis for interconnecting the four approaches. I first examine the relevance of Anzaldúa's borderlands and crossroads metaphors to the sociological realities of the lives of women of color and then theorize the crossroads of texts by women of color.

Critical Backgrounds: The Four Dominant Approaches to Texts by Women of Color

Theorizing Multicultural Conflicts: Western-Based versus Ethnic-Specific Approaches

The first two dominant approaches to texts by women of multicultural backgrounds arise out of the general arena of multicultural literary studies. Western-based critical approaches, which tend to be revisionist, understand and evaluate ethnic texts according to traditional paradigms and categories. Ethnic-specific critical strategies, on the other hand, emphasize ethnic-specific contexts in interpreting texts by women of color. For example, Western-based approaches to Maxine Hong Kingston's *The Woman Warrior* might consider the text as a challenge to Western autobiographical traditions or apply postmodern readings to the complexity and multiplicity of the narrator's subjectivity. Ethnic-specific readings might emphasize *The Woman Warrior*'s relationship to a Chinese American tradition of filiation and affiliation as thematic and rhetorical strategies (see D. Li, "Filiative") or locate the narrator's identity in Chinese historical figures such as Fa Mu Lan, the legendary warrior woman.

Western-Based Approaches to Literature by Women of Color: The most influential imperative in reimagining literary education comes from Gerald Graff's widely recognized "teach the conflicts" pedagogy, a call for involving students in the conflicts of literary studies to enable them to better negotiate our culturally diverse world (*Beyond* 12). Though perhaps the most significant contribution to date to multicultural pedagogy, "teach the conflicts" now tells only part of the multicultural story. In advocating that we make conflicts the center of pedagogy, Graff complicates the "either/or choice we have been offered between teaching Western or non-Western culture" (14), concluding that in our culturally diverse society a wide range of cultures and values should be taught. It is at the "*points of intersection*" with the dominant culture, Graff argues, that we should be teaching or understanding multicultural writing, as his example using Joseph Conrad's *Heart of Darkness* and Chinua Achebe's *Things Fall Apart* demonstrates (15, emphasis mine). The call by revisionists such as Graff to teach at the points of intersection with the dominant culture has led to the inclination to teach multicultural texts from Western-based approaches.

Well-known scholars such as Paul Lauter, Gregory Jay, Jane Tompkins, Barbara Hernnstein Smith, and Harold Kolb, among many others, were at the forefront of this movement, arguing for a broadening of the literary canon and questioning the criteria for literary value. No doubt, recent understandings of how texts exist within rather than apart from their cultural contexts have expanded the study of literature from purely textual matters to the broader social, political, cultural, and economic arenas. Yet, a significant portion of multicultural criticism has tended to focus on reading, understanding, and evaluating works by way of the same conventions used for approaching canonical literature. Consequently, many pedagogical approaches to multicultural texts tend to be revisionist—examining these texts *within* or *against* conventional paradigms and critical categories. These approaches value noncanonical works in terms of how they interact with canonical texts, generally ignoring elements present in the noncanonical texts if they are not present in the others.

Jacqueline Bacon's "dialogical" approach (a reference to Mikhail Bakhtin's *The Dialogic Imagination*) will serve as an example. In the dialogical approach, canonical and noncanonical texts are taught side by side to enable students to interrogate cultural constructions of race and ethnicity (Bacon 511). Reading a text such as Toni Morrison's *Beloved* against traditional renderings of American slavery, she argues, enhances students' understanding of the issues in this text, especially Morrison's attempts to rewrite the experience of slavery from an African American perspective.

While this is certainly true, such an approach neglects more culturally-based readings of *Beloved,* such as against the backdrop of the African folklore tradition, the African American jazz tradition, or the slave narrative tradition. Moreover, can we ignore feminist and African American feminist concerns? Barbara Rico and Sandra Mano argue that revisionist approaches "privilege the more established, more canonical work," making the canonical work "the central subtext" so that the noncanonical works become "other versions of that story" (103). As a result, these approaches deemphasize diversity, tension, and cultural difference (103). Reading multicultural texts through Western-based prisms too readily ignores non-Western contexts, thus reinscribing the very constructs teachers and scholars of multicultural literature seek to subvert.[11]

The problem is evident, for example, in *Storyteller*, if examined with a strictly revisionist approach focusing only on the autobiographical genre; in Amy Tan's *The Joy Luck Club* if studied solely as a subversion of the traditional, Western novel form; in Alice Walker's *Possessing the Secret of Joy* if approached solely as a form of the multiple narrator novel;[12] or in Walker's *The Color Purple* if read only against the context of the epistolary form or the conventional success story. Indeed, revisionist readings have led to charges of appropriation by some ethnic scholars. The end result for students is a superficial at best, misinformed at worst, understanding of the cultural traditions represented by and in the texts they read.[13] Those who argue for new theoretical approaches to multicultural literature claim that without them, multiculturalism will amount to nothing more than perpetuation of hegemonic structures and exclusionary practices. These critics demand that texts by people of color be read and understood on their own terms.

Ethnic-Specific Approaches to Literature by Women of Color: Opponents of Western-based approaches to multicultural texts argue that traditional categories of understanding, evaluating, and/or teaching literature are inadequate for these texts and preclude the application of new aesthetics and categories. Although new texts by women of color have been added to syllabi and curricula, they often elude traditional categories of discourse and evaluation; thus new categories are necessary, or multicultural texts will continue to be marginalized and the pioneering efforts to diversify the canon will be undermined. Can we value, for example, simplicity rather than complexity of language and meaning in a text like *The House on Mango Street?* Must a text be dense and ambiguous to be canonized? Must a literary work achieve unity and resolve its tensions, as formalist criticism insists? Will a text necessarily deconstruct itself, as deconstructionist criticism expects? Many critics of current approaches to multicultural texts insist that new interpretive strategies that reflect the diverse literary and cultural traditions of the texts are necessary so that students and teachers can break out of the box of familiar ways of reading literature.

One response to the call for new interpretive strategies has been the development of a general rubric of multicultural discourse, a criticism that defines, understands, and evaluates ethnic writing within a generalized multicultural tradition. JanMohamed and Lloyd, for example, posit a "minority discourse" they define as the "theoretical articulation of the political and cultural structures that connect different minority cultures in their subjugation and opposition to the dominant culture" (Preface ix). Rather than homogenizing ethnic groups, they argue, a minority discourse provides a sense of solidarity among marginalized people from a variety of oppressed groups who are linked by their minority status.

A general multicultural discourse has not, however, dominated approaches to texts by people of color. Ironically, by basing minority discourse on the common thread of "subjugation and opposition to the dominant culture," JanMohamed and Lloyd may inadvertently lead us back to the trap of traditional critical categories and revisionary writing by ignoring ethnic-specific contexts. As such, we run the risk of ghettoizing, essentializing, tokenizing, and stereotyping. When instructors treat ethnic writers as part of the larger group "minority," instead of as belonging to particular cultures and ethnicities, they inadvertently promulgate a patriarchal, assimilationist view that, according to Barbara Hiura, "erase[s]" difference (qtd. in Kafka, "Multicultural" 181). David Van Leer likewise claims that "truth is shared no more universally among minorities than it is between them and the dominant culture," for "cultural position always informs meaning" (228). Van Leer further argues that focusing on the similarities between ethnic groups obscures cultural specificity, overemphasizes hegemonic oppression, and causes the group to appear "primarily as passive and reactive" (225). Patricia Bizzell argues that many of the so-called "universal themes" approaches of multicultural anthologies tend to only portray people of color as victims, leading to resistance and defensiveness in the classroom ("Negotiating" 165). Finally, treating all ethnic groups as one big group can mask features of the text that emerge out of specific cultural contexts. For these reasons, general multicultural rubrics have not dominated approaches to multicultural texts, despite a general acceptance of the term "multicultural" to refer to texts by nonwhite writers as well as the emergence of multicultural criticism as a subfield within literary studies.

The primary opposing response to Western-based readings of multicultural texts has been ethnic-specific interpretive frameworks, the second dominant approach to multicultural women's texts and the second braid of teaching at the crossroads. John Maitino and David Peck, for example, call for new criteria, emphasizing the uniqueness of American ethnic literatures and the strength of their cultural and historical context, as they urge instructors to bring these contexts into the classroom (Introduction 5-16). Contextual criticism and pedagogy provide students with cultural understanding beyond one writer's vision, so instructors can avoid leading students to believe one writer speaks for all ethnic groups or individuals. Various scholars emphasize the importance of ethnic-specific knowledge for understanding and teaching ethnic texts.[14] For example, an awareness of the Flying Africans legend, a traditional oral African narrative, enriches our reading of Morrison's *Song of Solomon* (see Wilentz). The supernatural elements in *Beloved* require more than just a suspension of belief within Morrison's fictional universe but an understanding of the supernatural in African cultural traditions. In Zora Neale Hurston's *Their Eyes Were Watching God*, the folkloric elements are inextricably connected to female consciousness and Black self-determination (see Crabtree). Readers gain a new perspective on the discovery processes of mothers and daughters in *The Joy Luck Club* when they have knowledge of Chinese cosmology and other traditional Chinese belief systems (see Hamilton). *Possessing the Secret of Joy* is so contextually and historically based that an understanding of female circumcision in African culture as well as African politics and history is crucial to appreciating both the text's literariness and polemic.

Theorizing Mainstream Feminist and Ethnic-Specific Feminist Critical Discourses

The third and fourth most dominant approaches to texts by women of color, mainstream and ethnic-specific feminist readings, arise out of the current debates within mainstream feminist and multicultural feminist studies. Mainstream feminist readings tend to approach texts by women of color through a revisionist perspective, with women's literary traditions that have been identified on the basis of white, middle-class writers, and within a general framework of patriarchal structures and women's oppression. Ethnic-specific feminist approaches, however, often emphasize the specific dynamics of male-female relationships and roles within a particular ethnic community, examine the multiple oppressions of women of color, and seek to understand the work within its cultural and literary context. In Walker's *The Color Purple*, for instance, Pa's sexual abuse of Celie can be interpreted through a mainstream feminist focus on male dominance and control of women, yet Pa's suggestion in the novel that his violence toward women is a result of his own victimization by racism, a contention I believe Walker rejects, obviously raises issues beyond white feminist critique. Moreover, issues of African American feminist consciousness bring significant perspectives to bear on the text, such as the new black woman who recreates herself through the creative, maternal legacy (see Walker, "In Search").

Mainstream Feminist Approaches to Literature by Women of Color—Women's Literary Traditions and Re-Visioning White Male Discourses: Mainstream feminist literary criticism has been groundbreaking not only for white women writers but for writers of color—male and female—as well.[15] Indubitably, the feminist project has led to increased opportunities for women writers of color in the classroom and in scholarship.[16] Moreover, feminist and multicultural studies share many similar concerns, including the exclusionary nature of the Western and American critical and literary canons, the reinterpretation of traditional texts to reveal racist and sexist biases and stereotypes, the recovery of excluded texts, and the reevaluation of canonical criteria and status in relationship to newly recovered texts. It is not surprising, then, that mainstream feminist criticism can inform our reading of texts by women of color.

Feminist criticism began by targeting the literary canon, the sources of literary authority, and the nature and function of literature as a discipline. In her landmark essay "Dancing Through the Minefield: Some Observations on the Theory, Practice, and Politics of a Feminist Literary Criticism," Annette Kolodny argues that literary history "is a fiction" (8) and the canon "is of our own making" (9). In response to the canon's exclusion of women writers and distorted images of women, feminist critics came to recognize the gender-based social and cultural constructions of a white, male, literary establishment. They recovered previously excluded writers, reread traditional texts, and discovered an "exclusively female tradition of writing," one which counters canonical images of women and enables women writers to rely on their foremothers in finding "their own distinctively female voices" (Ewell 48). Elaine Showalter and others began to identify recurring patterns, themes, problems, and images passed from generation to generation of literary women. They argued that women are a subculture, unified by values, conventions, experiences, and behaviors and that the distinct qualities of women's writing grew out of women's continuous "struggle against the cultural and historical forces that relegated women's experience to the second rank" (1118).

From this perspective, literature by women of color might be studied within the contexts of women's literary traditions. For example, the circular structure of Sandra Cisneros' "Woman Hollering Creek" places this text in a tradition of women's identity narratives, while *Possessing the Secret of Joy* is informed by the feminist thematic of mother-daughter relationships.

A second prominent feature of mainstream feminist literary criticism is "re-vision—the act of looking back, of seeing with fresh eyes" (Rich 1038), expressed most pointedly by Adrienne Rich in her influential article "When We Dead Awaken: Writing as Re-Vision." Sandra Gilbert and Susan Gubar, editors of the landmark *Norton Anthology of Literature by Women* (1985), note the "exuberant variety yet strong continuity" of women's writing in English, a female literary tradition that has "coexisted with, revised, and influenced male literary models" (Preface xxvii).[17] Such language implies that women's lives have been defined entirely by their embeddedness in patriarchal systems of domination. Still today, Barbara Frey Waxman, applying poststructuralist insights to the ways we can approach writing by women of color, favors revisionist approaches, asserting that "confronting, resisting, interrogating, re-visioning" constitute the "vocabulary of the feminist theorist" (150). Diane Freedman echoes these claims by asserting that what others have identified as the "female mode," "associative, nonhierarchical, personal, and open-ended" forms of writing, counters traditional academic (or white male) discourse (3). Both Waxman and Freedman claim that this revisionist approach includes those ethnic women writers who take on the role of "poet-critics," "chal-leng[ing] the critical canon with their 'common' language and hybrid, alchemical forms" (4) and gaining "discursive power" (11). Revisionist readings lend themselves to interpreting *China Men* with reference to feminist rewritings of the conquest myth, or to the subversion of fairy tales like "Cinderella" and "Rapunzel" in *Mango Street*. Revisionist readings of Toni Morrison's *The Bluest Eye*, to use another example, might focus on American standards of beauty, while study of Judith Ortiz

Cofer's *Silent Dancing* could examine the text's intertexuality with the Western *kuntslerroman* tradition, such as the thematic and structural connections with such canonical texts as James Joyce's *A Portrait of the Artist as a Young Man.*

Moreover, mainstream feminist approaches may challenge patriarchal oppression in ways which may not be entirely applicable for women of color because ethnic communities experience patriarchal oppression in culturally specific ways. For Chinese American women, racist immigration laws in the United States have often combined with longstanding patriarchal traditions in China to produce particularly volatile gender relationships among Chinese American men and women, reflected both in criticism and in literature. Such contexts provide insights to understanding the narrator's father's violent bursts of language as well as deafening silences in Kingston's *China Men* and *The Woman Warrior* and Pearl's ultimate understanding of her father's abusiveness toward her mother in Amy Tan's *The Kitchen God's Wife.*

Furthermore, the gynocratic history of many Native American cultures complicates mainstream feminist approaches focused on challenging patriarchal oppression. Readers of contemporary Native American women's literature often ascribe political stances to references to female deities and figures that may not be politically constituted. In Silko's "Yellow Woman," a story within *Storyteller*, for example, the female protagonist is often understood by readers as a stifled housewife and mother even though such a reading may not be culturally informed. However, when one has knowledge of the central role of women in many Native American cultures, as well as the Yellow Woman legend, more culturally informed readings are possible.

Contesting Mainstream Feminist Practice—Ethnic-Specific Feminist Approaches to Literature by Women of Color: Recently, many feminist scholars have identified problematic relationships between mainstream feminist scholarship and American women of multicultural backgrounds: "difference has replaced equality as a central concern of feminist theory" (Fox-Genovese 232). Specifically, these scholars charge that mainstream feminist theory and practice, founded on a normative view of gender, inadequately accounts for race, ethnicity, sexual orientation, and class as complicating factors in the lives of ethnic women who, according to Chela Sandoval, "somehow exist in the interstices between the legitimated categories of the social order" (4). Feminist scholars of color look to frameworks that recognize these multidimensional and interconnected aspects of the oppression of women of color.[18]

These changes in feminist scholarship have influenced feminist literary studies as well. In recent years and continuing still today, mainstream feminist literary criticism has come under fire from many feminists of color who argue that it excludes and/or misrepresents women of color in scholarship and pedagogy and ignores the specific concerns of women writers of color. Because women's literary traditions have been drawn from a body of work whose authors are generally white, privileged, and heterosexual, many feminists—primarily women of color—have contested feminism's exclusionary practices and essentializing tendencies. Feminist scholars of color point to the paradox of mainstream feminist criticism's perpetration of exclusionary practices against women of color simultaneous with its critique and resistance of these practices in the white male literary establishment. Still others accuse white feminists of co-opting the writing of women of color to bolster their own careers (see duCille; Kanhai).

Despite the tremendous contributions of feminist literary theory to both women's and multicultural studies, mainstream feminist approaches alone can constrain readings of literature by women of color. Insulated from the ways in which race and class shape gendered lives, mainstream feminist practice often obscures or oversimplifies the nature of gender relations, oppression, and alienation in the experiences and writing of women of color from all ethnic backgrounds.

Indeed, many women of color share feelings of sisterhood with other ethnic women, believing that commonalities across cultural and racial barriers are as important as differences. Such an alliance affords women of color power and voice, and the general rubric of a multicultural feminism has distinct political advantages. Cherríe Moraga and Anzaldúa point to the political necessity of such a movement and emphasize the connectedness among women of color "between these seemingly irreconcilable lines" ("Between" 106), a connection constructed by issues of race and power: "Only *together* can we be a force" (Anzaldúa, "La Prieta" 209).

Yet despite these important political and intellectual alliances, distinct ethnic feminist critical communities have also emerged as a way to combat tendencies to substitute racial essentialism for gender essentialism. As Moraga and Anzaldúa note: "Cultural differences get subsumed when we speak of 'race' as an isolated issue" ("Between" 105). Clearly, women of color experience their racial identity differently; thus African American, Asian American, Latina, and Native American feminist critical communities, to name a few, have emerged as distinct and strong entities, even though they share many features in their histories and development. Despite important overlaps with mainstream feminist theory, criticism, and pedagogy, ethnic-specific feminist discourses on literature provide unique critical and pedagogical perspectives on the writing by women of color.

In *The Bluest Eye*, for example, readers might approach beauty from the perspective of the black female—what is beautiful in African and African American culture? *Mango Street*'s obvious references to traditional fairy tales are further informed by Chicana stories, myths, and legends, such as the legendary figure of La Malinche. In *Silent Dancing*, the narrator's journey as a writer/artist is profoundly influenced by the female community in Puerto Rico, her childhood recollections, the Puerto Rican tradition of female storytellers, and the stories told to her by her mother. Mother-daughter relationships in Walker's *Possessing the Secret of Joy* take on global dimensions if we interpret the text in light of her *In Search of Our Mothers' Gardens* and understand Walker herself as the mother who breaks African women's legacies of pain (Pollock 39). In a similar vein, the female protagonist in "Woman Hollering Creek," Cleofilas, is ultimately empowered to resist her abusive relationship not only through mainstream feminist attitudes or activism but through the enabling legacy of the legendary Mexican and Chicano figure, La Llorona, the weeping or wailing woman (see Carbonell; Mullen).

At the Crossroads of Critical Perspectives: Both/And, Not Either/Or

In the in-between space of these four critical perspectives is a new and transformative critical and pedagogical approach to texts by women of color. Both Western and ethnic-specific contexts can inform readings of these texts, so ignoring either perspective would be foolish and shortsighted. In suggesting that we read the classics and contemporary multicultural literature together, Kristina Chew asserts that "ethnic literature is a part of Western literature" as it draws quite substantially on the classical tradition, "reus[ing] traditional motifs, characters, and literary structures" (62). She argues that we cannot wholly sever multicultural literature from the Western tradition, that it is not "an altogether *sui generis* creation of completely new and original forms and themes" (62). Likewise, Bizzell cautions us against assuming that all people of color speak in one tongue, referring to Victor Villanueva and bell hooks' testimony that their writing styles have been "enriched by a variety of sources" ("Negotiating" 169). From this both/and perspective, the structural pattern of *Their Eyes Were Watching God*, for example, is not only informed by retrospective narration but imitates the "frame" convention of oral storytelling. Teaching at the crossroads incorporates these approaches so that they constantly play off one another in a multicultural dialogue.

Similarly, both mainstream feminist and ethnic feminist critical approaches can illuminate texts by women of color. Mainstream feminist critical practice has paved the way for the voices of women of multicultural backgrounds. Moreover, it still has much to offer these texts in terms of the feminist enterprise to interrogate, resist, and re-vision patriarchal structures, forms, discourses, and critical practices. Mainstream feminist criticism offers us a way to approach gendered relations in texts by women of color, yet ethnicity and class intersect with gender in complex ways for which critical approaches must account. *Their Eyes Were Watching God* is thus informed by mainstream feminist critique, through its exploration of the constraints of a traditional marriage, intraracial sexism, and male violence, but it must also be interpreted through the lens of black working-class women and the black female community (see Jordan). *The Woman Warrior* might be productively read within a tradition of women's autobiography—the female self constructed by the experience of gender and the mother-daughter relationship. Moreover, like many other ethnic feminist discourses, *The Woman Warrior* is double-voiced, engaging in a simultaneous critique of Chinese patriarchy and white racism. At the same time, Chinese myths, legends, family histories, and talk-story, in large part handed down through the narrator's mother, add a vital dimension of Chinese feminist specificity. Chinese female legendary figures such as Fa Mu Lan, Ts'ai Yen (a second-century poet, scholar, and musician held captive for twelve years), and even the narrator's no-name aunt contribute to the narrator's transforming female consciousness. Feminist readings must simultaneously represent the concerns of women of color, generally, as well as those of specific ethnic feminist communities. With a both/and perspective in mind, I turn to theorizing how we might teach literature by women of color at the crossroads of critical perspectives and cultures.

Teaching at the Crossroads

A Theoretical Framework for Teaching Literature by Women of Multicultural Backgrounds

As I have suggested, the four dominant approaches to texts by women of multicultural backgrounds—Western-based, ethnic-specific, mainstream feminist, and ethnic-specific feminist—derive from the critical conflicts resulting from the broadening of the canon and the inclusion of new kinds of texts in scholarship, research, and teaching. In the following pages, I will outline the rationale for the theoretical framework I call "teaching at the crossroads," which brings these four approaches together in constant engagement and dialogue.[19]

Like literature, theory and criticism are embroiled in politics and are value-laden; thus, each of the four approaches described in this chapter represents specific cultural and ideological positions. Years ago, Wayne Booth helped us to understand that all literary texts use persuasion and make arguments (see *Rhetoric)*. Moreover, as Mikhail Bakhtin has argued, fiction, like all discourse, is saturated with multiple discourses that compete with and interanimate one another. Discourse participants construct meaning not in isolation but through exchange and interaction. Bakhtin's concept of *heteroglossia*—the stratification of languages within a language—helps us to appreciate further that a text consists of diverse cultural elements. Together, these theories support the notion that texts by women of color comprise intersecting discursive sites, with embedded and conflicting cultural and rhetorical systems.

Teaching at the crossroads encompasses these sites. As a meeting place of cultures, traditions, and discourses, texts by women of multicultural backgrounds address the controversies and embody the dialogues of the various cultures and accompanying theoretical positions they speak to and through (and which speak to and through them). As such, these texts provide a theoretical framework by which to teach them. By teaching at the crossroads we connect theory with pedagogy and heed the conflicts within the texts.

Women of Color at the Crossroads of Cultures

The notion of the crossroads, interconnecting the various critical approaches to texts by women of color, arises out of the shape of women of color's experiences in the United States. Both women's studies and ethnic studies appeared and expanded as disciplines in the 1960s and 70s, but not until the late 1980s was curricular attention paid specifically to women of color, impelled by advancing knowledge in the various disciplines as well as the increase of women and minorities in higher education. The turn to "difference" in feminist studies in conjunction with the infusion of multiculturalism into the academy has led to this important critical attention to American women of color.[20] This work in women's and gender studies, as well as that found in theoretical literary studies, informs my pedagogical approach. The crossroads model emerges out of and makes available to students the social positions out of which texts by women of color are created.

U.S. women of color share certain sociological, historical, and political realities that influence their lives and writing. Although the feminisms of women of color vary in many ways, institutionalized racism and the struggles against racial oppression unite them. While the feminist movement has significantly improved white women's social status and economic opportunities, women of color remain far behind. Marginalized by white male and ethnic patriarchal structures, women of multicultural backgrounds are "caught between competing and unstable systems of male domination" (Anderson 7). Intersecting forms of domination produce both privilege and subordination, oppression and opportunity, for "power is the cornerstone of women's differences" (Zinn and Dill, "Theorizing" 327); white women have more of it, women of color have less. Women of color are more likely to be unemployed, receive the lowest wages, and live in poverty as single mothers (Zinn and Dill, "Difference" 4). Moreover, advances by white women in economic, social, and political arenas result in part from the availability of women of color in low-wage jobs (Anderson 6).

From Cherríe Moraga and Gloria Anzaldúa's *This Bridge Called My Back* (1981) to recent literary and sociological studies of women of color, there is widespread agreement that women of color "experience multiple oppressions simultaneously" (Anderson 9). Thus women of color exist in distinctive social locations that position them at the crossroads of various cultural oppressions. Many sociological studies of women of color point to the intersecting cultural systems that define these multiple positionalities. Zinn and Dill assert that for women of color, "gender is part of a larger pattern of unequal social relations; how gender is experienced depends on how it intersects with other inequalities" (Introduction 3). Clearly, women of color live in the crossroads of intersecting oppressive systems, and their complex identities, constructed out of the fluid borders of race, class, and gender must inform critical and pedagogical approaches to their written work.

Finally, Anzaldúa's borderlands metaphor, which she uses to theorize the experience of the *mestiza* in the U.S., is deeply relevant to other women of color. Writing about the experience of Chicanas and Mexican women immigrants in the U.S., Anzaldúa describes them as living in the borderlands, a "vague and undetermined place created by the emotional residue of an unnatural boundary"(*Borderlands* 25). Women of color exist between many cultures, alienated from each: "Alienated from her mother culture, 'alien' in the dominant culture, the woman of color does not feel safe within the inner life of her Self. Petrified, she can't respond, her face caught between *los intersticios*, the spaces between the different worlds she inhabits" (42). Like the *mestiza*, women of color often negotiate their existences in the invisible spaces created by multiple, intersecting systems of domination.[21]

However, Anzaldúa also describes the *mestiza* as a survivor, someone who grounds her identity in Indian women's history of resistance (43). She survives the indignities and oppressions of the borderlands and realizes its possibilities through her ability to "live *sin fronteras*/be a crossroads" (217). Within the crossroads, the *mestiza*—and by extension the woman of color—has choice and agency: "to feel a victim where someone else is in control and therefore responsible and to blame (being a victim and transferring the blame on culture, mother, father, ex-lover, friend, absolves me of responsibility), or to feel strong, and, for the most part, in control" (43). In the crossroads, the *mestiza* must create a safe space for herself. Such a space is possible through the creation of a "new *mestiza* consciousness" in the borderlands (99). *Mestiza* identity is multiple, flexible, and transformative.

While much of the sociological research emphasizes the multiple oppressions women of color experience, I see the crossroads as a positive, inspiring metaphor for the affirmative experiences in the intersections of cultural traditions. In fact, many women writers of color turn the materials of oppression into the sources of their art, and pass on that inspiration to their readers. Teaching at the crossroads allows teachers and scholars to move away from reading, interpreting, and teaching texts by women of color exclusively through the lens of oppression, victimization, and/or opposition to hegemonic structures, an approach which "omits any space for action (as opposed to reaction), creativity, cultural, or even individual/communal autonomy" (Davenport 53). At the crossroads of these texts, we learn about cultural traditions, beliefs, and practices—some positive, some negative—that meaningfully shape the lives of women of color in the U.S.

Teaching at the Crossroads of Critical Perspectives

The power of women of color to create new, positive identities in the intersections of cultures informs teaching at the crossroads. The crossroads of these texts, what Homi Bhabha calls the "in-between," have transformative power: "The borderline work of culture demands an encounter with 'newness' that is not part of the continuum of past and present. It creates a sense of the new as an insurgent act of cultural translation. Such art... renews the past, refiguring it as a contingent 'in-between' space, that innovates and interrupts the performance of the present" (7). It is in the "in-between" of critical perspectives, of cultures, of disciplinary structures, and of pedagogical practices that fresh and transformative activities can occur. Like the *mestiza* who "reinterprets history and, using new symbols...shapes new myths" (Anzaldúa, *Borderlands* 104), scholars and instructors of multicultural women's literature must work in the "in-between" of conflicting theoretical spaces and shape new myths. It is in this juncture—a critical and pedagogical borderlands—that we can situate practices for teaching multicultural women's literature. By theorizing the conflicts and connecting them with the cultural positions inside these texts, we create new, transformative pedagogical spaces in the crossroads.

What does it mean, in practical terms, to teach at the crossroads of texts by women of color? It means choosing primary or core course texts by women of color, selecting a focus for each text (a theme, issue, textual feature, or dominant question), and then seeking out relevant cultural and critical contexts based on the four critical strands and the multiple cultural perspectives they represent. From there, instructors choose what I call "crossroads texts": a nexus of texts that comprise the critical and cultural crossroads of the primary text under consideration and which themselves might serve as primary texts in other courses with other purposes. The crossroads model does not prescribe a particular number or type of primary texts or crossroads texts, nor does it prescribe the particular foci of the primary texts. However, this model's crucial distinction from other critical approaches is that it requires the instructor to assign priority to a few texts by women of color and to subordinate the reading of other texts—some by women, some by men, some by white writers, some by writers of color—to students' understanding of the primary texts. In so doing, it underscores for students the provisional nature of the relationship between and among texts as well as the ways in which meaning and value are contingent upon purpose and context.

For example, earlier in this chapter I discussed some of the various critical and cultural contexts—literary and nonliterary—of Kingston's *The Woman Warrior*. Let's say I have chosen this text as a primary course text, and I have chosen to focus on the narrator's developing sense of identity, which is a common critical approach to this text. After researching the various contexts relevant to *The Woman Warrior* as an identity narrative, I would assign various reading selections—crossroads texts—based on their critical and cultural intersections with the primary text.[22] For example, I might assign excerpts from Henry Thoreau's *Walden* to highlight *The Woman Warrior*'s structural pattern in relationship to identity, the ways in which Kingston's text challenges the line between fiction and nonfiction, and the masculinist rationalism of documentable "truth" (see Johnston; Melchior), as well as the stable self that emerges in canonical male autobiography. I might assign Frank Chin's *The Chickencoop Chinaman*, a "canonized" Chinese American text which sheds light on male-female relationships in *The Woman Warrior*, helps readers understand the narrator's relationship with her father, and also provides a literary historical context from which Kingston, as an Asian American woman writer, positions herself. Other possibilities include women's identity narratives with particular emphasis on silence in women's texts, some more straightforward and linear and some more resistant to such patterns. Examples might include Hisaye Yamamoto's "Seventeen Syllables,"

Tillie Olsen's *Tell Me a Riddle*, and some poetry by Emily Dickinson. Jade Snow Wong's *Fifth Chinese Daughter* would work nicely to situate *The Woman Warrior* in a tradition of Chinese American autobiography. I would also want to incorporate readings from some of the Chinese myths and histories upon which Kingston draws as she shapes her imaginative consciousness and finds the means to combat ethnic and gender oppression, such as poetry by Ts'ai Yen, including the epic poem "The Eighteen Laments." Additionally, to further illuminate the role of Kingston's legendary swordswoman Fa Mu Lan in the second chapter of *The Woman Warrior*, I might include the warrior song of Lady Mu from the Chinese classic *Book of Songs*, completed around 600 B.C.[23]

Teaching at the crossroads thus recognizes the complexity of an ethnic woman writer's positioning within a wide range of cultural and discursive systems. These intersections are meeting places for cultural traditions and practices that simultaneously bleed into one another. Because literature is part of a complex social, political, and cultural nexus rather than autonomous and self-enclosed, it both produces and reflects the larger society from which it originates. As products of multiple cultural and literary influences, women writers of color traverse these various discursive and cultural systems, both reinforcing and challenging them. "Multicultural" indicates a plurality of intersecting cultures, sites of negotiation, contest, and connection, and texts by women writers of color, themselves illustrative of these conflicts, demand that we read them on their own terms. We should not choose among the various cultural and critical perspectives in reading/teaching, but should consider them all in dialogue with one another, to "teach at the crossroads."

Teaching at the crossroads broadens the longstanding notion of "literary tradition" in terms of a work's formal and aesthetic relationship with preceding and succeeding texts, joining literary traditions with their cultural, social, and political contexts. Theories of intertextuality insist that a text exists not as a self-enclosed entity but within a complex matrix of other texts. Contemporary critical theories have expanded our notion of "text" to encompass any signifying structure, so we can appreciate an "intertext" as any literary text, literary tradition, historical moment, or cultural practice. Intertextualists often cite T.S. Eliot's seminal essay "Tradition and the Individual Talent" to convey the power of literary interactions: "not only the best, but the most individual parts of [a poet's] work may be those in which the dead poets, his ancestors, assert their immortality most vigorously" (48). But Eliot conceived of *the tradition* as a white, male, Western one. An ethnic woman writer's "historical sense," to use Eliot's term (49), is more encompassing, drawing from a vast array of literary and cultural traditions, for texts by women of color exist within complex networks of literary, social, political, economic, and cultural systems.

Donald Keesey claims that the intertextual critic favors "studying the monuments themselves" as the best way to learn the conventions, dismissing literary study based on other disciplines (263). But such an approach is based on a narrow conception of "the monuments" and their relationship to culture. When Western tradition was considered *the* tradition (subsuming Greek, English, American, etc.), cultural factors seemed unimportant, presumably shared by everyone who wrote or read the texts. But once we acknowledge a number of traditions—cultural and literary—we cannot assume this shared basis. Literature is a function of language and of other literary texts, but it is likewise a function of a variety of intersecting cultural, political, and social forces. Louis Renza remarks that even in current criticism a focus on the ways literary works "comprise revision or updating of their textual antecedents...perform[s] a conservative cultural function," enforcing the "homogeneity and continuity of the Western 'literary' tradition" (186), but that a broadened conception of influence allows for "other voices—other texts—even to those other disciplines themselves supposedly influencing the study of literature" (201). By employing this broadened perspective on intertextuality, instructors become part of the process that allows other voices to be heard and canonical practices, structures, and paradigms to be transformed.

Among these other voices are multicultural women's texts. Eliot's remark in "Tradition and the Individual Talent" that literary tradition "cannot be inherited, and if you want it you must obtain it by great labour" (49), however narrow Eliot's conception of *the tradition*, reminds us of the tremendous effort involved in understanding any literature, including literature by women of color. It is difficult to break from familiar patterns, and it is humbling to venture into areas outside one's own expertise. But we must try. The multiplicity of cultural influences on these texts demands tremendous effort to teach them competently and compassionately. As instructors, we have a duty to take on this multiplicity. Otherwise, we homogenize these texts, their writers, and their cultural groups, reinscribing the unequal relations of power we seek to redress.

Western, ethnic-specific, mainstream feminist, and ethnic-specific feminist readings can unlock the complexities of texts by women of color in meaningful ways. However, a critical pedagogical approach that combines these perspectives as they intersect and illuminate each other can provide a more enriched and informed understanding of the complexities faced by women of color in contemporary America. In this intertextual matrix, students can negotiate the discursive conditions of multiple cultures. Morrison's innovative use of language in *Beloved* can be interpreted from the perspective of poststructuralism, but does this perspective ignore traditional African beliefs in the supernatural? The male-female relationships in *Beloved* can be read according to a mainstream feminist benchmark of male power, but what about the complexities added by the systematic oppression of African American males in a white racist society or the sexual exploitation of slave women and the attendant stereotypes still perpetuated today? Gloria Naylor's *Linden Hills* is richly informed by Dante's *Inferno*, but its meaning is likewise deepened through the perspectives of black sisterhood (see Andrews) and the guidance of African ancestors (see Puhr). The mother-daughter conflicts in *The Joy Luck Club* are both universal and culturally informed, as attested to by Jing-mei Woo's final acceptance of her Chinese mother and her own Chinese heritage. Like the women who write them, these texts are multiplistic, complex, and diverse. In turn, they demand interwoven, interdependent, critical strategies.

Teaching at the Crossroads

Teaching at the crossroads is thus a call for a new kind of critical approach to texts by women of color. In a speech to faculty, staff, and students at Lehigh University on April 26, 2001, Anzaldúa spoke of the parallels between writers and any other individuals in the process of creating, and I would like to extend her remarks to instructors at the crossroads of critical perspectives. In the transformative "in-between space," instructors negotiate and arbitrate between various and diverse belief systems or theoretical perspectives, and transform the disparate pieces into some kind of cohesive form.[24] Like the "artistic revolution" Anzaldúa experiences in the act of writing, teachers can work through resistance, rebellion, and breaking down and, finally, rebuild. Anzaldúa suggests that in the transformative space, reality becomes visible. In these spaces, what she calls "cracks," we can see through the dishonesties to the truths, and we come away with new perspectives. It is thus incumbent upon each of us, to again use Anzaldúa's words, to "scramble around and make the pieces fit" (Speech). That is the work of teaching at the crossroads.

Incorporating such an approach is challenging for those instructors willing to "scramble around and make the pieces fit." In the next chapter, I discuss the practical considerations and broader implications on curriculum and pedagogy of this new theoretical framework. I will suggest, finally, that in order to accomplish the potentially transformative work at the crossroads of texts by women of color, institutional and disciplinary changes must likewise occur.

3 The Crossroads in the Classroom: Curriculum and Pedagogy

> En unas pocas centurias, *the future will belong to the* mestiza. *Because the future depends on the breaking down of paradigms, it depends on the straddling of two or more cultures.*
>
> —*Gloria Anzaldúa, "La conciencia de la mestiza"*

The Implications of the Crossroads in the Classroom

English studies is experiencing a pivotal moment, a "time when the very nature of the discipline is being called into question, when what is to be taught and how it should be taught are in dispute" (Levine 10). In part, English studies' soul-searching can be attributed to the changing face of higher education generally in an age of technology and job-oriented students. Traditional liberal arts degree programs are threatened as many colleges and universities shift funds to programs that focus on careers. Nationally, English programs, which witnessed rising enrollments during the 1980s, incurred a 12 percent decrease from 1993 to 1997 (see O'Neill). In this time of the "profit-protocol" (J. Williams 747) of higher education, where "students have been unabashedly reinvented as consumers, as shoppers at the education store, buying a career-enhancing service" (747), literary studies' role in educating college students is profoundly uncertain.

Certainly economic factors and ideological changes in higher education have contributed to the uncertainties facing literary studies today. But the questions in the discipline—about how and what we teach, about the meaning of teaching and learning literature—run deeper.[25] Literary studies has been unable to respond to these questions because literary value and the value of teaching literature are themselves contested within the discipline, in large part because of the canon wars. There is little doubt that curricular diversity has increased, attested to by the inclusion of nontraditional literature on syllabi, in anthologies, in journals, and in books. But an increasingly loud constituency attacks this diversity as substandard, charging that quality has been replaced by "representation."

Literary specialists committed to a diverse canon, however, face their own questions and challenges. Recognizing the pernicious nature of previously held, narrow aesthetic criteria, they are reluctant to make any kinds of literary or cultural judgments, for fear of being labeled ethnocentric and/or imperialist (see Berthoff; Dasenbrock, "Why Read"). In such a climate, how does the discipline, as well as individual instructors in the classroom, assert the importance of literary study?

The questions posed to literary studies by multiculturalism seem at times not only divisive but destructive, potentially wreaking lasting harm on the discipline. Yet, I believe that multiculturalism's impact on literary studies, while admittedly tumultuous, has brought about opportunities for critical reflection of pedagogies, critical methods, curricular issues, disciplinary structures, and other institutional contexts that can reinvigorate the teaching of literature and the value of literary study. More so than the Great Books, multicultural literature offers opportunities for students to engage the diverse cultures and values of the United States and to interrogate the terms of living in a multicultural society.

In this chapter, I focus on the implications of teaching at the crossroads for both curriculum and pedagogy. Whether one believes that curriculum has been subsumed by debates over pedagogy, or pedagogy has been subsumed by debates over curriculum, what becomes clear is that both are enormously significant to teaching literature by women of color. Moreover, they are inextricably interwoven, as Goebel and Hall suggest: the "new canon" represents, as they see it, not only a set of texts, fixed or changing, but also "comprehensive curricular change and an expanding repertoire of self-reflective teacher knowledge and strategies" (Introduction xiv). Both the what and how of teaching literature by women of color have far-reaching importance.

In many ways, similar issues of curricular content and teaching methods were faced by feminist scholar-teachers whose past (and current) struggles can inform some of the issues faced today by scholar-teachers of literature by women of color. In 1986, Paula Treichler observed that "simply adding women to existing institutions (curricula, disciplines, committees, research protocols, etc.) will not bring about sufficient change" (67-68). Instead, she argued, women's studies must engage in a different journey, one which "entails the reconstruction of human knowledge and human existence" (68). Teaching at the crossroads thus continues this reconstructive work—the "breaking down of paradigms" (Anzaldúa, *Borderlands* 102)—dismantling and rebuilding curricula and pedagogy in new ways. Transforming English studies means including women writers of color on reading lists *and* finding new and appropriate ways to teach these texts. It also might mean using fresh insights to rethink issues in literary studies more generally.

The Curriculum at the Crossroads

Arguably, curricular change has already taken place in literary studies, as attested to by the inclusion of texts by men and women of color in college classrooms, even in courses once devoted to the traditional canon. Moreover, courses devoted specifically to ethnic and ethnic women's literature exist in many colleges and universities. Yet, despite these important changes, significant questions over text selection remain. Teaching at the crossroads addresses some of these issues.

In addition, curriculum, as I define it, refers to the ways texts are grouped in a course according to a conceptual framework. The implications of multicultural literature on course designs have begun to be explored (see Bizzell, "Negotiating," "Contact Zones"; Foster; Lanier), but I believe course designs are central to curricular issues and demand extensive, creative consideration. In the pages that follow, I will discuss the crossroads model as it impacts course design, particularly what is known as the "coverage" model, as well as course rubrics. Finally, I will suggest that the implications for teaching at the crossroads may extend even further—to ways of thinking about literary texts more generally.

Text Selection

Text selection is among the most important issues raised by multicultural studies, generally, and literature by women of color, specifically. However, Susan VanZanten Gallagher argues that teacher-scholars today seem more concerned with teaching methodologies than with text selection, especially in their own classes (55). I think she is probably right. On the positive side, less attention to text selection would seem to suggest that texts by women of color are regularly included on class reading lists. The major anthologies' inclusion of diverse authors and texts provides instructors a variety of choices, including works by women of color, and for many instructors, simply including these texts in their classes is sufficient. But the matter is not that simple: Which texts should be included? Which texts will be replaced? On what bases should these choices be made? What are the implications of these choices? Teaching at the crossroads addresses these crucial questions as it engages two significant, interrelated issues with potentially far-reaching impact: (1) what Gallagher calls the "pedagogical canon," and (2) questions of literary value.

The pedagogical canon, "texts that are taught in college and university settings" (54), is, as Gallagher rightly points out, widely influential in terms of how we represent the American literary and cultural landscape to students, even more so than what John Guillory calls the "imaginary canon" (qtd. in Gallagher 54), a widely debated set of the "best" literary texts. Simply put, the texts we select in our classrooms—rather than what we debate in our scholarship—influence students' understanding of multiculturalism, diversity, oppression, and privilege.

Instructors' text selections, therefore, have concrete ramifications. By bringing new perspectives to text selection, teaching at the crossroads broadens the pedagogical canon and subsequently furthers the dialogue on literary value and excellence. As it reinscribes or resists inclusions and exclusions of texts and writers, the pedagogical canon determines who is and is not included in American literary histories. In choosing texts, instructors make assumptions and determinations about literary criteria—wittingly or unwittingly—and thus about both the pedagogical and imaginary canons. Instructors' selections of texts make implicit and explicit assumptions of the value (and lack thereof) of specific texts. Through careful and reflective text selection, instructors can more *deliberately* than in the past contribute to the creation of a new pedagogical canon, one that is both inclusive and subject to ever-expanding standards of artfulness and literariness, and which remains fluid and open to change.

Such questions over text selection were confronted first by feminist critics who sought to transform the traditional canon. In her landmark article "Treason Our Texts" (1983), Lillian Robinson articulates the "*agony*" (120) of feminist critics torn between including works based on traditional standards of literary excellence and the necessity of redefining these criteria and definitions, a "debate that will have to be engaged":

> For there comes a point when the proponent of making the canon recognize the achievement of both sexes has to put up or shut up; either a given woman writer is good enough to replace some male writer on the prescribed reading list, or she is not. If she is not, then either she should replace him anyway, in the name of telling the truth about the culture, or she should not, in the (unexamined) name of excellence. (121)

Denis Donoghue's charge that the selection criteria in the *Norton Anthology of Literature by Women* (1985) "are not critical at all" but are "political and sociological" (qtd. in Benstock 169) foreshadows similar criticisms leveled against the editors of the *Heath Anthology of American Literature*, as, for example, when Richard Ruland writes, "the Heath anthology shows little concern for what can be called 'literariness,' nor does it say much about how students are to recognize it when they see it" ("Art" 354).[26]

Of course, questions and debates over literary value—how to define it, what constitutes it, and why we should teach a given work—remain, impacting curricular choices. In the question posed by the title of her well-known work, "'But Is It Any Good?': The Institutionalization of Literary Value," Jane Tompkins argues that a text's engagement with the social and political is never separable from its literary excellence. However, at the 2001 MELUS (The Society of the Study of the Multi-Ethnic Literature of the United States) Conference, MELUS President Bonnie TuSmith called on scholars of multi-ethnic literatures to be more critical in their evaluations of ethnic literature; we have gone "overboard," she asserts, on inclusiveness and have shirked our responsibilities to the aesthetic and artistic attention to these works.[27] Multi-ethnic literature, she argues, should not be read merely for its cultural information, politics, or historicism. TuSmith calls for open dialogue, honest assessment, and accountability in insisting that teacher-scholars apply critical judgment to multi-ethnic texts.

Teaching at the crossroads lends itself to deliberate consideration of text selection and the accompanying issues of literary value. In this model, primary course texts are completely at the discretion of the instructor and will be influenced by a variety of factors: instructor personal preference and familiarity, students, course designation and level, local and national interests, academic capital, student accessibility, text availability, representation, and aesthetics. However, one governing factor in primary text selection, whether we like it or not, is the text's "canonical" status, mainly because instructors—many of whom will not be experts in multiple traditions—often need to draw on other scholars' research on primary texts in order to select crossroads texts which are at play at the critical and cultural intersections of these primary texts.[28] Such scholarship points us to the various crossroads texts pertinent for the classroom. In teaching *Beloved*, for example, Chauncey Ridley's scholarship was invaluable in my understanding of African folklore traditions' role in *Beloved*, and Kashinath Ranveer's analysis alerted me to specific issues of African American feminist identity in the text. Ana María Carbonell's study of Chicana mythical and legendary figures Llorona and Coatlicue in Cisneros' "Woman Hollering Creek" has enriched the way I read and teach this text. Christine Berg's work on Gloria Naylor's intertextual connections to Walt Whitman and other canonical texts has helped me teach the Western-based contexts of Naylor's novels, including *The Women of Brewster Place* and *Linden Hills* (see "Giving Sound"; "Methods").[29]

Primary text selection is significant, but it is at the crossroads of these texts by women of color that the most influential work on the pedagogical canon and issues of literary value can occur. First, teaching at the crossroads broadens the pedagogical canon, since the primary course texts themselves help to determine crossroads texts. Patrocino Schweickart explains the act of reading and interpretation as one in which the "texts set the agenda for the discussion. This agenda is negotiable—but it is not irrelevant" (6). In this way, a substantial part of the process of selection—and the power that goes with it—belongs to ethnic women rather than white men, as has traditionally been the case in the Western and American canon. That is, when Whitman appears on the syllabus as a crossroads text to aid in understanding Naylor (*not* as a benchmark against which to evaluate the literariness of Naylor's text, which might occur, explicitly or implicitly, in a typical "American Literature" course, for example), power dynamics are reversed.

Selection of crossroads texts is also determined in part by the instructor's choices about the focus of the primary texts. That is, instructors must decide which specific textual features, among an infinite number of choices, they want students to study in a particular primary text, such as genre, language, or identity. The crossroads model compels sustained inquiry of a particular textual feature in order to highlight the interplay(s) of critical and cultural contexts. The model also addresses the practical issue of time restraints, and the virtual impossibility of focusing more broadly on multiple texts in a single course. Of course, as will become more clear in chapters 4 and 5 when I provide examples of the crossroads approach, demarcating and separating one textual feature from the others to which it is inextricably connected is itself somewhat artificial. While in these chapters I will discuss each of the texts separately, I want to emphasize that I usually organize my courses so that primary texts speak to one another in some capacity. For example, I often teach at the crossroads of genre in both *Mango Street* and *Storyteller* during the same semester to have these texts converse with each other, as well as with the various other crossroads texts. This configuration allows some of the crossroads texts to overlap, thus simplifying some of the practical issues in choosing crossroads texts. Similarly, Silko's *Ceremony* and Morrison's *Song of Solomon* work beautifully together as primary texts speaking to one another about their male protagonists' journeys inward, to home and to culture. Most significant, by bringing the texts together in this way, I try to emphasize both their connectedness and their differences. Let me emphasize, however, that the primary text's "negotiable agenda" does not eliminate the instructor's powerful role in text selection. Indeed, instructors have great leeway, depending on their purposes and goals for the course. The crossroads model compels us, in ways that anthologies may not, to be more cognizant and reflective of these choices.

I will describe different crossroads scenarios for *Beloved* to illustrate how the crossroads would be different depending on the textual feature centered in classroom study. In the example of *Beloved* at the crossroads of identity, which I detail in chapter 5, I use postmodern readings, male and female slave narratives, African tales of badness, and other relevant readings to provide various interpretive perspectives on the protagonist's identity. At the crossroads of genre, however, *Beloved*'s crossroads texts might include historical texts, such as those related to the Margaret Garner story (the slave woman upon whom Sethe is based); Western renderings of slavery, such as Harriet Beecher Stowe's *Uncle Tom's Cabin*; Flying Africans folkloric traditions (see Wilentz); male and female slave narratives; and texts on African American female epistemology (see Collins). Considerations of language at the crossroads of *Beloved* might include postmodern readings on language, jazz traditions (see C. Hall; Keizer), theories of feminine language identified by feminist theorists Helene Cixous and Julia Kristeva, African traditions of the supernatural, and slave narratives. A study of the character Beloved at the crossroads would include historical readings, African traditions of the supernatural, Cixous' and Kristeva's theories of feminine language, and texts on African American female epistemology (see Collins).

Selecting crossroads texts also engages instructors in issues of value. In 1982, Elizabeth Meese called on feminist critics "to determine new, inclusive standards for literary excellence" and to "formulat[e]...revised criteria for inclusion rather than the abandonment of all standards" (17). Meese argued that feminist critics had not yet developed critical modes appropriate for prose forms—essays, letters, journals, diaries, and oral narratives—and that feminist critical modes should arise from "female epistemology" (18). Likewise, critics of multi-ethnic women's literature have work ahead of them to discover and create critical modes relevant to and originating from the texts themselves.

Teaching at the crossroads helps guide us in this direction. For example, returning to my discussion of the various crossroads scenarios for *Beloved*, it becomes clear that many of these crossroads texts raise questions of value related to African American and African American feminist aesthetics. How do African folktales or African American jazz and blues traditions influence how we might understand the artistic choices in *Beloved*? How might they compel a different set of aesthetic standards without forcing us to abandon standards altogether? "*El Corrido de Gregorio Cortez*," which I teach at the crossroads of genre in *Mango Street*, surely extends notions of literary value, and more important, invites all of us, including students, into the process of defining such criteria. When teaching at the crossroads of *The Woman Warrior*, the diverse aesthetics in this text, along with *Walden*, *The Chickencoop Chinaman*, "Tell Me a Riddle," Emily Dickinson's poetry, and poetry by Ts'ai Yen, raise enormously useful questions about literary value for students. In my classes, students often question me about the class packet and handouts of the readings I provide, wondering why we are not using an anthology. Such questions provide further occasion to address canon issues as well as to reinforce the theoretical basis of teaching at the crossroads.

No doubt, putting together a coherent set of intertextual readings (literary and nonliterary) to illuminate the intersecting traditions in a particular text requires a great deal of planning and creativity. Usually, this means going outside traditional anthologies and collections of literary works. One solution is to use a "class packet," but these require copyright clearance and thus can take time to obtain, and permission is not always granted, which can mean last-minute scrambling around for a replacement or putting a reading "on reserve" in one's campus library. Publishers are also making it possible for instructors to put together their own "anthologies" of course readings by creating larger pools of texts which, as they expand, may be useful for the crossroads model. For example, McGraw Hill's *Primis* series and Pearson Custom Publishing's *The Mercury Reader* enable instructors to exert greater control over classroom text selection than traditional anthologies, for the instructor works with the publisher to put together a set of readings from a list of works made available by the publisher. *LitPacks Online*, by XanEdu, currently only has one packet available but is working toward more. I cannot predict whether or not these resources will be useful or limiting, but I do want to point out that these and other Web resources may eventually be an additional way to design crossroads courses. In my experiences, some combination of these resources has been sufficient, enabling me to include the appropriate crossroads texts in my courses.

Let me use my experiences teaching at the crossroads of genre in *Mango Street*, which I cover in chapter 4, as an example of putting together a set of crossroads texts. For an approximately four-week unit of the course, readings include *Mango Street*, Tomás Rivera's *...y no se lo tragó la tierra (...And the Earth Did Not Devour Him)* and Kate Chopin's *The Awakening*. In a class packet, I also included a short excerpt from Edward Stewart and Milton Bennett's *American Cultural Patterns;* William Faulkner's classic story "Barn Burning"; Madonna Kolbenschlag's "A Feminist's View of 'Cinderella'"; Lorna Dee Cervantes' "Heritage" and "Visions of Mexico While at a Writing Symposium in Port Townsend, Washington"; Carmen Tafolla's "La Malinche"; a transcribed version of "*El Corrido de Gregorio*

Cortez" (from Américo Paredes' *With His Pistol in His Hand);* and excerpts from Rodolfo Gonzáles' *I am Joaquín/Yo Soy Joaquín.*[30]

I am planning to teach Silko's *Ceremony* next year and have begun to imagine the direction I might take studying this text at the crossroads. If, for example, I choose to focus study of *Ceremony* on the protagonist Tayo's healing journey inward, to home and culture, I would devise a set of readings that would include some or all of the following, depending on other circumstances of the class. Mark Twain's *The Adventures of Huckleberry Finn*, featuring the quintessential white male protagonist who "lights out" in search of self, would situate *Ceremony* in the canonical tradition of American journey narratives. I would likely include Native American writer N. Scott Momaday's *House Made of Dawn*, in which the alienated protagonist Abel, like Tayo in *Ceremony*, learns that survival and meaning lie in his Indian heritage. As TuSmith remarks, Silko "rewrites Momaday's novel in some ways" (*Relatives* 104), so including this text at the crossroads of *Ceremony* positions Silko within the contemporary Native American male tradition. In a class packet, I would likely include women's narratives such as Joan Didion's "On Going Home," which reveals what many feminist writers and critics have identified as women's need for attachment rather than separation. I might also include other texts by Native American male writers stressing the notion of tradition as a healing form, such as in the writing of Simon Ortiz. The class packet might also include the Keres folktale about Tayo, a boy whose pet eagle carries him into the sky where he meets Spider Woman and then returns to his people bearing gifts (see Todd), as well as a reading on the relationship between spirituality and sexuality in Pueblo culture, such as Silko's essay "Yellow Woman and a Beauty of the Spirit," to illuminate the significance of Tayo's relationship with Ts'eh.[31] To emphasize Silko's relationship to other Native women writers, I might bring in a short story by Louise Erdrich, such as "The Red Convertible" from *Love Medicine*, which involves two brothers, one of whom has returned from the Vietnam War. Finally, because of the communal emphasis in ethnic literature generally (see TuSmith, *Relatives*), numerous texts, such as Toni Cade Bambara's "Sweet Town" or "The Lesson," would serve to emphasize the interconnectedness between Silko's *Ceremony* and a tradition of literature by women of color.

Course Design: Text Grouping

Grouping texts according to some kind of conceptual framework is a second crucial issue addressed by the crossroads model. Perhaps even more so than with text selection, it is in course design that teaching at the crossroads might be most transformative, in introductory and "survey" courses as well as in more specialized courses, such as "Women Writers" or "African American Literature." It may even give us an opportunity to reconsider pedagogical strategies for canonical texts as well as a fresh look at what it means for a student to major in English studies. Like the *mestiza*'s dependence on "the breaking down of the paradigms" (Anzaldúa, *Borderlands* 102), it may be time for these models to be "busted up" (Bizzell, "Negotiating" 164).

Canon expansion has yet to impact in any significant way traditional course designs. Typically, multi-ethnic and other noncanonical works are added to traditional groupings, such as literary periods, genre, theme, historical periods, or geographical regions. However, some scholars have noted the disadvantages of "ADD[ing] ONE" or "ADD[ing] ON" (Foster 197): "We cannot re-form American literature by consuming fewer works by dead white men, increasing our intake of women's texts, and adding a new category or two to our literary plates" (197). Simply adding an ethnic text into a curriculum without considering its literary or cultural contexts as well as its theory or aesthetic is unacceptable. Adding a multicultural text or two to a traditional grouping merely tokenizes and devalues it since that text's aesthetics may not fit neatly with those in the traditional grouping, as Patricia Bizzell's example of Harriet Jacobs' *Incidents in the Life of a Slave Girl* in a traditional category of "American Renaissance" texts such as Nathaniel Hawthorne's *The Scarlet Letter* attests. Moreover, creating new literary periods specifically for ethnic texts (in anthologies or in courses) ghettoizes these texts ("Negotiating" 164).

Another common approach to grouping texts, the "universal themes" course design, has also come under fire. Many critics, including Bizzell, Gary Olson, and Julie Drew, argue that while on the surface, thematic grouping attributes equal value to canonical and noncanonical texts, such approaches can too easily minimize or trivialize cultural difference. My main concern with a universal themes approach is that instructors' choices are imposed on the texts without the texts having any say in interpretive strategies, forcing interrelatedness among various texts without researching the traditions and interconnections among them.[32] Too often, these approaches rely on anthologies and thus limit an instructor's choices.

In the crossroads model, text grouping does not follow either the add-on or universal themes approach. Rather, grouping occurs as a result of the instructor's objectives for crossroads study. Certainly, as I have already discussed, the instructor must make decisions about primary text selection based on what he/she wants to accomplish in the course. If I choose to teach at the crossroads of identity, for example, I will choose texts by women of color that lend themselves to identity issues. Moreover, I must make decisions about specific ethnic communities to include in the course. As I will discuss later in this chapter, because teaching at the crossroads demands intensive, focused study of primary texts, the model does not lend itself to including as many ethnic "representatives" as in more traditional survey courses in ethnic literature.

Once primary text selection is made, crossroads texts selection (and thus overall course design) is determined in large part by the texts themselves. Once I decide upon a theme or textual feature, such as identity, and primary text, such as *Song of Solomon*, I do not look for poems, short stories, plays, or excerpts of novels in an anthology that I might use for the course. Rather, I study *Song of Solomon* and the scholarship on it, carefully, and let them lead me to relevant readings. Although I make choices among these readings, I would argue that these choices are driven by other factors than in traditional course designs, such as accessibility, availability, length, or quantity.

Course Design: The "Coverage" Model

One other important issue of course design is what has come to be known as the "coverage" model for teaching literature—a representative sampling of the canon, often taught via anthologies. Many scholars have noted the limitations of this approach, especially in introductory courses. Douglas Lanier traces the coverage model's history to the conception of literary study as "curatorial"—the preservation of the most worthy literary texts (199).[33] As Martha Cutter observes, however, changes in notions of literary excellence have not dismantled the coverage model (what she calls the survey course) but have made it even more unmanageable—"overstuffed"—with teachers wanting or feeling obligated to cover as much as they can—the "great writers" in addition to the recently added minority and women writers (120).

Teaching at the crossroads, which is not a coverage model, does not lend itself to quantity or breadth. Rather, the model requires focused study of specific texts and the crossroads texts to which they lead; the driving forces are depth (focused study of the primary texts) and range (variety of crossroads texts) rather than coverage. I am not suggesting that the crossroads model eliminates instructors' difficult decisions about coverage altogether. For example, I make choices about how many primary texts to use and, subsequently, how many crossroads texts can be covered in such a time frame. Moreover, choices must be made about how many and which ethnic groups to "represent" in the course. In a multicultural literature course last semester, I chose three primary texts: *The House on Mango Street*, *China Men*, and *Storyteller*. With this decision, I omitted African American texts as primary texts, although I did include two African American texts as crossroads texts, which is problematic on the one hand, but instructive on the other. Certainly, there is a pressure, perhaps for good reasons, to include the four most "visible" ethnic groups, to refer again to Amy Ling's designation, on course syllabi, not only in general survey classes but especially in classes specifically designated as "multicultural," "diverse," or "alternative," as is the course title at Penn State. My decision to include these works without an African American primary text was based on the ways in which I wanted the three other texts to "speak to" one another as stories of development as well as on practical constraints like time. I have considered whether the decision might feel exclusionary to any African American students in the class, but I believe that because the decision-making process was made visible to my students, the few African American students in the class did not feel excluded. Decisions about "representation" and "coverage" must be seen anew, with an awareness that "representation" claims completeness but, in fact, can never be complete.[34] Representation was not an aim in my course, because it is utterly unattainable. Teaching at the crossroads points to "representation's" incompleteness and opens possibilities for students to have conversations about what these choices mean. Issues of "coverage" still exist, requiring instructors to make choices, but these issues exist differently.

The coverage model is also criticized for its lack of attention to students' reading and interpretive strategies. Typically organized by genre, theme, historical periods, geographical regions, formal devices, or, more recently, ethnic groups, the coverage model stresses variety and quantity but, Lanier argues, hinders students' interpretive and critical applications by feeding them one text after another without any consideration of reading strategies. Teaching at the crossroads, however, offers a different approach, one that encourages students' awareness not only of reading strategies but of writing strategies as well. By reading ethnic women's texts through multiple perspectives, students learn about a range of critical and interpretive strands. Moreover, they gain a sense of the writers' rhetorical strategies as they relate to various cultural and literary traditions. Teaching at the crossroads thus acknowledges the ways in which theory operates in the classroom.

Finally, teaching at the crossroads compels some adjustments on the part of instructors and how we are typically accustomed to teaching literary texts. First, it requires in-depth study of specific, crucial issues or elements of a text to highlight the intersecting conflicts and cultures within. By focusing attention on one textual feature, we inevitably leave others out, which can be discomforting, yet also liberating, because it allows for enriched exploration of a particular textual element.[35] Instructors must become comfortable with knowing they have made students' experience with one textual feature both richer and more representative of the text's overall construction.

Instructors must also be willing to allow students time to delve into the various interpretive positions and spend time in these important intersections. Crossroads study involves sustained inquiry of one primary text and others to which that text directs us—focused intellectual work that can be quite beneficial to students. Marshall Gregory makes an important point about students' intellectual development, and how the traditional approach's attempt to cover too much information can actually be detrimental to students' learning: "what students need is time to make mistakes, to correct them, to fail and try again—and they need teachers who can help them view each failure as merely interim, as merely a *halt* in forward progress, not as a terminal judgment on their abilities" (76). Clearly, the crossroads model allows students time to revisit and thus reflect on, with new and varied information, the texts under study. The exercises included in appendix A offer sets of discussion questions designed to stimulate this intellectual process.

Rethinking Course Rubrics

Teaching at the crossroads similarly raises important curricular issues of course rubrics and categories. Is the course a general survey of American literature, an African American literature course, an "Alternative Voices" course such as Penn State's, a women's literature course, or something else? Is it a first-year general education course or an upper-level seminar? In the discussion that follows, I will suggest that the type and level of the course impact the use of the crossroads approach as well as suggest ways to adapt the model to these various rubrics. Perhaps more significant, I will also suggest that the crossroads model might encourage new ways to approach traditional, embedded course rubrics.

Teaching at the crossroads, because it draws on diverse texts that traverse all kinds of boundaries, has flexibility that allows for its implementation in all kinds of courses. Regardless of the type of class offered, the integrity of the theoretical framework for teaching at the crossroads remains; it is adaptable because its theoretical foundations are clearly articulated. In order to convey the various configurations a crossroads course might take, I will describe the ways I have used this approach in a general survey of American literature, a general education class called "Alternative Voices in American Literature," as well as a "Women Writers" course. In doing so, I hope to convey the flexibility of the model.

In the general introduction to American literature course, I chose to focus on the protagonist's journey toward selfhood using *The House on Mango Street* as the primary text (in chapter 4, I provide an extensive discussion of teaching *Mango Street* at the crossroads of genre). *Mango Street* led to various and diverse crossroads texts, including, among others, J.D. Salinger's *Catcher in the Rye*, various Ernest Hemingway "Nick Adams" stories, F. Scott Fitzgerald's *The Great Gatsby*, William Faulkner's "Barn Burning," John Barth's "Lost in the Funhouse," Kate Chopin's *The Awakening*, Paule Marshall's "To Da-Duh, In Memoriam," Gary Soto's "Black Hair" and "Mexicans Begin Jogging," and Lorna Dee Cervantes' "Beneath the Shadow of the Freeway." Even though canonical texts outnumbered texts by women of color, some students nevertheless expressed disappointment, even resentment, that a text by a woman of color was so prominent. Most students, however, seemed to like the way the texts connected with one another and allowed them to rethink earlier interpretations and points of view. Teaching at the crossroads gave these students the opportunity to question and challenge their preconceived notions of canonical American texts.

I have taught "Alternative Voices in American Literature" a number of times, each time configuring it a bit differently. Generally, however, I have used two to four primary texts by women of color and a variety of crossroads texts. Because of the "Alternative Voices" designation, I do weigh the course more heavily to writers of color, but I do not omit white writers altogether—male or female. Each time I have taught the course, I have varied the textual features under consideration, from genre and identity, as discussed in the next two chapters, to structure, language, and community and identity. One semester, I chose to focus on memory and the role of the past in *Beloved*, primarily because I wanted to include August Wilson's *Fences* on the reading list since the local community theater was presenting this play. Again, the model is flexible and adaptable.

In the "Alternative Voices" class, students expect "diversity," given that the course fulfills a general education diversity requirement. Thus, students were somewhat less resistant in this course to texts by people of color. Indeed, they were initially surprised by the inclusion of canonical texts in the course, but I believe most came to understand the theoretical perspective of the course and the interconnectedness among the texts. Some students even addressed the appropriateness of these texts in their written work. Two students' final essays argued about whether or not including two Faulkner stories in an "alternative voices" class was justified.

My plans for a general education course called "Women Writers" could include a "traditional" course design, such as a chronological depiction of the history and stages of feminist criticism and women's writing through representative texts. I could also design the course according to ethnicity, literary tradition, or genre. Instead, I will center the course around two primary texts by women of color, including Alice Walker's *The Color Purple*. I chose *The Color Purple* because one of my objectives in the course is to connect women's literature to the practical and real needs of poor and working-class women (both women of color and white women) in the nation, as well as in the local community, and to integrate service learning into the course. As such, I intend to focus study of *The Color Purple* at the crossroads of domestic violence, and the various cultural and literary traditions informing treatment of the issue in this text. Crossroads texts include William Faulkner's "Dry September," Richard Wright's "Long Black Song," Charlotte Brontë's *Jane Eyre*, Charlotte Perkins Gilman's "The Yellow Wallpaper," poetry by Adrienne Rich, Harriet Jacobs' *Incidents in the Life of a Slave Girl*, Zora Neale Hurston's *Their Eyes Were Watching God*, excerpts from Audre Lorde's *Sister Outsider*, and Cisneros' "Woman Hollering Creek." The emphasis is obviously on white and ethnic women writers, most prominently African American women writers, but significant male-authored texts are included as well in order to illustrate Walker's interaction with the white male and African American male literary traditions.

Let me state unequivocally that I deliberately choose to put texts by women of color at the center of my courses in literature and, relatedly, I am aware that the crossroads approach to texts by women of color gives short shrift to the crossroads texts. In describing identity as relational, as "always in this in-between zone, the *nepantla* or borderlands," Anzaldúa states that depending on the circumstances, certain aspects of her identity take "center stage" (qtd. in Reuman 12). In my teaching, I consciously choose to give "center stage" to texts by women of color and believe I am practicing a form of "curricular affirmative action" (J. Hall 4). Since for so long texts by women of color have been pushed out and excluded, I feel very comfortable about bringing them to the center of instruction in a deliberate effort to challenge and dissolve biases and prejudices that have long kept these voices on the margins. As Susan Lanser observes, "if one does not want to marginalize what has been marginal, one must centralize it instead" (61). The crossroads model gives white men, white women, and men of color time and space to be "silent for a spell, while [we] read, study, and listen to women of color" (Ward 214). Even more importantly, it acknowledges, in some sense, Anzaldúa's desire that whites who attempt to fight for social justice "come to see that they are not helping [people of color] but following [their] lead" (*Borderlands* 107).

I should point out, too, that the crossroads model does not only bump texts by whites from the center to the margins in courses which would traditionally rely heavily on the canon, such as "Introduction to Literature." The crossroads model brings texts written by white men and women into courses such as "African American Literature," exploring intertextual relationships within African and African American men's and women's cultural and literary traditions, but not ignoring mainstream feminist perspectives. To use another example, teaching at the crossroads brings texts by white men and women as well as by Chicanos into a "Chicana Writers" course, where I would emphasize Chicana texts, but would not ignore the various cultural and literary contexts that comprise their crossroads. Thus texts by white women, Chicanos, and other writers of color would be included on the class reading list. Even in a "Chicana Novels" course, I would include more Chicana novels than other kinds of texts, but I would not limit the course to Chicana novels. The crossroads model thus challenges course rubrics and opens up various "traditional" and nontraditional courses to multiplicities.

My experience has been that, overall, students respond favorably to the crossroads model. I began this book by discussing the "perils" of teaching texts by women (and men) of color, about the kinds of student responses that can be troubling and challenging. I certainly do not mean to suggest that the crossroads model eliminates these challenges, for it does not. It can be difficult and frustrating to teach texts by women of multicultural backgrounds in classes filled largely with white students, to face student resistance, defensiveness, guilt, and confusion. But we must acknowledge the tremendous challenge we put to students when we ask them to reconsider their deeply-held beliefs and views of the world. This is particularly true for the students in my classrooms, a largely homogenous group from Berks County, Pennsylvania. Most (certainly not all) students in my courses take "diversity" courses to fill "diversity" requirements, and many of these students bring prejudices and stereotypes to the classroom.

What must it be like for students, "crossing from one world to another" (Anzaldúa, qtd. in Reuman 5)? As Beverly Clark, et al. tell us, "personal connections give life and meaning to theory" (133), so that each student's personal connections to the texts we introduce will differ. The majority of my students are middle-class whites, but of course, not all middle-class whites are the same. For each student, what happens in the intersections of divergent critical perspectives will vary. Overall, however, students seem to like seeing texts come together in meaningful ways, to leave the class with a sense not only of the continuities and discontinuities of the texts they have read, but a broader picture of what it means to live and write as a woman of color in American society.

I want to end this section on curriculum by addressing two broader issues raised by teaching at the crossroads. The first issue is related to coverage, but specifically as it applies to the traditional English major. What does it mean for a student who graduates with a degree in literary studies? Certainly notions about what it means to "cover" English studies in both graduate and undergraduate programs have undergone revisions. Stephen Greenblatt and Giles Gunn remarked in 1992 that the sweeping changes in the discipline have made impossible "a unifying, totalizing grasp of our subject"(2). Moreover, David Chapman's, Jeanett Harris', and Christine Hult's 1995 study of English programs likewise illustrates that departments of English and the traditional literature emphasis were being "reinvent[ed]" by various writing concentrations, options, or tracks (422). Nevertheless, English undergraduate programs typically attempt to "cover" the field of English for English majors through historical, periodized groupings and categories. The crossroads model may have implications for rethinking this paradigm as it calls into question such issues as coverage and representation.

Second, the notion of the crossroads, derived from Anzaldúa's theories of women of color, may paradoxically speak to traditionally canonical texts as well. That is, in the same way that people of all genders, races, ethnicities, and sexual orientations have embraced borderlands identity, even if their borderlands differ from others', we might re-see textuality more generally. Theorizing about women of color and their texts gives us a new perspective from which to re-see and reconsider traditional texts, which must also be crossed-over, even if the intersections themselves may be comprised differently. Teaching at the crossroads may indeed be a way to approach all literary texts, as well as the various positionalities and discourses intersecting between and among them.

Pedagogy at the Crossroads

Because the curriculum will not "*automatically* impose its benefits on students" (71), as Gregory asserts (nor, I might add, its harms), teaching at the crossroads has important implications for general issues of pedagogy as well. Feminist theorists and teachers grappled with similar questions as they sought transformative ways to teach new and unfamiliar canons and texts. The crossroads framework for teaching texts by women of color reinforces the necessity of revising traditional classroom practices and it also raises new issues. In discussing some of these issues, I will pay particular attention to the relationship between scholarship and teaching, decentered and process methodologies, and, finally, what it means for the instructor at the crossroads.

At the Crossroads of Scholarship and Teaching

According to George Levine, while the profession has begun to realize the important and inextricable connections between pedagogy and literary scholarship, in practice, we remain "two nations" (13). Most institutions (especially research institutions) do not "count" books on teaching as scholarly work. Similarly, teaching lower-level literature courses is not a mark of success in the discipline. Levine, Goebel and Hall, and others point out that many schools do not typically require that faculty reflect on teaching practices; indeed, they discourage it through either a research emphasis that devalues teaching or, at the other end of the spectrum, heavy teaching loads.

However, I certainly see signs that the research/practice gap in literary studies is beginning to shrink, as more and more teacher-scholars, as well as institutions, acknowledge the urgency and professional responsibility of reflective, theoretically-informed teaching.[36] The "burgeoning dialogue" (Goebel and Hall, Introduction xv) between research and teaching in literary studies can be attributed to numerous factors, including the impact of literature by people of color on the discipline.

I firmly believe in the research-practice connection and am committed to being accountable for the theoretical assumptions underlying what and how I teach. Teaching and scholarship are, for me, inextricably connected, each stimulating the other so that the work I accomplish in each arena informs the other. In my view, there is no more important place to "test out" theories of literature, especially as they relate to texts by women of color, than the classroom. If our critical approaches to these texts do not make reading them a meaningful, even transformative, experience for students, then we need to reconsider our theories. Our approaches should stimulate our students' creative, intellectual, political, and ethical thinking; so, too, should their questions and comments do the same for us.

I believe that teaching at the crossroads is theoretically informed and, subsequently, contributes to narrowing the longstanding research/pedagogy split in literary studies. Levine argues that while Graff's "teach the conflicts" model, discussed in chapter 2, potentially brings together theory, criticism, and pedagogy and addresses literary studies' teaching/research split, "there is very little critical or empirically based writing that works out in some detail what teaching the conflicts—however theoretically attractive on the surface—might entail" (11). And, Levine continues, even when such work has been done, scholars have been more interested in the theoretical, rather than practical, dimensions of the conflicts. The crossroads model, a theoretical and pedagogical enactment of conflicts, satisfies Levine's vision of how we might put Graff's model into practice. Teaching at the crossroads is both theoretically *and* critically based, thus bringing together various forms of scholarly and pedagogical work. In a similar vein, the crossroads model also answers Levine's call to "reimagine" (12) lower-level teaching to make it "intellectually interesting to faculty" and coherent with their literary scholarship (13). It is simply not possible to effectively implement this model without some degree of scholarship, for the texts themselves demand such work at their crossroads.

Decentered and Process Methodologies in the Classroom at the Crossroads

Teaching at the crossroads invites the decentered and process-oriented methodologies generally advocated by multiculturalists. Influenced by critical pedagogy, feminist pedagogy, and composition studies, most multiculturalists recognize how such instructional approaches, as students participate in making knowledge, provide more meaningful learning contexts than traditional classroom approaches.[37] These instructional methods underscore the ways that knowledge, the canon, and the curriculum or syllabus can be socially constructed. They invite students to be active thinkers rather than passive recipients of political correctness and the multicultural mission, promoting students' development of critical thinking abilities as they assume greater responsibility for their own learning. Decentered, process-oriented methodologies are particularly appropriate for literature by women of multicultural backgrounds, which demands new contexts for learning. In classrooms in which students read literature by women of color, teacher and student together construct meaning and value. Yet, the embracing of innovative instructional practices does not mask the challenges these practices present for instructors. Rather, it illuminates them, presents additional challenges, and offers some potential redress.

Teaching at the crossroads necessitates that instructors find ways for students to understand and enter the cultural and critical debates of multicultural and feminist literary study. We can achieve these objectives by helping students ask the same kinds of questions scholars and instructors ask, particularly when it comes to issues such as canonization and literary value. I often bring the crucial conflicts of multicultural and feminist literary study into the classroom through a variety of readings and active and collaborative learning assignments, before or at the same time as we read the primary texts by women of color.[38] Appendix A includes some of the assignments I have used to raise these issues. For instance, canon issues become more clear when students consider the literature assigned in their high school classes and collectively construct a sample canon. Using a variety of assignments, such as comparing and contrasting these texts with books they have read on their own or writing a "defense" of a work the literary world has not accepted as worthy of canonization, students enter the debates of literary value and excellence. They interrogate artificial hierarchies and constructions imposed by language and culture, formulate answers to questions of canonization, literary value, and cultural difference, and work toward developing new, expanded criteria of value.

Additionally, I bring students to the debates over literary excellence by paralleling some of the issues with their more immediate concerns. For example, in one assignment students read Tompkins' "'But Is It Any Good?': The Institutionalization of Literary Value" in conjunction with Allan Bloom's "Music." In class work and writing assignments, students respond to Bloom's article, which assails rock music, and thus consider the issues of musical and artistic "excellence" in relationship to literary studies. I also use variations of James Laughlin's collaborative project, which asks students to construct an anthology of an aspect of American popular culture (such as music, sports figures, television programs, etc.), paralleling students' conflicts with literary specialists' as a way to speak to the conflicts of literary studies.

From these larger debates, we move to the specifics of the crossroads framework, and I am up front with my students about my approach to the texts in the course, even using some of my own written work and excerpts from Anzaldúa's work as classroom reading material. Moreover, as we complete our study of specific core texts, I always assign a writing/discussion exercise to bring together students' work at the crossroads of the text. Rather than simply asking students to interpret texts, the assignments in the course ask students to engage theory, not only by questioning and examining criteria for literary excellence and by questioning the selection of texts in the course, but by questioning the crossroads model and its theoretical commitments as well as the various theoretical and critical approaches to the literature. Like Lanser, I try to emphasize theory as an "open process of inquiry" rather than content to be mastered (58), still acknowledging that students must learn content and grasp theory before they can apply, question, critique, and transform it (59). Echoing Lanser, I teach from multiple theoretical perspectives so students can "negotiate a place from which to stand or at least to understand" (60). At the crossroads of texts and of my classrooms, critical and cultural voices dialogue.

The crossroads approach brings with it certain advantages for addressing some other crucial concerns of teaching literature by women of color, including the paradox created by the bringing together of decentered methodologies and the critical need for students to have background and contextual knowledge of unfamiliar cultures and ways of seeing the world. Sandra Jamieson warns of these difficulties: "classes we once devoted simply to texts must now also teach their historical and cultural contexts, and finding a satisfactory balance is not easy" (139). The intersection of decentered pedagogies with cultural unfamiliarity raises numerous questions. How much time do we devote to cultural contexts rather than literary analysis? How do we bring these contexts into the classroom in ways that do not undermine innovative classroom methods? How do we avoid simplistic, reductionist, or stereotypical answers to questions of cultural differences? How do we avoid the traps of stereotype, tokenism, and reductionism for even those with the best intentions, and begin to lead students to broad-based understanding and respect? We must be wary of how generalizations about any culture can be potentially more detrimental than productive, but how much information about cultures should we give to students? These are all critical questions that have no definitive answers.

The crossroads model does not eliminate the problem of cultural contexts and background knowledge, but it does offer some redress. Specifically, by teaching at the intersection of Western-based, ethnic specific, mainstream feminist, and ethnic-specific feminist critical strands, we actually bring in various contextual components through the crossroads texts themselves. For example, I teach about the slave narrative tradition with respect to *Beloved* by including all or part of Frederick Douglass' or Harriet Jacobs' narrative on the class reading list. To help students understand Kingston's references to female infanticide in *The Woman Warrior*, I bring in cultural and historical readings. I use poetry by Walt Whitman, Wallace Stevens, and T.S. Eliot to help students discover Naylor's intertextual relationship with the canonical tradition (see Berg, "Giving Sound"). I bring CDs of various blues music to play in class when we study the influence of the blues tradition on the language and structure of *Beloved* or *Their Eyes Were Watching God*.

I should point out that the crossroads model does not require instructors to become experts of every text; indeed, it recognizes the impossibility of this task. I do most of my literary research in literature by women of color, but I can never expect to have the depth of knowledge of someone who spends all of her or his time with a particular author or even ethnic literary tradition, and instructors who are not members of a specific racial or ethnic group may never fully understand every cultural context within a given text.[39] The more I teach texts by women of multicultural backgrounds and the more I read the extensive critical scholarship on these texts, the more I know and can provide for my students. At the same time, I am becoming more accustomed (though not "comfortable" necessarily) saying "I don't know" when students ask me about specific cultural information with which I am unfamiliar.[40] I also use such instances as "teaching moments," bringing classroom discussion back to issues of canons, multicultural texts, and cultural difference, and also often ask the inquirer to try to find answers to his/her question through research. I work very hard to bring these cultural contexts to students' readings of texts by women of color, but I have also learned that the richness and density of these texts defy complete understanding.[41] Joseph Trimmer's "cautionary tale" warns instructors of trying to do too much, of becoming experts on all cultures and contexts and taking the excitement of exploration away from students, asserting that multicultural literature is a "*process*," a "new method of inquiry that encourage[s] students to mount their own expeditions through the history and literature of other cultures" (256).[42] But I have also seen the other side: students' utter confusion and frustration with texts that seemingly alienate them in their difference. Achieving precisely the right balance is difficult.

Decentered methodologies also raise issues of classroom power relations, which the crossroads model begins to address but does not resolve. Multiculturalists tend to agree that rather than transmit specific content to students through a set of sacred texts, instructors should elicit students' participation in the process of creating and defining what that content will be. Most instructors of literature probably agree that we no longer expect students to find *the meaning* of a particular text, nor do we expect to impart a specific, prescribed meaning to them. Instead, we ask students to interpret and make meaning of a text, which does not mean that a text means whatever a student/reader wants it to mean but rather that we evaluate students' interpretations on their clarity, originality, insight, and rhetorical effectiveness. In this context, students are not passive recipients of traditional notions of truth and objectivity, but apprentice scholars who participate in the making of meaning.

Yet, how much power should students have in controlling the direction of the class? Should students be involved in constructing the syllabus itself (Bower 224)? William Savage claims that classroom discussion is successful only to the extent that we "find ways to empower students to set the agenda, to lead the class towards their own interests" (294), but are students' interests necessarily in their best interests from an academic and intellectual development standpoint, as well as in the best interests of the larger objectives of multicultural education? Given the resistance and apathy of many students to multicultural education, how practical is it for us to give our students so much autonomy?

Specifically, the crossroads model raises the question of how much guidance the teacher's selection of texts and crossroads texts provides to students. To what extent should students control their own reading and interpreting? I certainly envision that in upper-level courses, students might determine crossroads texts. Through their research projects, students might extend the various crossroads texts beyond those chosen by the instructor. In the lower-level courses I have taught, discussion questions (such as those provided in appendix A) guide students as they work their way through these issues. But are the questions loaded, in the sense that the "answers" to something like "La Malinche" are preordained? Is there a way to argue that it's not a crossroads text? Am I still the "teacher-expert, whose questions are designed to solicit specific answers" (Lanser 58)?

Anzaldúa's description of her "struggle as a human being" as one of "striving to balance" while "letting the see-saw take turns going down" (qtd. in Reuman 18) is an apt metaphor for the crossroads model, which must be flexible, allowing for the shifting of its "multiple selves" (Reuman 18) and striving for balance, which is not always easy to attain. It is crucial that in presenting this model for teaching texts by women of color, I do not replace one orthodoxy with another. In the end, I believe the model provides students with a set of questions, not answers. It does not claim that we can discern authorial intention and literary meaning, in any narrow sense. But it does embody the critical stance put forth by Schweickart, one that recognizes the interaction between the reader's subjectivity and the text's objectivity, that establishes a middle ground—an intersection, if you will—between the subjectivity of the reader (and a community of readers) and a text's power to shape the reader's response. In arguing that most reader-response theories are androcentric, Schweickart also claims, rightly I believe, that the theory of feminist reading she describes allows for political and social change, for it allows for resistant reading (6-7). The text is not irrelevant, but neither does it ensnare the reader in a text's objective structures.

Within the text's flexible agenda exists a great deal of ambiguity, as the borderlands metaphor suggests; in writing by women of color this often stems from the intersecting and frequently competing cultural systems at play in the text. The crossroads model embraces ambiguity and contradiction in its design, for it juxtaposes various interpretive stances even as it is guided, in part, by the text. Within this model there are multiple ways of reading, but they work in conjunction with—not in opposition to—

one another. Thus we identify in constantly shifting, varying degrees. Likewise, the model itself is perpetually shifting, changing shape as instructors modify, build from, and even transform it.

Conclusion: The Instructor at the Crossroads

The challenges posed at the crossroads of texts by women of color should not deter us from teaching them. We must acknowledge that none of us has all the answers to these sometimes daunting questions, but we must pursue them in the name of professional and ethical responsibility. As Trudy Palmer observes, "we are bound to make mistakes as we put into place the structure and goals of multicultural literacy" (221). The ambiguities come with the rejection of grand narratives and the acknowledgment that each day we are still learning about what it means to teach and exist at the intersections of race, gender, and class.

Let me return for a moment to Anzaldúa's see-saw metaphor, which is fitting for the instructor at the crossroads, particularly one who, like myself, is a cultural outsider. As Obioma Nnaemeka describes it, such a teacher "finds himself or herself situated at the congruence of different and often contradictory cultural currents. This point of convergence where the teacher stands has its privileges and rewards, but it is also fraught with danger" (306). This "ambiguous site" in which we "stand astride…our culture and other cultures" (306) is described by Nnaemeka as "standing at the crossroads of cultures" (306). I see such a space as potentially transformative, a space from which we can envision and invent the new paradigms, structures, and rubrics I have described. It is incumbent upon us to use the transformative possibilities the crossroads space provides, to cross borders as we work toward social change.

Among its many important themes, Anzaldúa's *Borderlands* is about how women of color create both individual and communal identity. Again, I see this as a fitting metaphor for the instructor at the crossroads, for each individual instructor must use the crossroads idea in his or her own way. Each teacher brings his or her own uniqueness to the crossroads space. The crossroads is available to any instructor committed to teaching texts by women of color. It can be intimidating, even scary, in this new and transformative space where important, far-reaching work can take place. But we can help one another learn from our mistakes as more and more instructors take on the challenge of teaching these texts.

4 | Teaching at the Crossroads of Genre in *The House on Mango Street* and *Storyteller*

Art is a struggle between the personal voice and language, with its apparatuses of culture and ideologies, and art mediums with their genre laws—the human voice trying to outshout a roaring waterfall.

—*Gloria Anzaldúa,* "Haciendo caras, una entrada"

In this chapter, I apply the crossroads model to two specific texts, Sandra Cisneros' *The House on Mango Street* and Leslie Marmon Silko's *Storyteller*, in order to illustrate how the model might look in practice. Specifically, I will describe ways to teach these texts at the crossroads of genre. Western generic issues—the Western *Bildungsroman* and Western autobiography, respectively—have dominated critical approaches to these texts. However, teaching at the crossroads illuminates the significance of other generic traditions to both texts.

As I explained in chapter 3, the crossroads approach is applicable to almost any feature or element of an ethnic women's text. Genre, however, is particularly germane, as it is appropriate for study in almost any given text and because it is an important site at which interpretive, critical, and cultural perspectives meet, intersect, and compete. Certainly, genre analysis helps us appreciate the ways in which form may shape the meaning of a work as well as to help readers understand the tradition(s) behind a text. But for years, literary critics dismissed texts such as slave narratives and diaries because they did not live up to the standards of canonized literary genres. Moreover, many texts by women and people of color have been similarly dismissed in their failure to meet certain generic requirements. However, contemporary critical theories have destabilized genre (along with everything else), exposing how issues of race, ethnicity, class, and gender shape genre and genre theory.

As Ralph Cohen asserts, recent theories have reconceived genres as sites of change, as "process[es] of textual change" (86-87) rather than as "fixed"

(86): "Members of a genre add, vary, modify, or abandon constituents so that the genre is modified by additional instances" (88), often for oppositional purposes. At the crossroads of texts by women of color, however, genres become not only sites of struggle—"the human voice trying to outshout a roaring waterfall" (Anzaldúa, "Haciendo" xxiv)—but of celebration of diverse cultures and traditions. By examining *Mango Street* and *Storyteller* through multiple perspectives of genre, students gain a rich appreciation of the various cultural and critical influences on these texts.

At the Crossroads of Genre: Teaching *The House on Mango Street*

Although it is a short, accessible text, *Mango Street* nevertheless embodies a complex web of intersecting and mutually informing discursive systems that may be exposed through critical literary and rhetorical analysis. Among the most prominent are generic traditions. The most dominant critical approach to *Mango Street* centers on the genre of the American *Bildungsroman*. Yet other generic traditions are at play in this text—the *corrido* tradition, the Chicana poetic tradition, and the tradition of fairy tales—so a focus on the conventional *Bildungsroman* can be limiting. Through examining the intersections of these generic perspectives of *Mango Street*, students gain greater understanding of the challenges Cisneros faces as a Chicana writer in U.S. society.

Since most students can easily relate to stories of development and since critical studies of *Mango Street* repeatedly interpret the text in this light, I like to begin classroom study of genre in *Mango Street* with the *Bildungsroman*. In this Western-based approach to *Mango Street*, students attempt to delineate the extent to which the text conforms to and resists *Bildungsroman* traditions. The *Bildungsroman*, a class- and gender-specific concept of identity formation derived in late eighteenth-century Germany, was reinvented in the United States by Benjamin Franklin's *Autobiography of Benjamin Franklin*, coinciding with the emerging national identity. The *Bildungsroman* genre met the ideological needs of the nineteenth century, reinforcing the country's sense of itself as a moral leader through the exemplary self-made individual at the center of *Autobiography*. Breaking from family and other ties, Franklin asserts the individualism at the heart of the American character, simultaneously reconciling the need for socialization and conformity. Despite the variety and breadth of the tradition, *Bildungsroman* texts do share certain characteristic patterns: the protagonist's passage from childhood through maturity and concomitant linear structure; the balancing of self-reflection and social interaction; the protagonist's spiritual crisis; the protagonist's ultimate recognition of self-identity and his/her place in the world; and the final emphasis on the ideology of individualism.

Students can read any of a number of classic American *Bildungsroman* texts, such as Franklin's *Autobiography*, Mark Twain's *The Adventures of Huckleberry Finn*, or J.D. Salinger's *The Catcher in the Rye*. Thomas Matchie argues that Cisneros' literary models include Twain's Huck Finn and Salinger's Holden Caulfield, "primarily because they are adolescents growing up in culturally oppressive worlds." He identifies "literary continuity" in Esperanza's child's language and the "paradigm of growth where a young person encounters an outside world, evaluates it in relationship to herself, and then forges an identity, something that includes her sexuality and the prominence of writing in her life." I often use William Faulkner's "Barn Burning" as a crossroads text. Alongside *Mango Street*, "Barn Burning" helps students begin to define *Bildungsroman* traditions. The final words of "Barn Burning," "He did not look back" (1565), suggest to many students (as well as scholars who have read and studied this Faulkner classic), the white, American male version of individualism and thus the white male *Bildungsroman* tradition. However, I ask students to question the story's implicit commentaries on American individualism. Though ostensibly Sarty Snopes "lights out" in the manner of Huck Finn, a "self-made" man in the making, his decision to inform DeSpain of his father's intentions may signal escape or break from his father and family in a gesture to the larger human community. Thus students come to understand that even "classic" notions of American identity can be interrogated and renegotiated. Esperanza's story differs from and intersects with Sarty's because even Faulkner, the white male "literary master," critiques the society that exploits and limits the opportunity of some of its members. "Barn Burning" represents the shameful conditions in which the Snopes family was forced to live and the systematic exploitation they faced.

As exercise 2, appendix A, illustrates, I encourage students to consider *Mango Street* in the context of "Barn Burning" and *Bildungsroman* traditions. As *Mango Street* traces the development of Esperanza Cordero from childhood through maturity, it revises *Bildungsroman* traditions, for Esperanza must contend with various cultural and discursive systems seeking to preclude her development as an autonomous woman and writer. The obstacles she endures and eventually overcomes differ in many ways from those of classic white male texts, as Esperanza's derive from the multiple oppressions of race, class, and gender. Facing poverty, discrimination, prejudice, and culturally-prescribed gender roles, Esperanza manages to define her identity as a writer and woman. However, the conflicting impulses of individualism and social responsibility in the classic *Bildungsroman* lie at the heart of *Mango Street,* for Esperanza seeks to balance her need for a space of her own and her desire to give back to her community. Cisneros' complexly-layered philosophies of individualism and collectivity, what Margot Kelley calls "the negotiations of characters and a culture 'caught in the transition' between the collective and the individual orientation" (65), can lead students to interrogate the ideological perspective she espouses in relationship to traditional American ideologies of individualism and the public good.

Unlike Sarty, who "lights out" on his own, Esperanza finds a different way to live within and beyond her community. Esperanza draws strength from her mother; family bonds of love sustain Esperanza as she questions the world around her and seeks her place within it. Even when she breaks free from the constraints of the Mango Street community, Esperanza's movement toward autonomy and agency differs in important ways from classic *Bildungsroman* stories. Esperanza's commitment to return to the Mango Street community revises *Bildungsroman* endings and the assertion of individualism as the driving force.

At the same time, *Mango Street* questions traditional American notions of progress. Esperanza must reject and reshape American cultural systems as she demythologizes culturally-defined notions of progress and the American Dream. "Barn Burning" stands in contrast—when Sarty sees DeSpain's mansion for the first time, he thinks: "Because, for all the twelve movings, they had sojourned until now in a poor country, a land of small farms and fields and houses, and he had never seen a house like this before. *Hit's big as a courthouse* he thought quietly, with a surge of peace and joy whose reason he could not have thought into words, being too young for that" (1557). Cisneros, however, critiques an American Dream that bombards young Chicano/as with its glorious images but denies them its possibilities. Esperanza's dream of a house outside the barrio derives from cultural definitions of progress, "the house Papa talked about when he held a lottery ticket and...the house Mama dreamed up in the stories she told us before we went to bed" (4). The house on Mango Street, however, "isn't it" (5), and Esperanza's response to her parents' declarations that this house is just temporary—"But I know how those things go" (5)—suggests the failure of the American Dream for Chicanos in the barrio and undercuts the ideology of mobility-as-progress: "We didn't always live on Mango Street. Before that we lived on Loomis on the third floor, and before that we lived on Keeler. Before Keeler it was Paulina, and before that I can't remember. But what I remember most is moving a lot" (3). The family "had to leave the flat on Loomis quick"(4) because of its dilapidation, ending up in the house on Mango Street. Moreover, Esperanza's "laugh out loud" about the mayor's failure to "make [Mango Street] better" suggests the failure of the democratic process for Chicanos in the barrio (107). But Esperanza's developing social consciousness may suggest a new role for individuals in a democracy.

Cisneros' critique of the ideologies and practices inherent in the white male *Bildungsroman* is undeniable. But its richness compels readings beyond those based in Western or American cultural and literary systems. Thus I include Tomás Rivera's *...y no se lo tragó la tierra (...And the Earth Did Not Devour Him),* the most canonized Chicano story of growing up, at the crossroads of *Mango Street.*

Many critics point to the intertextual relationships between *Mango Street* and *...y no se lo tragó la tierra,* particularly the manner by which they assert certain Chicano values. Engaged in the political and resistant tradition of Chicano literature, both works challenge the individualist ideology of capitalism by exposing its dark side: child laborers and families denied basic human needs. The commonplace "we can achieve if we try hard and work hard" may not work for those who confront socioeconomic and political forces beyond their control. *Mango Street* and *...y no se lo tragó la tierra* root the individual self in the Chicano community. Cisneros' house motif unravels rather than reinscribes the individualist, material orientation of the American Dream, as she uses the house to represent unrealized basic human needs as a result of poverty, hate, and oppression. Similarly, *...y no se lo tragó la tierra* emphasizes collective values, as the protagonist shares his textual space with a rich interplay of Chicano voices, from the migrant workers on the broken-down bus to the children who died in a fire while their parents were in the fields. Exercise 3 illustrates how I use group work and writing assignments to encourage students to examine the intertextual relationships between *Mango Street* and *...y no se lo tragó la tierra,* especially both texts' critique of the rugged individualism of "Barn Burning."

From here, the class moves to the women's *Bildungsroman* tradition, which includes such literary forebears as Charlotte Perkins Gilman's "The Yellow Wallpaper" and Kate Chopin's *The Awakening.* This mainstream feminist critical approach to genre points to how *Mango Street* interrogates and re-visions patriarchal practices and hegemonies that repress Chicanas while simultaneously reinforcing the conventions of the female form of the genre.

Many feminist critics point out how women writers of the *Bildungsroman* subvert male patterns, adapting the genre to women's concerns. While the male protagonist typically breaks from the father and family in a linear development process, the female's journey is often circular, worked out in terms of family and communal relationships (see Matchie). Furthermore, female versions of the *Bildungsroman* have historically underscored the heroine's lack of autonomy and self-determination, "consigning her to either a conventional marriage or death" (Midalia 90).[43] As a result, women's journeys in these texts tend to be nonlinear, interrupted by the difficulties of growth. Images and language of entrapment pervade these texts, suggesting that women's breaks are more difficult due to prescribed gender roles.

While postmodernism has seen the demise of the white male *Bildungsroman*, revised forms of the genre have been widely used by white women, men and women writers of color, and other disenfranchised groups who use it to "express...their struggle for individuation and a part in the American dream, which society simultaneously proffers and denies to them" (Braendlin 75). Postmodernism's destabilization of the coherent Self is countered by women's striving for a self-consciousness—however contingent—in a society which continues to deny female identity as equal to male. Defying postmodernist malaise and meaninglessness, including language's inability to order chaos, these writers—including Cisneros—equate writing/language with power: to name, to exist, to thrive. To occupy the language of the oppressor is to cast a victory; Cisneros subverts both language and genre to reshape cultural myths that dehumanize and marginalize Chicanas.

At the crossroads of genre, then, it is important to introduce students to some of the most influential female *Bildungsroman* stories to begin to identify some of the patterns common to that genre, such as circular structure and a typical ending of death or marriage. Chopin's *The Awakening* serves this purpose, and exercise 4 demonstrates how I encourage students to examine *The Awakening*'s major themes before we consider it in relationship to *Mango Street. The Awakening* involves the story of Edna Pontellier's spiritual and sexual awakening, as she "begin[s] to realize her position in the universe as a human being, and to recognize her relations as an individual to the world within and about her" (14). Searching for self-definition in a time when women are defined largely in terms of domestic roles, Edna cannot easily reconcile how to balance her responsibilities to her sons and to herself. Not a "mother-woman" (9), Edna is constrained by the conventions of her society, particularly with respect to gender limitations. Thus her awakening is shadowed by images of darkness and death: "An indescribable oppression, which seemed to generate in some unfamiliar part of her consciousness, filled her whole being with a vague anguish. It was like a shadow, like a mist passing across her soul's summer day" (8).

Similar images of confinement abound in *Mango Street;* Esperanza describes herself as a "balloon tied to an anchor" (9), and Esperanza's great-grandmother and her place by the window symbolize female oppression:

> She looked out the window her whole life, the way so many women sit their sadness on an elbow. I wonder if she made the best with what she got or was she sorry because she couldn't be all the things she wanted to be. Esperanza. I have inherited her name, but I don't want to inherit her place by the window. (11)

This image of women confined and sitting by the window recurs throughout the text. Mamacita, one of the women on Mango Street, "sits all day by the window" and "won't come down," dreaming of her life in Mexico (77). The windows on Esperanza's house are "so small you'd think they were holding their breath" (4) and had "wooden bars Papa had nailed on…so [the children] wouldn't fall out" (5). They protect (thereby reinforcing some of the justifications for women's prescribed roles in Chicano culture), yet also confine.

But the place by the window in *Mango Street* also suggests the possibility of freedom, particularly of the imagination. Esperanza wonders whether Sally shares her dream of a "nice" house with "big windows" that "would swing open" and "all the sky would come in" (82-83). But when Sally marries, her husband "doesn't let her look out the window" (102), and she is no longer free to imagine. But Esperanza grabs hold of this freedom to imagine and, as she matures, she breaks from traditional values that relegate women to subservient roles, even while she affirms a collective consciousness and solidarity. Unlike Edna, who commits suicide, Esperanza breaks from the traditional tragic endings of women's *Bildungsroman* stories, the circularity of her text suggesting communal commitment rather than futility. Resisting Western notions of individualism and the individual self, Esperanza leaves her community so that she can gain the power she needs to transform it upon her return. Her individuality and autonomy are rooted in the collective, communal good. In the second-to-last vignette, "A House of My Own," Esperanza's vision remains egocentric: "A house all my own. With my porch and my pillow, my pretty purple petunias. My books and my stories" (108). But in the final section, as Esperanza envisions her departure from Mango Street, her vision broadens and the stories "inside [her] head" (109) become communal: "They will not know I have gone away to come back. For the ones I left behind. For the ones who cannot out" (110). Her "break," therefore, will never be absolute.

Mainstream feminist critique also underscores how *Mango Street*'s intertextuality with the traditional Western fairy tale challenges the objectification of women in popular culture's construction of the perfect, desirable woman. Esperanza contrasts fairy tale romances with the lives of women around her as a way to to deconstruct their power and envision another way to live. Recurring throughout the text, the "Cinderella" myth takes on a dark side; in "The Family of Little Feet," for example, Cisneros subverts the popular tale's focus on Cinderella's dainty feet. In these popular renderings of "Cinderella," it is Cinderella's feet, as they slide gracefully into the glass slippers, that win her the Prince. In Cisneros' text, sexuality is threatening: "Bum man says, Yes, little girl. Your little lemon shoes are so beautiful. But come closer. I can't see very well. Come closer. Please" (41). In "Chanclas," her shoes embarrass Esperanza—"my feet scuffed and round, and the heels all crooked that look dumb with this dress...my feet are ugly" (47). The child Esperanza has internalized the messages of female beauty and worth inscribed in these mythologies, but the developing woman and writer will shed them: "They all lied. All the books and magazines, everything that told it wrong" (100). Esperanza comes to realize that the imprisonment implied in these tales and the lives of the women around her is not the destiny she wants for herself.

Exercise 5 examines *Mango Street* through the lens of traditional fairy tales and Cisneros' renderings of them. In this unit of the course, I introduce students to a broad overview of feminist criticism, moving them from its earliest stages of recovery and reevaluation and the identification of literary traditions (such as the female *Bildungsroman*) through its current emphasis on difference. I use Adrienne Rich's widely cited "When We Dead Awaken: Writing as Re-vision" as a springboard from which students can interrogate Cisneros' re-visioning of traditional fairy tales in *Mango Street*. Additionally, I bring to our discussion feminist critiques of fairy tales, such as Madonna Kolbenschlag's "A Feminist's View of 'Cinderella.'" Finally, students bring these components together in writing assignments that ask them to consider *Mango Street* in relationship to contemporary Cinderella stories, such as Disney's recent "multicultural" film version, starring Brandy.

However, because race and class intersect with gender, Esperanza's revisioning does not only center on white culture's construction of the ideal woman. Esperanza must also break Chicano cultural codes about women's roles as she refuses to accept gender-determined limitations. Thus Cisneros critiques Chicano constraints on Chicana identity and agency; Esperanza must free herself from Chicano patriarchal structures that "don't like their women strong" (Cisneros 10). It is at this point that I introduce the class to the simultaneous critique of both white oppression and Chicano patriarchal attitudes, a common feature of Chicana writing.

Since the intersecting forces of race and class on gendered lives complicate feminist critique, I use this opportunity to circle back to *...y no se lo tragó la tierra* through a Chicana feminist lens. Cisneros wields her critique at the gender limitations which are implicit in Rivera's text. As many scholars have noted, the women in *...y no se lo tragó la tierra* tend to be passive, even "crazy." While the males make some attempt to overcome their hardships (as in "The Portrait"), the women, many of whom are devout Catholics, seem to passively accept their circumstances. Most of the women remain submissive, leading these scholars to observe that Rivera's critique of white oppression is tainted by Chicano patriarchy. Arguably, even Rivera's male protagonist reinforces the status quo, apparently unwilling to subvert the system he's been recalling. In the final scene of the text, the boy heads back home, realizing he "hadn't lost anything" but instead "had made a discovery" (152). What he has discovered, according to Raymund Paredes, is that "the gift of life, even in the harshest circumstances, is to be profoundly cherished" (1107). Cisneros rebukes such passivity by creating a protagonist committed to helping her community break the bounds of white oppression, extending her critique beyond Chicano patriarchal oppression to the hegemonic structures that reinscribe poverty, exploitation, and oppression. Exercise 6 encourages students to examine the extent to which the passivity of Rivera's protagonist reinforces the values of the dominant culture, particularly those supporting patriarchy, and to what extent Cisneros critiques Rivera's text.

To underscore the significance of these kinds of critiques in Chicana discourse, I turn from the *Bildungsroman* to the intersections of the Chicano *corrido* tradition and Chicana feminist practice. The *corrido*, a narrative poem used in response to Anglo American encroachment into the South Texas valley in the latter half of the nineteenth century, has deeply influenced Chicano literature. These heroic songs about social resistors, beginning with the "master narrative," "*El Corrido de Gregorio Cortez*" ("The Ballad of Gregorio Cortez"), are rooted in patriarchal tradition. In the classroom, I use both "*El Corrido de Gregorio Cortez*" and Lorna Dee Cervantes' poem "Visions of Mexico While at a Writing Symposium in Port Townsend, Washington" to depict how Chicana poets appropriate and dissolve these male narratives into their writing by "seiz[ing] the narrative voice back, to subvert the homogenizing and dominant male narrative by claiming control of the narrative herself" (McKenna 195).

"*El Corrido de Gregorio Cortez*" relates the story of Gregorio Cortez, accused by a white sheriff of horse stealing. Unable to understand English, Cortez becomes involved in an altercation with the sheriff that ends up wounding Cortez's brother and killing the sheriff. Cortez flees across Texas but gives himself up at the Mexican border because of reprisals against his family. Américo Paredes' influential study of the Cortez *corrido, With His Pistol in His Hand: A Border Ballad and Its Hero*, analyzes how the ballad and the legend have created the hero and, how, in a cyclical fashion, they keep one another alive as a central facet of Mexican American cultural identity. It is a song of resistance and pride:

> Then said Gregorio Cortez,
> With his pistol in his hand,
> 'Ah, so many mounted Rangers
> Just to take one Mexican!' *("El Corrido")*

Many Chicana feminist critics view the *corrido* tradition as exclusionary of women. In "Visions of Mexico," Cervantes finds agency not in Mexico or male-constructed political borders, but by re-visioning Cortez's pistol with her pen and creating a space for a more complex subjectivity that does not ignore gender (McKenna 203). For the speaker of the poem, both the "land" (l. 22) and the "chant of an epic corrido" (l. 23) "ripple through [her] veins" (l. 22). Coming from a "long line of eloquent illiterates" (l. 24) whose anger is "an utterance more pure than word" (l. 27), the speaker will "steal" words (l. 62) and "gather [her] feathers/for quills" (l. 66-67).

The class then circles back to *Mango Street*'s intertextual relationships with the *corrido* tradition against the backdrop of Chicana poetry's resistant and revisionist stance, as exercise 7 illustrates. Like Cervantes, Esperanza will resist with her pen, committing herself through her writing to the communal good, even though Chicana writers face enormous obstacles, as Elena Poniatowska, one of Mexico's best known women writers, explains: "To be a Chicano is not easy, but to be a Chicana is even harder. To be a writer in Mexico is not easy, but to be a woman writer sometimes makes no sense at all. A Chicana writer in the United States gets the worst of both conditions: being a woman and a Chicana aspiring to become a writer" (43). But Esperanza fights her "own quiet war" (Cisneros 89) through education and writing, for she looks to positive female models who promote her interest in writing to resist the images and influence of those victimized and subjugated. In *Mango Street*, Esperanza's mother tells her, "I could've been somebody" (90), while urging Esperanza to "take care all your own" (91). It is Aunt Lupe who listens to her stories and poems and tells Esperanza to "just remember to keep writing" for "it will keep [her] free" (61). Alicia "is young and smart and studies" at a university "because she doesn't want to spend her whole life in a factory or behind a rolling pin" (31-32). Esperanza's literary voice emerges through her individual and collective experience, and the self-empowerment that results is also communal and individualized. She is like the four strong elm trees outside her window—"four who reach and do not forget to reach" (75) but require one another for sustenance: "Let one forget his reason for being, they'd all droop like tulips in a glass, each with their arms around the other" (74-75). Her writing enables her to pass down her power to alter Chicanas' lives.

Carmen Del Rio asserts that contemporary Chicana writers, especially poets, celebrate the mother/daughter bond and then extend it to all women, acknowledging the central role that bonds among women play in their lives (441-44). Where she once thinks, "There is nothing *I* can do" (Cisneros 85) to help Minerva escape the vicious cycle of abuse from her husband, finally Esperanza's dreams of "[her] own house" take on a collective nature: "But I won't forget who I am or where I came from. Passing bums will ask, Can I come in? I'll offer them the attic, ask them to stay, because I know how it is to be without a house" (87). Esperanza will return to tell their stories. As Jacqueline Doyle suggests, Cisneros breaks from traditional women's paradigms when, "through naming herself and her community, Esperanza returns both to accept and to alter her inheritance" with "her most conspicuous alliances" being "ethnic and local" (21). Reconstructing Virginia Woolf's "room of one's own," according to Doyle, Esperanza's "house of my own" simultaneously represents an "escape from the barrio, a rejection of the domestic drudgery of 'home'" and "a solitary space for her creativity, and a communal expression of women's lives" (22). She has learned the power of her imagination to transcend difficult circumstances both for herself and those around her.

In class, we continue with Chicanas' appropriation of Chicano patriarchal discourse through other Chicana poetic traditions. Yvonne Yarbro-Bejarano explains the often-innovative formal and linguistic qualities of much Chicana writing as "the search…for a language that consciously opposes the dominant culture" (142), for the Chicana feminist writer connects her writing to "the political situation of all Chicanas" (139).[44] Excluded from "literary authority," many Chicana writers appropriate this authority from their own cultural traditions, including oral storytelling, which "challeng[e] the dominant male concepts of cultural ownership and literary authority" and "reject the dominant culture's definition of what a Chicana is" (141). As they "derive literary authority from the oral tradition of their communities," Yarbro-Bejarano argues, many Chicanas in turn "commit their stories to writing" (141).

To emphasize these cultural traditions, I turn to the reconstruction of La Malinche in Carmen Tafolla's "La Malinche" and Rodolfo Gonzáles' *I Am Joaquín/Yo Soy Joaquín*. I begin the unit with background information about La Malinche's historical significance and cultural meaning. La Malinche, an Aztec woman who was Hernán Cortés' interpreter, translator, and mistress during the Spanish conquest of the Aztec empire in the sixteenth century, has been traditionally viewed as the quintessential symbol of betrayal in Mexican popular mythology. In the Chicano Movement of the 1960s, Chicanos appropriated the term *"malinche"* to apply to Chicanas who married Anglo men, who sought higher education, and who allied themselves with feminism (Pratt, "Yo Soy" 175).

In response, many Chicana writers have resymbolized La Malinche to explore the conflicting relationship between struggles for gender equality and struggles for racial equality that permeate contemporary Chicano criticism. These contemporary Chicana writers have remade her into a symbol of victimization—as opposed to collaboration—and thus resistance (175). Tafolla's poem "La Malinche," which begins with the line "Yo soy la Malinche," rewrites Malinche's story while simultaneously responding to Gonzáles' classic Chicano text, which asserted a masculinist nationalism, relegated Chicanas to secondary roles as supporters of men, and ascribed to women a passive role as the object of men's sexual gratification (see Del Rio). The strong assertion of identity and pride in this epic poem is rooted in Mexican heritage as well as through a description of Chicano heroes—Pancho Villa, Joaquín Murrieta, Alfego Baca, and the Espinoza brothers. Linking these heroes to the leaders of the Chicano Movement and to a sense of the past, Gonzáles exhorts the leaders and followers of the Chicano Movement to resist assimilation and assert ethnic pride in the face of oppression:

> Here I stand
> Poor in money
> Arrogant with pride
> Bold with Machismo
> Rich in courage
> and
> Wealthy in spirit and faith. (15) …
> And now the trumpet sounds,
> The music of the people stirs the
> Revolution,
> Like a sleeping giant it slowly
> rears its head (19) …

I am the masses of my people and
I refuse to be absorbed.
I am Joaquín (20)

In her assertion of Chicana feminist agency, Tafolla combines Chicana identity, Chicana feminism, and nationalism. Tafolla re-visions Malinche to retrieve her sense of agency, to disassociate herself with betrayal, and to pass her vision to her Chicana sisters:

But Chingada I was not.
Not tricked, not screwed, not traitor.
For I was not traitor to myself—
I saw a dream
and I *reached* it. (Tafolla, l. 50-54)

Students connect *Mango Street* to "La Malinche" and *I Am Joaquín/Yo Soy Joaquín* through assignments such as that described in exercise 8. Like the Malinche of Tafolla's poem, Esperanza refuses to be passive and instead, like the four elm trees, reaches for new possibilities and new visions. Moreover, she rejects the notion of herself as a traitor. Del Rio asserts that the Chicano male has sought to "keep [the Chicana] silent and passive when it comes to any criticism of the Chicano and his sexual oppression of her" (432), so to speak out, then, risks a "double marginalization," an "exile" from both the Chicano and dominant culture (433). Esperanza, like her creator, Cisneros, refuses to remain silent about Chicano patriarchal oppression and how it constrains women's lives.

However, Cisneros does not superfluously critique Chicano males. Indeed, she displays a simultaneous empathy for Chicano males, who are also oppressed and victimized by the dominant culture. In exercise 9, I include an assignment in which students are asked to think about the stereotypes they hold of Chicanos and then consider how Cisneros works to dispel them. Cisneros' depiction of Esperanza's father and their deep love is probably the most compelling example. The vignette "Papa Who Wakes Up Tired in the Dark" is a moving tribute to a father's humanity: "And I think if my own Papa died what would I do. I hold my Papa in my arms. I hold and hold and hold him" (57). Cisneros also unravels stereotypes of poor Chicano males, particularly when Esperanza reflects on the "stupid people" who fear the men in her neighborhood: "We know the guy with the crooked eye is Davey the Baby's brother, and the tall one next to him in the straw brim, that's Rosa's Eddie V. and the big one that looks like a dumb grown man, he's Fat Boy, though he's not fat anymore nor a boy" (28). Clearly, however, Cisneros does not idealize the men around her, as the vignette "There Was an Old Woman She Had So Many

Children She Didn't Know What to Do" illustrates. Rosa Vargas' "bad" kids, abandoned by their father, are spinning out of control—"without respect for all living things, including themselves"(29)— and are likely to continue the cycle of neglect and abuse they have endured.

Teaching *Mango Street* at the crossroads of genre thus brings together, in mutually illuminating ways, the four dominant critical approaches to texts by women of color. Exercise 10 illustrates how I ask students to reflect on their experiences with the text. From Western notions of the *Bildungsroman* and specific texts like "Barn Burning," students can see the extent to which Cisneros is schooled in the American canon and manipulates it for her own purposes. But clearly *Mango Street* is not this simple, encompassing, as it does, the important, transformative space that allows both Esperanza and Cisneros to go beyond Western constraints on Chicana writing and identity. Thus women's *Bildungsroman* traditions such as *The Awakening* and the quintessential Chicano *Bildungsroman ...y no se lo tragó la tierra* broaden students' perspectives as they examine *Mango Street* beyond the bounds of white male paradigms. The Chicano *corrido* tradition and traditional Western fairy tales further broaden students' understanding. Finally, *Mango Street* must also be interpreted through a Chicana feminist lens, from Chicana poetic traditions that revision "*El Corrido de Gregorio Cortez*" to the appropriation of La Malinche. At the crossroads of genre, *Mango Street* becomes a complexly layered work of art that explores the political dimensions of personal experiences and emphasizes Chicanas' agency without situating them only as victims of white or Chicano oppression.

At the Crossroads of Genre: Teaching *Storyteller*

Teaching Leslie Marmon Silko's *Storyteller* presents a number of dynamic critical and pedagogical opportunities. A hybrid text composed of poetry, prose, photographs, and oral tales, *Storyteller* challenges the ways we have been taught to read literary texts. Consequently, much of the critical scholarship on *Storyteller* gravitates toward the familiar: examining the text in the context of the American autobiographical tradition, a tradition defined by privileged white males who tend to be known for their public achievements, including, among others, John Adams, Henry James, Mark Twain, Benjamin Franklin, Jonathan Edwards, Walt Whitman, and Henry David Thoreau. Such a narrow definition essentially eliminated women writers and men of color from the autobiographical canon. It is certainly reasonable and illuminating to read *Storyteller* against the backdrop of canonical autobiography, but it is also limiting. By focusing solely on

Western considerations of *Storyteller*, we reduce this work to a comparison with traditional critical categories and fail to broaden our notion of literary value. As Jennifer Browdy de Hernández writes, "the contemporary Native American autobiographer must grapple with complex relationships of tribal culture and mainstream culture, which interact representationally in such a way as to leave neither culture unchanged" ("Writing" 56-57). By teaching *Storyteller* at the crossroads of genre, we transform ourselves (as readers and teachers), our pedagogy, and our students' understanding of the text.

Western-based autobiographical readings of *Storyteller* tend to focus on the autobiographical subject: the extent to which she exists as the center of the text, whether she ultimately achieves a sense of identity, and, finally, the nature of that identity. To reinforce the weight of the autobiographical tradition within and against which Silko interacts, I bring Western canonical texts such as Franklin's *The Autobiography of Benjamin Franklin* to the classroom. Exercise 11 includes discussion questions designed to stimulate comparisons between *Autobiography* and *Storyteller*. Intricately connected with our nation's emerging identity, Franklin's work embodies and resolves the conflicting impulses of the individual's desire for autonomy and independence with the need for socialization and conformity that we see, in different forms, in *Storyteller*. How Silko works from and resists the ideologies inherent in Franklin's autobiography complicates students' understanding of Silko's autobiographical identity.

From our study of *Autobiography* we move to a study of the autobiographical subject in *Storyteller*. Exercise 12 includes assignments that ask students to consider whether this text is an autobiography, according to the tradition represented by Franklin's text. First, is there an autobiographical subject? Silko does not begin *Storyteller* with recollections of her birth or early childhood, as is customary in Western autobiographies (Krupat, *Voice* 163). Indeed, the first two sentences of *Storyteller* occur in the third person, perhaps a deliberate attempt to divert the focus from herself: "There is a tall Hopi basket with a single figure/woven into it which might be a Grasshopper or/a Hummingbird Man. Inside the basket are hundreds/of photographs taken since the 1890's around Laguna" (Silko 1). Not until the third sentence does the narration switch to first person, when Silko writes "My grandpa Hank" and "my father" (1). Arguably, from the outset, Silko attempts to divert attention from the individual autobiographical subject, and the book itself embraces a more collectivist viewpoint.

However, we can reasonably suggest that Silko adopts an autobiographical stance in the role of storyteller. She begins *Storyteller* by describing a Hopi basket filled with photographs. In the third stanza of the opening section, the narrator tells of the interconnectedness of stories she remembers and the photographs in that basket, and she claims ownership: "It wasn't until I began this book" (1). Even in the parts of *Storyteller* that seem nonautobiographical, Silko nevertheless appears at times, however indirectly. The italicized lines within the verse stories, as in the example below, conceivably constitute her instructions to the reader, her voice filling in context:

> Once there was a young Laguna girl
> who was a fine hunter
> who hunted deer and rabbits
> just like the boys and the men did.
> *You know there have been laguna women*
> *who were good hunters*
> *who could hunt as well as any of the men.* (82)

Here, Silko the storyteller asserts her identity as a writer of cultural and familial narratives, intervening to educate the reader about women's roles as hunters in Laguna culture.

Next, my students consider *Storyteller*'s structure, since Western-based interpretations of *Storyteller* as autobiography also point to its nonlinear, fragmented structure as a challenge to the genre, which tends to be linear and unified in the autobiographical subject's movement toward self-discovery. From a Western perspective, *Storyteller* seems like a pastiche of disparate ideas and voices rather than the story of an individual narrator. It includes a variety of narrative styles, from oral storytelling to verse, prose, and photographs. Exercise 13 includes a series of questions that ask students to consider the structural development of *Storyteller* and the autobiographical subject, particularly in relation to Franklin's *Autobiography*. Arguably, Silko defies traditional autobiographies about artists by failing to demonstrate a "developmental or evolutionary dimension" to her choice of becoming an artist (Krupat, *Voice* 164). However, we can trace Silko's development by studying those chapters that do explicitly relate to Silko's personal life. In so doing, one can detect a discernible movement toward an acceptance and understanding of the narrator's role as a writer-storyteller. In "I always called her Aunt Susie," the second entry in *Storyteller*, Silko portrays Aunt Susie as a kind of mentor, someone to listen "to all [her] questions and speculations" (4). Aunt Susie "had come to believe very much in books/and in schooling," but, unable to write because of poor eyesight, passed on her stories orally (6); the narrator tells the "small part" she "remembers," in some sense translating her aunt's voice into her writing: "I write when I still hear/her voice as she tells the story" (7). In a reprinted letter in *Storyteller* dated 1975 discussing the stories "they" told her, Silko writes, "But I understand now," how they spoke of landscapes she knew only as "dry and covered with tumbleweeds," but which she can now pass on to her own grandchildren so that they too can have visions of the land the way it used to be: "the fields of wild asters and all the little toads that sang in the evening" (170). This moment of recognition of herself as a storyteller comes in the middle rather than the end of the text, opposing the linear development of the Western autobiography. But a developmental process exists nevertheless in the backtracking and alternate perspectives provided through the non-autobiographical passages and the photographs that add to its complexity.

Next, the class moves from considering the autobiographical subject's developmental process to the nature of her identity as writer-storyteller. Krupat suggests that *Storyteller*'s title announces the familiar Western pattern of "discovering who one is by discovering what one does, the pattern of identity in vocation" ("Dialogic" 59). However, he distinguishes *Storyteller* from Western autobiographies because in Pueblo culture the vocational storyteller has an important function that the Western storyteller lacks: "to be known as a storyteller is to be known as one who participates, in a communally sanctioned manner, in sustaining the group" (59). Thus we turn next to the oral tradition and a consideration of the traditional role of the artist in tribal society in maintaining the link between symbols and social processes, a role that "many Native American writers continue to assume" (Jahner 8), and one which might help explain Silko's role as storyteller. Oral tradition has played a crucial role in sustaining Native American culture. The autobiographical narrator and other characters in *Storyteller* hold on to their heritage while being pulled toward the dominant culture, by force, necessity, choice, or some combination of these. Ultimately, the role Silko adopts as both writer and storyteller may constitute her small part in sustaining tribal values:

The storyteller keeps the stories
all the escape stories
she says "With these stories of ours
we can escape almost anything
with these stories we will survive."
(247)

To enrich students' understanding of this possible interpretation of Silko-as-storyteller, I use texts that emphasize the artist's role in tribal culture. Appropriate crossroads texts include Linda Hogan's autobiographical essay "The Two Lives," which explains role of the poet-storyteller as cultural/historical: "Telling our lives is important, for those who come after us, for those who will see our experience as part of their own historical struggle. I think of my work as part of the history of our tribe and as part of the history of colonization everywhere" (233). Another essay, Diane Glancy's "Two Dresses," stresses the role of the artist in contemporary tribal culture: "Poetry is a ghost dance in which one world seeks the other. Though the two worlds are opposed, they long to be united. Poetry is a road, a highway" (172). Bridging two worlds, poetry also provides "a sense of self as whole even though fragmented. It gives voice" (170).

Exercise 14 illustrates a series of questions for students as they explore Silko's connection to the cultural tradition of Native American artists in two poems and an essay by Simon Ortiz. The poem "My Father's Song" underscores the need to pass down stories through the generations, while "The Poems I Have Lost" stresses the relevance of old stories in making sense of one's world, especially in the face of loss and fragmentation. Ortiz's essay, "The Language We Know," tells of the "unspoken vow" (191) of the storyteller to use language to resist injustice. Clearly, Silko's role as storyteller continues an important cultural tradition that carries with it a larger cultural purpose, as Ortiz's works suggest.

Ortiz's emphasis on the collective leads us to reconsider *Storyteller*'s autobiographical subject's rejection of an individualistic stance through the context of Native values of collectivism rather than individualism. Krupat argues that the Native American notion of the self is best understood as existing "only in relation to the coherent and bounded whole of which [it is] a part" ("Native" 174).[45] As opposed to the monologic models of the self offered in Western autobiographies, predominant Native models of the self are dialogic, Krupat suggests, achieved through "particular placement in relation to the many voices without which it could not exist" (*Voice* 133). In the introduction to their collection of autobiographical essays by American Indians, Brian Swann and Krupat describe the difficulty faced by the writers they asked to contribute to the collection, citing one contributor who stated, "You should realize that focusing so intently on oneself like that and blithering on about your own life and thoughts is very bad form for Indians" (qtd. in Swann and Krupat, Introduction xii). To emphasize the role of collectivist worldview in Native American autobiography, I turn to the oral tradition and other forms of preliterate autobiography. Hertha Wong identifies the earliest Native American autobiographical forms, a body of work she calls "communo-bio-oratory" (22). These preliterate autobiographical forms, including naming rituals, stories that continually update an individual's life through recurrent naming, and the coup story, a personal narrative of male deeds of bravery, inform the broader Native American autobiographical tradition, despite the fact that most of these early forms were performed by men. Although related to individual achievement, these stories remained incomplete until tribal members "share[d] in the creation of a new self-image and a new personal narrative for the one counting coups" (24). They inform an understanding of *Storyteller* because the audience's participation in meaning-making and the flexible nature of individual identity may be important lines of influence. Native American autobiography comprises "intra-cultural collaboration" because the tribe contributes both passively (through transmission of codes and expectations) and actively "by joining in the storytelling, singing, and dancing, thereby accepting, affirming, and exalting the individual/tribal identity" (20). Even singular male narratives of bravery expressed artistically—painted on garments, tipis, or shields—were done collaboratively. We see this thread carried on in *Storyteller*, where Silko roots her identity in family, community, and culture. Preliterate forms of autobiography can be included in the classroom through Web sources as well as books or through research assignments, as exercise 15 illustrates.[46]

From preliterate autobiographical forms we move to the tradition of *written* Native American autobiography, which also underscores the collective nature of tribal culture while simultaneously illustrating how Silko, as a contemporary writer, has different concerns as well. These written texts emerged in the nineteenth century as a result of contact with white colonizers. The function and production of Native American autobiographies cause them to be bicultural and composite, sharing certain characteristics with *Storyteller*. Among these characteristics is a representation of the self as neither prioritized nor valorized, reflecting Native culture's general deemphasis on individuality and self-assertion. Nineteenth-century autobiographies establish the collective humanity of Indians for a white audience that perceives them as less than human.

Two nineteeth-century Native American written autobiographies, William Apess' *A Son of the Forest: The Experience of William Apess, a Native of the Forest* (1829) and George Copway's *The Life, Letters, and Speeches* (1850), work well at the crossroads.[47] Exercise 16 includes a series of discussion questions through which students can examine *Storyteller* in light of these nineteenth-century works. Apess attempts to establish his authenticity through his devotion to God and through his ancestry while, in a different time and place, Silko interrogates the issue of authenticity itself. Apess' text chronicles white injustices toward Indians, but his is less a story of personal identity than one of spiritual salvation. Copway's autobiographical narrative resembles *Storyteller* in terms of its mixed form, blending the oral storytelling tradition with historical and personal narratives. But like Apess, Copway finds it necessary to establish his authority and his educated status for his white readership, thus including literary quotations, speeches, and published letters. As in *Storyteller*, the autobiographical subject in *Life, Letters, and Speeches* seeks a balancing role to mediate between white and Indian culture, casting himself as the "embodiment of both the noble virtues from the savage past and the Western European culture from the civilized present" (Ruoff 256). Both writers confront the challenges of writing to a white audience while attempting to preserve tribal values, though students can interrogate their assimilative tendencies. Although both Copway and Silko seek to affirm the humanity of Native Americans in the face of white hatred and oppression, they take different paths—culturally and rhetorically—determined in large part by their historical circumstances.

Next, we examine contemporary Native American autobiographies, such as Jim Barnes' "On Native Ground" and Joy Harjo's "Ordinary Spirit," both short accessible pieces in Swann's and Krupat's *I Tell You Now*. Like Silko, these writers trace materials from the past in an effort to heal the pain of loss, both personally and culturally. Barnes' essay catalogues the "scars of loss" (87): the land, home, and Indian languages. For Barnes, poetry is "affirmation" of loss (94). Harjo describes how, in the midst of writing, "the world gives way" and her grandfather, an "old, old Creek," stands before her: "I tell him that it is writing these words down, and entering the world through the structure they make, that has allowed me to see him more clearly, and to speak. And he answers that maybe his prayers, songs, and his belief in them has allowed him to create me" (266). The questions in exercise 17 encourage students to look at the thematic interconnections between *Storyteller* and these contemporary Native American autobiographies that likewise emphasize collective values and the role of writing/storytelling in contemporary contexts.

Of course, Harjo's essay leads us to a consideration of feminist and Native American feminist perspectives in interpreting *Storyteller*. I remind students of our experiences reading Franklin's *Autobiography*, pointing out Nancy Walker's observation that Ben Franklin assumed himself as a role model for other men, not women (240). Thus we turn to mainstream feminist readings of *Storyteller*, locating the text in a women's tradition of autobiography and a challenge to patriarchal values and systems of dominance.

I begin with background information on women's autobiographical traditions through Estelle Jelínek's landmark study of autobiography, *Women's Autobiography: Essays in Criticism* (1980), which centers on the exclusion of women from canonical autobiography. As one of the earliest studies of women's autobiography, Jelínek's analysis focuses primarily on the influence of gender on the autobiographical self, ignoring race, ethnicity, class, sexuality, geography, and political location. Because critical theories of autobiography have generally connected value with significant historical events from which women have largely been excluded, Jelinek focuses on the social bias inherent in evaluating women's life stories. He asserts that women's autobiographies "may constitute, if not a subgenre, then an autobiographical tradition different from the male tradition" as they challenge traditional aesthetic criteria (Introduction 6).

To emphasize the revisionist nature of *Storyteller*'s generic conventions, I assign excerpts from articles by Linda Danielson, who argues that Silko engages in the kind of re-visioning of the white literary establishment's notion of literature and the canon that pervades feminist criticism, appropriating canonical conventions and forms for her own purposes: "in effacing her own authorship, crediting the community, mixing once-sacrosanct genres, and abjuring linear structure—in short, by denying the standards and customs of white male-dominated literary criticism—Silko reclaims the making of books from the white male critical establishment" ("Grandmother Spider's Web" 330). Jelínek points out that the linearity and wholeness of men's autobiographies reflect the linearity of their lives toward a goal of success, while women's texts are irregular, fragmentary, and disconnected, representing how women's prescribed domestic roles have precluded similar definitions of success (Introduction 17). A more recent study by Janice Morgan also notes that those features of modern and postmodern male-authored texts that are representative of self-consciousness —fragmentation, discontinuity, and duality—are not new in women's writing or in women's autobiography but have existed all along as "alternate and, to some extent, oppositional strategies of self-representation" (7).

In the classroom, I use excerpts from Gertrude Stein's *The Autobiography of Alice B. Toklas* to illustrate this common feature of women's autobiography. Stein's text exhibits the discontinuous, fragmentary, and nonchronological nature of women's autobiographical texts, comprised largely of anecdotal portraits of her artist friends that she provides piecemeal throughout the narrative. Moreover, Stein's text is also nonchronological within and between chapters. According to Jelínek, Stein rejects linear and chronological narrative form both to project her "scorn for the usual autobiographical mode" and for the literary world that refused to recognize her, to reflect the chaos of the era, and to disguise her lesbianism (*Tradition* 136). From a revisionist feminist perspective, *Storyteller*'s generic differences from the male form of autobiography similarly respond to white patriarchal oppression and the silencing of Native women's voices. The assignment in exercise 18 encourages students to examine *Storyteller*'s structural differences in light of Danielson's analysis and in conjunction with *The Autobiography of Alice B. Toklas*. Through a feminist lens, *Storyteller*'s fragmented nature seems typical of women's autobiographies.

However, Danielson also presents a tribally-informed feminist perspective of *Storyteller*'s structure, claiming it is like a spiderweb, derived from Keresan mythological traditions of female deities like Thought Woman and Grandmother Spider. According to Danielson, *Storyteller* is thus a "coherent work about how tribal people survive" ("Storytellers in *Storyteller*" 21), for Silko connects the last story to the first to emphasize "the ongoing life of the people" ("Grandmother Spider's Web" 351). Radiating strands of the spiderweb-like structure cluster around specific themes, and these themes are connected to one another through the lateral threads that focus on storytellers and storytelling.

To illuminate this tribal feminist perspective, Keres myths and legends and contemporary poems dealing with Spider Woman can be brought into the classroom, as exercise 19 illustrates. Keres creation stories and ceremonial practices center on Spider Woman, whose relation to her people influences much of the contemporary writing by Native women.[48] In Native American legend, earth and humankind originated in the mind of Grandmother Spider, and woman is central to all life forms: "At the center of all is Woman, and no thing is sacred...without her blessing, her thinking" (Allen, "Grandmother of the Sun" 13). Native American feminist approaches to *Storyteller* and Spider Woman in particular suggest that the autobiographical subject's identity is rooted in the traditional, integral role of Native women in tribal cultures. The centrality of the Spider Woman image attests to women's creative power, and much of contemporary Native women's literature points to this creativity.[49] As Susan Scarberry suggests, Spider Woman is the "inspiration" through which American Indian poets "weave verbal images into verse for the good of their people" (100). Allen's poem "Grandmother" is a wonderful example to use in the classroom, for the poet appropriates the creative powers of Spider Woman as the creative inspiration for her own art and for bringing together her people: "After her I sit on my laddered rain-bearing rug/and mend the tear with string" (l. 19-20).[50] Additionally, James Welch's "Snow Country Weavers" can help illuminate the ways in which *Storyteller*'s spiderweb structure suggests a bringing together of the people who comprise the narrator's story.[51]

Spider Woman's central role in many Native myths compels us to examine the role of women in tribal cultures more generally as a way to understand the autobiographical stance in *Storyteller*. Exercise 20 includes assignments which ask students to explore Native women's traditional roles as well as how contact with the dominant culture has altered the gynocratic nature of many tribal cultures and influenced Silko's and other Native women's writing, using Linda Hogan's poem "The Women Speaking" as a crossroads text. Devon Mihesuah claims that in the face of mass oppression and destruction, women "have been just as crucial [as men] to the economic, social, religious, and political survival of tribes" (21). Allen concurs: "Like our sisters who resist in other ways, we Indian women who write have articulated and rendered the experience of being in a state of war for five hundred years" (Introduction, *Spider* 1-2). She claims a political and personal objective to the literature of Native American women, resisting obliteration of a people and their traditions.

Thus Silko's role as storyteller continues women's longstanding tradition of sustaining Native culture. Throughout *Storyteller*, women's voices abound, voices from which Silko draws strength and the confidence to become a writer-storyteller. First-person accounts in *Storyteller* are mostly stories about her family, and Silko identifies herself in terms of family and the community through the oral and cultural traditions incorporated into the work. Women's voices, a great tradition of female storytellers, fill the text—Aunt Susie and Grandma A'mooh, in particular, who told Silko and her sisters stories "about the old days" (Silko 35). Creative female deities from Keresan mythology, Grandmother Spider and Thought Woman, play an integral role in Silko's journey to become a storyteller, as in "COTTONWOOD *Part One: Story of Sun House*," "COTTONWOOOD *Part Two: Buffalo Story*," and "Yellow Woman." This notion of relationality is also a good example of how tribal feminist perspectives complicate feminist theorizing. Mary Mason, one of the earliest and most influential theorists of women's autobiography, argued that "the self-discovery of female identity seems to acknowledge the real presence and recognition of another consciousness, and the disclosure of female self is linked to the identification of some 'other'" (210). But Silko extends the notion of literary foremothers to include creative deities and males. Silko fills her text with male storytellers like Grandpa Hank, links her own art with her father's photography (Silko 160-61), and says she "owe[s] a great deal" to poet Simon Ortiz (170).

Finally, then, we turn to the tradition of Native women's autobiography as our last perspective through which to examine generic issues in *Storyteller*. Kathleen Sands notes many similarities between Native women's autobiography and women's autobiography as an entire genre, including the tendency to be disconnected and fragmentary (281). Allen maintains that "much of women's culture bears marked resemblance to tribal culture"

("Kochinnenako" 243), and Browdy de Hernández identifies the tendency of Native women's autobiography to be discontinuous and polyphonic as "also typical of the Native American oral tradition" ("Writing" 45).[52] The overlapping of women's and tribal cultures can be confusing for students as they examine *Storyteller* in these contexts, but they can also be illuminating. As Browdy de Hernández asserts, Native women's autobiographical texts such as *Storyteller* "are uninterested in joining the feminist fray" but do resist and oppose white oppression ("Writing" 50). The status of women in Native cultures precludes the assumption that an assertion of female power should be read against the benchmark of male power (48). Thus, she argues, Silko "does not challenge the Law of Genre directly" but "shifts the text on to different ground, into a textual space" where neither Western nor traditional Native laws of genre apply ("Laughing" 34).

The body of work of Native women's autobiography, which as of this writing includes over one hundred and thirty texts (Sands 273), exhibits characteristics common to the genre of women's autobiography as a whole (such as a different negotiation of the public/private split), as opposed to men's. But there are also differences between women's autobiographical texts in general and Native women's autobiographies specifically. Sands claims that, like other women's autobiographies, *Storyteller* combines fragmented memory with narrative, but it diverges from this tradition because it "makes no claim to be verifiable or to develop a comprehensive history of a life" (284). Sands calls *Storyteller* a "new kind of autobiographical text" (283) in which Silko "uses fragments of personal narrative to bind together traditional expression of collective cultural memory with her contemporary fictional and poetic versions of those stories central to the identity of Laguna people" (283).

Numerous crossroads texts enable the study of *Storyteller* through the prism of Native women's autobiography. Diane Glancy's *Claiming Breath*, like *Storyteller*, disrupts students' expectations of what autobiographies should be. However, this text is more overtly feminist in its challenge to hegemonic structures, especially those that silence and marginalize women. Also effective is Allen's "The Autobiography of a Confluence," in which Allen links her subjectivity to a larger network of land, people, and history. Most important, it is stories that link them all together. She describes herself as living in "the confluence" (145), a space where cultures come together. Additionally, Beverly Hungry Wolf's *The Ways of My Grandmother* blends various narrative voices so the end result is, like *Storyteller*, a multivocal text.

I like to circle the class back to Harjo's autobiographical text "Ordinary Spirit," this time from a tribal feminist perspective, as exercise 21 illustrates.

"Ordinary Spirit" is more directly autobiographical than *Storyteller*, but Harjo likewise weaves together personal and cultural histories and stories—the "Old creek" (her grandfather), the spirits of her ancestors, and the white woman with the "starved" soul—in creating her story (270).

Silko and Harjo bridge not only the worlds of the personal and the collective, but also those of Native and white. As mixed-blood, contemporary writer-storytellers, Silko and Harjo find new roles for themselves as "mediator[s] or interpreter[s] between the conflicting cultures represented in [their] mixed blood," helping these cultures find a sense of wholeness as well, a role Janet St. Clair claims is typical of mixed-blood writers (51). Patricia Riley further notes that *iyeska*, the Lakota term for mixed-blood, connotes dual roles: the *iyeska* is both the interpreter between Native and white worlds and "between the world of spirits and of human beings" (231). Harjo reconciles these worlds in her essay:

> I walk in and out of many worlds. I used to see being born of this mixed-blood/mixed-vision a curse, and hated myself for it....I have since decided that being familiar with more than one world, more than one vision, is a blessing, and know that I make my own choices. I also know that it is only an illusion that any of the worlds are separate. (266)

In the final paragraphs, Harjo reminds us that her poem-making is part of a larger process of creation: "It is now very late and I will let someone else take over this story.... It is not the last song, but to name anything that, only means that I would continue to be amazed at the creation of any new music" (270). Likewise, Silko remembers Aunt Susie's and Aunt Alice's different renderings of the same stories—adding one's imagination to a story changes it into a "new story with an integrity of its own, an offspring, a part of the continuing which storytelling must be" (227). Most important, both writers participate in meaningful cultural rituals and traditions that emphasize and celebrate their Indianness, embracing the past as a means of resistance and survival: "to give voice is to give back to those who could be forgotten" (Perreault 127).

In the introduction to *New Voices in Native American Criticism*, Krupat emphasizes his hope that "ethnocriticism," a critical discourse constructed on both Western and indigenous values and knowledge systems, is possible (Introduction xx). In a similar way, Allen explains her own theoretical, "tribal-feminist," approach as tribal *and* feminist, claiming deep interconnections among them both ("Kochinnenako" 237). Tribal feminist critique acknowledges that the "central role of woman is harmonizing spiritual relationships between the people and the rest of the universe by empowering ritual activities" (239). It also recognizes the profound influence of patriarchal colonialism on tribal life, how it distorts social and spiritual relationships and how, as Allen asserts, colonization "misinform[s] both the colonized and colonizer" (240).

By teaching at the crossroads of *Storyteller*, instructors honor both Krupat's and Allen's calls to recognize the varied influences on Native American writing. In the example I described on teaching at the crossroads of genre, I begin with Western notions of autobiography, using Franklin's *Autobiography* as the representative text. Clearly, this text sets certain patterns that Silko writes both within and against. From there, the class turns to Native American generic contexts such as oral storytelling and poetry, preliterate autobiography and nineteenth- and twentieth-century written autobiography to bring new perspectives to Silko's autobiographical stance. We then turn to mainstream feminist perspectives, both in terms of Danielson's revisionist stance and in relation to the tradition of women's autobiography, using *The Autobiography of Alice B. Toklas* as the crossroads text. Finally, the class examines how Native contexts and gynocratic systems have influenced feminist theory and thus shed new light on Silko's role as writer-storyteller, focusing on Spider Woman's and women's recurring roles in Native women's texts and, specifically, autobiographies. Exercise 22 offers students the opportunity to bring these perspectives together through Allen's notion of "confluence," the linking together of cultures, of present and past, and of land and borders.

Through preserving and telling stories, Native culture and traditions continue, despite systematic outside efforts to destroy them. As Ortiz claims, "story is to engender life" ("Part I" 67). But as instructors and students of this literature, we have a responsibility to listen—and to learn. Jeanne Perreault asserts that white critics (and I would extend this to instructors and students) must attend to Native texts not from the position of colonizer but from a perspective of resistance and transformation; thus we must allow the texts to speak and reject the "ideological freight" that predetermines what "minority" discourse should be, allowing for ambiguity (134). Silko affirms Ortiz's claim about the role of stories in "The Storyteller's Escape": "With these stories of ours/we can escape almost anything/with these stories we will survive" (247). In the old teller's "best" story about her own escape, she worries that "without this story" (252) she will be forgotten. We must listen, with an open mind, to Silko and her antecedents' calls, allowing the different versions and multiple interpretations to be heard. In so doing, we will forget neither the stories nor the people.

5 | Teaching at the Crossroads of Identity in *Beloved* and *China Men*

Art is about identity, among other things,
and her creativity is political.
—*Gloria Anzaldúa,* "Haciendo caras, una entrada"

For many women writers of color, to resist invisibility, to achieve a sense of self, to "strip off the *máscaras* others have imposed" and "become subjects in [their] own discourses" (Anzaldúa, "Haciendo" xvi), is language's power. Thus, despite the postmodern destabilization of the self, and in some cases as a part of it, many women writers of color use language to construct self, however multiply inflected across cultural, racial, class, gender, historical, and sexual lines. In this chapter, I focus on the struggle for identity in Toni Morrison's *Beloved* and Maxine Hong Kingston's *China Men* to offer another example of teaching at the crossroads. In *Beloved*, I show how various cultural and critical contexts can be used to illuminate Sethe's quest for identity in the aftermath of her life as a slave. In *China Men*, I center my analysis on the stories of the narrator's male ancestors.

At the Crossroads of Isolation and Identity: Teaching *Beloved*

Morrison's award-winning novel *Beloved* can alienate students through its textual difficulties and graphic depictions of slavery. However, by teaching at the crossroads, we can meet some of these challenges and make students' experience with *Beloved* productive and educational. In the following pages, I will focus on one compelling feature of this text: Sethe's search for identity in her life after slavery.

Sethe's quest for psychic and spiritual wholeness lies at the center of *Beloved*. From a Western-based perspective, postmodernism's interrogation of "grand narratives" sheds light on Sethe's process of (re)discovery. One significant strand of postmodern theory examines the manner by which language controls and determines meaning, and contests the idea that names stand for "reality" or "truth." Thus as part of a postmodern tradition, Sethe's quest for (re)development hinges on her attempts to reclaim a sense of personal worth and wholeness from white America, to shed the definitions of woman and mother that have stripped her of her dignity.[53] In appendix A, classroom exercise 25 asks students to consider how we might explain the process through which Sethe learns that the words of her oppressor do not construct her, because this identity is "derived from a discourse determined not by self but by other" (B. Marshall 11).[54] Sethe's sense of self was utterly destroyed the moment she overheard Schoolteacher listing her "human" and "animal" characteristics, as she finally tells Denver. It was at that precise moment that Sethe became aware of how she was viewed by the dominant culture, as represented by Schoolteacher, who chastises his nephew for mishandling Sethe as he would mishandle his horse or hound. Stripped of her humanity, even under the so-called humane treatment by the Garners, Sethe's emptiness is reinforced when Paul D learns that Sethe killed her baby: "'You got two feet, Sethe, not four,' he said, and right then a forest sprang up between them; trackless and quiet" (165). Both Schoolteacher and Paul D destroy Sethe's sense of identity, leading her to conflate her "self" with white society's conception of her as animal-like. For Sethe, healing can occur only if she can reject the definers' definitions.

In a similar vein, *Beloved* belongs to a postmodern tradition that resists "totalizations, absolute Identity, absolute Truths," the "grand stories or explanations which make sense of the world according to one overarching truth" (B. Marshall 6). From this perspective, we might view Sethe's killing of her baby girl as a challenge to white society's claim to Truth about slave mothers.[55] For Sethe, at the center of this challenge is the act of infanticide that has come to define and haunt her, an act condemned by a white society which could not understand the depth of her trauma. Sethe is judged harshly by Western standards of morality, represented by the newspaper clipping Stamp Paid shows Paul D. He knows that "whatever was written on it should shake him" (Morrison 154), and even though he cannot read the words he initially insists to Stamp that "It's a mistake somewhere 'cause that ain't her mouth" (158). As Dana Heller suggests, Paul D's inability to read the newspaper account of the infanticide indicates that "the 'literate' culture's interpretation of her act is, and by necessity should remain, far removed from his own." But wrestling with demons of his own, Paul D succumbs, temporarily, to Western standards of judgment, and abandons Sethe and her family. But Sethe, who knows how to read only seventy-five words, "knew that the words she did not understand [in the clipping] hadn't any more power than she had to explain" (Morrison 161). Although Sethe seems to acknowledge that even "definitions [that] belonged to the definers" (190) were not always wrong, such as when Sixo stole from Schoolteacher as a matter of pride rather than need, such definitions fail to recognize the specific circumstances surrounding the infanticide.

But the question of an alternate morality, distinct from the grand narratives of Western tradition, brings up the issue of cultural relativism, which students explore through excerpts from James Rachels' *The Elements of Moral Philosophy*. As exercise 24 illustrates, I frame the discussion around issues of relativism: Is Morrison asking her readers to reject universal notions of truth and embrace a relativistic philosophy, or is she arguing for universal notions of morality? Initially, students tend to view Sethe's behavior as immoral, and they justify their judgments by the African American community's ostracism of Sethe and her family. They also point to her own sense of guilt and desperate need for self-forgiveness as well as the profound consequences of her actions: her baby girl's death and subsequent reincarnation as the ghost haunting 124 Bluestone, the loss of her two sons who ran away from home, and the lonely life she leads with her only remaining child, Denver. Sethe's loss and guilt are profound, even though she feels justified in her behavior, that it was a moral response to unthinkable circumstances. Sethe tells Paul D "it worked" (Morrison 164), since none of her children were returned to slavery, and she responds to his "Maybe there's worse" with "It ain't my job to know what's worse. It's my job to know what is and to keep them away from what I know is terrible. I did that" (165). The moral ambiguities of Sethe's infanticide provide critical opportunities to explore postmodern notions of morality and truth.

Sethe must also cast off the perverted "mother" identity imposed upon her by the slave system that denied her the love of her own mother and precipitated the act of infanticide that has come to haunt her. In order for students to re-see Sethe's actions as she pieces together the experiences from her past, and to begin to understand why she would commit violence against her own child, other readings and historical information are useful. Many students will need to learn about the slave system that capriciously stripped children from mothers and fathers at will, valuing money over human life and regarding slaves as nonhuman. The slave system systematically and without remorse destroyed slave families, for slave parents had no rights to their children, who could be taken from their parents and sold, for slaves were economic commodities rather than human beings.

Against this backdrop, Sethe's desperate need to save her child from slavery's horrors and to fill the gaping hole of her sense of identity result from the lack of bonding between Sethe and her own mother. Sethe's only roots are on the "chokecherry tree" which scars her back (79). As a slave child, Sethe "sucked from another woman whose job it was" (60), recognizing her own mother only by the burnt cross under her breast. Sethe was denied the right to be "a daughter which is what [she] wanted to be and would have been if [her] ma'am had been able to get out of the rice long enough before they hanged her and let [Sethe] be one" (203). Killing her daughter repeats a legacy too painful to remember but that now compounds her own guilt: "She threw them all away but you. The one from the crew she threw away on the island. The others from more whites she also threw away. Without names, she threw them" (62). In like fashion, Baby Suggs' freedom "didn't mean a thing" because her eight children were gone from her:

> in all of Baby's life, as well as Sethe's own, men and women were moved around like checkers. Anybody Baby Suggs knew, let alone loved, who hadn't run off or been hanged, got rented out, loaned out, bought up, brought back, stored up, mortgaged, won, stolen or seized. So Baby's eight children had six fathers. What she called the nastiness of life was the shock she received upon learning that nobody stopped playing checkers just because the pieces included her children. Halle she was able to keep the longest. Twenty years. A lifetime. Given to her, no doubt, to make up for *hearing* that her two girls, neither of whom had their adult teeth, were sold and gone and she had not been able to wave goodbye. (23)

The legacy of slave children ripped from their mothers—of being used like pawns in someone else's game—profoundly influences how readers might justify Sethe's actions.

But Sethe's crisis of motherhood results as well from the brutal act she committed against her own daughter, even if out of love. She is wracked with guilt, and the latter half of the novel, which many students find disturbing, centers on her desperate need to "take care of and make up for" (243): "I won't never let her go.... I'll tend her as no mother ever tended a child, a daughter" (200). Now that Beloved has returned to her, Sethe "can sleep like the drowned, have mercy" (204), having wanted to lay in the grave with her baby girl but having been unable to do so because she had her three other children to care for. As exercise 25 illustrates, students can examine the extent to which Sethe can "be the unquestioned mother whose word was law and who knew what was best" (242).

However, postmodernism's destabilization of the subject problematizes Sethe's larger journey, her need to "claim...ownership of that freed self" (Morrison 95), and thus compels alternate readings of Sethe's identity development. Indeed, feminist theory itself contests some postmodern ideas, particularly the critique of the liberal humanist ideology of representation and identity, since identity and subjectivity have been denied women for so long. The application of postmodern theories to African American texts such as *Beloved* is highly contested. As Arlene Keizer asserts, "The challenge for those coming out of slavery was how to exercise their choices in becoming new people, African Americans; how to create themselves from the conflict of two cultures, one of them dedicated to denying the existence of the other." She argues that verbal and musical improvisation allowed slaves to reaffirm their humanity. While not arguing for the recovery of an "essential African American subject," Keizer notes that "all fragmented subjects may not feel the same way about their fragmentation." Ultimately, she says, this black subjectivity Morrison creates is "between essentialism and postmodern fragmentation."

My students consider these issues in relationship to *Beloved*. Denver emerges as a strong young woman, with an emerging "self to look out for and preserve" (Morrison 252). Baby Suggs' self is lost because of the tragedies she has endured, but its loss suggests its ability to exist: "the sadness was at her center, the desolated center where the self that was no self made its home. Sad as it was that she did not know where her children were buried or what they looked like if alive, fact was she knew more about them than she knew about herself, having never had the map to discover what she was like" (140); in freedom, Baby Suggs keeps her name because it is "from [her] husband" (142). Even the inconclusiveness of Sethe's self-identity as the book ends—her questioning, "Me? Me?" to Paul D's insistence that "'You your best thing, Sethe'" (273)—likely has more to do with her spiritual journey toward wholeness in the face of a brutal and traumatic past than with a postmodern conception of fluid identity. If he "put[s] his story next to hers" (273), "will the parts hold" (272)? We sense that however arduous a process it might be, Morrison does believe Sethe can "claim...ownership of that freed self" (95).

At the crossroads of identity, the implementation of additional perspectives is necessary, including African and African American cultural and literary contexts. One good place to start is the African American slave narrative tradition, which many scholars have cited as the origin of an African American literary tradition. Slave narratives had to tell the lives of slaves to a culture that viewed them as subhuman, and these texts are informed by their authors' "quest for voice and their desire to 'know their names' and to affirm self(hood)" (Owusu 73).

Reggie Young claims that African American slave narratives have influenced "the continued development of the African-American literary tradition," for as these narratives convey, "the path African Americans must take toward freedom is one paved by the acquisition of literacy" (360). By virtue of their being written, slave narratives claim African Americans' humanity as they "challenge the intellectual rationale behind their enslavement" (363). By constructing slaves as less than human, white America could convince itself that slaves did not deserve the rights, privileges, and status of human beings. Because the myth remains, Young argues, an embedded part of American culture, the majority of literary works by African Americans "should be viewed as slave narratives of varying types," for African American writers are "still writing themselves into being" (369).

In the classroom, excerpts from Frederick Douglass' *Narrative of the Life of Frederick Douglass, an American Slave,* allow students to revisit Sethe's process of healing and self-discovery from an African American perspective. Exercise 26 provides assignments that ask students to consider *Beloved* in this tradition. Clearly, Morrison's text continues the tradition of African Americans writing themselves into being. Not only does the text stress literacy as a means for Denver's emerging self, but the text itself writes slaves into American history from new perspectives, challenging the white renderings of slavery ensconsed in American literary history. Like Douglass, Morrison challenges the rationale that justified slavery with the profound moral question posed by the infanticide at the novel's core. From this perspective, the act of infanticide calls into question not only the logic of the act itself, but the logic of the slave system. Indeed, Morrison may ask readers whether Sethe's behavior is not more logical than slavery itself, and the enslaved more moral than the enslavers. The ambiguities surrounding the infanticide—an act of love rather than utter cruelty of slavery itself—turn moral questions back on both the system and the text's readers.

The impact of the infanticide on Sethe's sense of personal worth is also illuminated from the perspective of African vernacular traditions. For students, Sethe's profound isolation from the community of African Americans in Ohio is easily explained by the act of infanticide. However, by bringing African vernacular traditions into the classroom, students can address this issue from alternate perspectives. This is where I use Chauncey Ridley's informative analysis of two folklore traditions: "big love" and "badness." Acknowledging that *Beloved* can be emotionally powerful for even "casual readers" (154), Ridley nevertheless emphasizes the importance of cultural knowledge, "suggesting that levels of meaning specific to the Pan-African vernacular tradition are constitutive of the novel's complete artistic performance and available to those readers willing to research and contemplate the specific Pan-African vernacular resources of great African American literary texts" (154).

"Big love," which is committed and invested, undermines the ideological and economic objectives of the slave system (Ridley 155). But Sethe can only love "big," what Paul D calls "too thick" (Morrison 164): "Unless carefree, motherlove was a killer" (132). Paul D ponders Sethe's kind of love: "For a used-to-be-slave woman to love anything that much was dangerous, especially if it was her children she had settled on to love. The best thing, he knew, was to love just a little bit; everything, just a little bit, so when they broke its back, or shoved it in a croaker sack, well, maybe you'd have a little love left over for the next one" (45).

Compounding Sethe's "big love" is "badness," characterized by violence as a means to defend one's autonomy. "Bad" was a term used by slaveholders for undisciplined slaves but subverted by slaves to mean good, since "what was bad for slavery was good for them" (Ridley 156). Mr. Garner, who encouraged his slaves to marry freely, to work one day a week for wages, and to use these wages to buy freedom, fostered Sethe's sense of autonomy. Ridley argues that the community, already put off by Sethe's self-autonomy and "big love," resents Sethe for "never doubt[ing] that she was correct in her effort to murder her children to protect them" (162).

In the classroom, I bring in excerpts from Ridley's article, and, as exercise 27 depicts, I ask students to find evidence for Ridley's claims.[56] Paul D thinks, "more important than what Sethe had done was what she claimed" (Morrison 164)—her pride in knowing she did the right thing. The crowd watching Sethe being taken by the sheriff feels "shocked" by the "clarity" of her profile:

> Was her head a bit too high? Her back a little too straight? Probably. Otherwise the singing would have begun at once.... Some cape of sound would have quickly been wrapped around her, like arms to hold and steady her on the way. As it was, they waited till the cart turned about, headed west to town. And then no words. Humming. No words at all. (152)

Sethe "insults" Baby Suggs' mourners by refusing to eat their food or to attend Reverend Pike's service (171). Stamp Paid admits to himself that "her outrageous claims, her self-sufficiency," which seemed to "demand" the "meanness" of the community, may have led him to expose Sethe's secret to Paul D (171).

Ridley argues that in tales of badness, black communities consistently abandon "bad" heroes at precisely the climactic moment of confrontation, and then immortalize them "in ritual retellings of their exploits" (Ridley 157). The Ohio community of ex-slaves abandons Sethe out of both envy and fear, for "badness" leads to intensified and random white violence against blacks, according to folk wisdom. If, as Ridley claims, we should view Sethe as a "sacrificial victim, ritualistically expelled to the periphery of a desperately vulnerable community," we can then understand why, "on the novel's metaphysical dimension, Sethe becomes a woman haunted by ghosts": the community has "burdened Sethe with their own nagging guilt and remorse accompanying their own histories of lost love" (162). For Ella, Sethe's crime was "staggering," but Sethe's "pride outstripped even that" (Morrison 256). But when Ella remembers the "hairy white thing" she refused to nurse that lived only five days (258), we cannot help but wonder about Ella's own feelings of guilt. The thirty women who perform the exorcism remember the time "playing in Baby Suggs' yard, not feeling the envy that surfaced the next day" (258)—"envy" that Sethe had the courage to save her child from the horrors of slavery. Only when they embrace her burden, when "the personal pride, the arrogant claim staked out at 124 seemed to them to have run its course" (249)—when Denver seeks their help—do they forgive her. When students begin to interrogate the community's response to Sethe in light of big love and badness tales, they can move beyond seeing the community's ostracism of Sethe and her family as an indictment of Sethe, and begin to consider the infanticide as a morally ambiguous act of rebellion against the institution of slavery.

From this point, I move students to mainstream feminist analysis to further complicate Sethe's isolation, pride, and need for healing in the context of male-female relationships. From this perspective, Sethe's identity development is partly a response to her abandonment by the men in her life, the lack of trust she has for men, and her need to prove she can be independent and protect her family in the absence of men. Indeed, Morrison has been both praised and maligned for her portrayal of African American men in many of her works, including *Beloved*. One particularly useful crossroads text at this point is "The Men in Toni Morrison," a chapter from Edward Jackson's *Images of Black Men in Black Women Writers, 1950-1990*. Referring to some critics' condemnation of Morrison's rendering of black men, Edwards writes, "at best, her portrayal of men is ambiguous; at worst, they are negative" (62), pointing to the example of

Halle's failure to protect Sethe from the mammary rape as an example of the open-endedness of Morrison's depiction of black men. I also like to use excerpts from an academic symposium on African American gender relations as a crossroads text to illuminate the divisive issues separating African American men and women as well as the ways in which scholars suggest these conflicts can be bridged (see hooks).

Students can examine how Morrison portrays African American men in *Beloved*, paying special attention to the significance of Paul D in Sethe's life, as exercise 28 entails. Kashinath Ranveer claims that Morrison's African American male characters tend to be weak, "incapable of living with dignity and respect," and she points to Halle as an example in *Beloved* (44). Until Paul D arrives to fill in the missing pieces, Sethe has no knowledge or understanding of Halle's fate, in particular his failure to show up for their family's escape from Sweet Home. But Paul D is able to fill in the gaps, and Sethe finds, to her horror, that Halle witnessed the theft of her breast milk by Schoolteacher's nephews, and "It broke him" (Morrison 69). Are we to see him as weak or unmanly, or are we to see him as another of slavery's victims? Sethe's response seems to indict him: "He saw them boys do that to me and let them keep on breathing air? He saw? He saw? He saw?" (69).

Halle's absence, regardless of what it suggests about his strength of character, has denied Sethe a healthy sexual and loving relationship with a man. Perhaps more significantly, it has forced her to raise her children without him. As the novel indicates, slave women were often the heads of households because of slavery's destruction of black families, but they did not "rule" the family as with matriarchal or female-dominated family units (Collins 52). Citing work by Deborah Gray White, Patricia Collins notes that the slave economy raised motherhood above marriage, for black women were necessary for the propagation of the slave labor force (51-52). Thus Paul D's arrival in Sethe's life might also be explained through a feminist lens. He calls attention to the fact that she has been without a man upon his arrival at 124 Bluestone:

> "No man? You here by yourself?"
> "Me and Denver," she said.
> "That all right by you?"
> "That's all right by me."
> She saw his skepticism and went on. (10)

I ask students about the extent to which Paul D brings something positive to Sethe's life or takes away from it, whether the beautiful image of the three shadows holding hands suggests that the family will benefit from his presence. Ultimately, we examine whether Sethe is better off with or without him. Certainly, Paul D's behavior during the course of the novel invites feminist analysis. Unable to be a loving and supportive partner for her, he sleeps with Beloved, abandons Sethe upon learning of the infanticide, and, with great cruelty reminds her of when Schoolteacher likened her to an animal: "Paul D dug it up, gave her back her body, kissed her divided back, stirred her rememory and brought her more news: of clabber, of iron, of roosters' smiling, but when he heard *her* news, he counted her feet and didn't even say goodbye" (189). Moreover, there is textual support for the assertion that Morrison is making a feminist statement. When Paul D comes to Sethe's work to tell her he's been sleeping with Beloved, he tells her "you won't like what I'm 'bout to say" (128). The narrative voice gives us Sethe's response: "Sethe looked at him steadily, calmly, already ready to accept, release or excuse an in-need-or-trouble man. Agreeing, saying okay, all right, in advance, because she didn't believe any of them—over the long haul—could measure up" (128).

But in the end, a feminist analysis would likely also compel us to judge Paul D with empathy and to consider whether Morrison believes Sethe is better off with or without him. Paul D's demons have led him to question his own sense of manhood. When he has wrestled with his own identity—with how he might define himself, rather than be defined by Mr. Garner as a Sweet Home man—then he can accept Sethe for both her weaknesses and strengths. Thus even though Sethe states it is "all right by me" (10) to be without a man, Sethe's and Denver's lives can be fuller with the love of Paul D. As their relationship develops, the narrative voice tells us "her story was bearable because it was his as well" (99), and Sethe is thus ready to "launch her newer, stronger life with a tender man" (99) as he "put[s] his story next to hers" (273).

When race and class issues intersect with gender, African American feminist theory can help students understand the specifics of black female selfhood and thus shed new light on Sethe's sense of identity. A useful crossroads text at this point is Ula Taylor's article on black feminism, "Making Waves." Taylor's historical and theoretical analysis of black feminist theory and practice, as well as her accessible language, make this an excellent classroom resource. As exercise 29 depicts, students examine *Beloved* through the prism of black feminist consciousness and stereotypes. Ranveer claims that *Beloved* "reflects African-American feminist consciousness effectively" as it traces Sethe's awareness of her subhuman status and her subsequent quest for freedom (42). It is when Sethe realizes what is in Schoolteacher's notebook, Ranveer argues, that she experiences the "true erosion of her very black female self" (43). When she runs from the plantation to attempt to secure her children's safety only to be found by Schoolteacher, Sethe murders her baby daughter and "retains her dignity as a human being" as she "moves from the state of total ignorance and unawareness about herself towards the state of total black feminist consciousness" (43). But this achievement is at a painful cost, which, Ranveer argues, is Morrison's point. Killing her baby restores her sense of agency and black womanhood, and although it was perhaps unjust and self-destructive, the infanticide nevertheless restored justice and self-respect in an immoral and unjust world (43). I also allow for another perspective, that it is Sethe's attack on Bodwin at the end of the novel, rather than the act of infanticide, that restores Sethe's black female selfhood: "He is coming into her yard and he is coming for her best thing.... And if she thinks anything, it is no. No no. Nonono. She flies. The ice pick is not in her hand; it is her hand" (262). Although Bodwin "had one clear directive: human life is holy, all of it" and worked diligently for the abolitionist cause, Morrison gives us some evidence that his motives were suspect: "Nothing since was as stimulating as the old days of letters, petitions, meetings, debates, recruitment, quarrels, rescue and downright sedition.... The Society managed to turn infanticide and the cry of savagery around, and build a further case for abolishing slavery. Good years they were, full of spit and conviction" (260). By attacking Bodwin, a representative of the system that destroyed her, Sethe regains her dignity and humanity.

Similarly, we can understand Sethe's agency in the context of the sexualization and stereotyping of African American women by the dominant culture during and after slavery. *Beloved* documents in graphic detail the sexual exploitation that accompanied the economic exploitation of African American female slaves. Citing studies by Angela Davis and Margaret Burnham, Collins points out that:

> Under such a system in which the control of property is fundamental, enslaved African women were valuable commodities. Slaveowners controlled Black women's labor and commodified Black women's bodies as units of capital. Moreover, as mothers, Black women's fertility produced the children who increased their owners' property and labor force. (51)

Black women's sexuality as commodity is revealed when Baby Suggs was promised in return for sex that she could keep her child (though the promise was reneged), and when Sethe paid for her baby's headstone with sex. Slave women were often abused sexually for their masters' pleasure, as when one of Schoolteacher's nephews steals Sethe's milk from her breasts while the other holds her down. *Beloved* thus deconstructs the myth that slave women willingly consented to sex with their owners and its accompanying stereotypes of African American women's promiscuity and passivity, which are still present today. Morrison's critique is wielded specifically at the slave system's dehumanization of slave women in treating them as breeders. Interesting crossroads texts to use at this point include "Slave and Mistress: Ideologies of Womanhood under Slavery," the second chapter of Hazel Carby's *Reconstructing Womanhood*, and texts that consider black women's sexuality as it is portrayed through popular culture. Taylor, for example, discusses the ways in which popular culture links black women's sexuality with violence in much rap music as well as in films like Spike Lee's *She's Gotta Have It*.[57]

Finally, an African American feminist perspective asks readers to examine Sethe's identity development in the female slave narrative tradition, and through this perspective we circle back to our work with Douglass' *Narrative*. To bring this context into the classroom, I include excerpts from Harriet Jacobs' *Incidents in the Life of a Slave Girl* (1861), the prototypical women's slave narrative, as well as excerpts from Winifred Morgan's analysis of the distinctions between male and female slave narratives. Morgan argues that male and female slaves experienced slavery differently and "tell different stories of resistance to their enforced servitude" (75), male narrators emphasizing the importance of literacy, and female narrators stressing the importance of relationships and the network of shared cooperation and interdependence among slave women. Male writers of slave narratives had to counter stereotyped representations of themselves as "boys," while women strove to oppose their prescribed status as victims or whores; thus, men often used literacy to prove their manhood, while women "demonstrated [their] womanliness and [their] shared roles with women readers" through establishing relationships with others (76).

As exercise 30 illustrates, students can examine these assertions in Jacobs' *Incidents*, which, as W. Morgan suggests, "depicts a network of relationships"—with her grandmother, parents, children, brother, uncles, aunt, and even her employers and abolitionist Amy Post—"on which she depends and to which she contributes" (84). Collins, citing studies by James Turner, Molefi Asante, and Linda Myers, speaks to the centrality of family and community in black women's lives, its roots in African cultural systems and experiences under slavery: "Afrocentric models of community stress connections, caring, and personal accountability" (223). For Jacobs, this network "assures her of her own worth" and "impels her to take a role in the larger world" (W. Morgan 84). By hiding for seven years in the crawl space over her grandmother's storage shed, Jacobs hopes to prevent her children from living the lives of slaves, conveying the destructive nature of slavery on familial and other relationships.

The reconstruction of family and community relationships is of particular importance to both *Beloved* and *Incidents*. Sethe's ostracism from the community of women in Ohio is central to her wounded soul; when they finally embrace her (as they shed their own guilt and remorse) Sethe's healing can begin. Furthermore, the need to preserve children's safety and keep them from lives of slavery is a common, crucial thread in both texts and can underscore the danger slave women faced with regard to losing their own children to the institution of slavery.

In her study of the varied literary influences on African American writers and texts, Tracy Mishkin suggests that "interracial literary influence"—usually positive, sometimes negative—exists for African American writers, despite the desire of some scholars to deny the existence of white writers' influence on African Americans (15). If we ignore outside influence we miss what the texts and the writers themselves say: "accepting that interracial influence means not that a black canon is not self-sufficient but that it did not grow in a vacuum" (15). In exercise 31, I include an assignment that culminates my students' work at the crossroads of identity in *Beloved*. Cross-cultural interrogation of Sethe's identity development includes postmodern notions of identity and the self in relationship to the grand narratives that have defined Sethe as woman, murderer, and mother; African American contexts of the slave narrative tradition and the black vernacular; a mainstream feminist critique of the men who have abandoned Sethe; and an African American feminist perspective that includes the unraveling of sexual stereotypes and the female slave narrative tradition. This pedagogical approach can illuminate the multiple intertextual influences on *Beloved*. By teaching at the crossroads of *Beloved*, we heed Morrison's call to listen to the voices in her text: "Perhaps a conversation, they thought, an exchange of views or something would help" (Morrison 4).

At the Crossroads of Identity and Masculinity: Teaching *China Men*

Maxine Hong Kingston's *China Men* is a powerful and important story of the experiences of Chinese American men in America, whose voices have long been silenced and ignored. It is also an extremely difficult text to teach and for students to understand, primarily due to its cross-cultural contexts.[58] *China Men* disdains conventional narrative strategies, presenting instead a collection of Chinese literary and cultural traditions, folktales and fables, historical documents, autobiographical accounts, and imaginative narratives. It contains multiple, contradictory versions of the same story, and has six main chapters and twelve interchapters. In the following pages, I will demonstrate how to teach at the crossroads of identity in *China Men*, focusing on the collective identity of Chinese American men through the stories of four generations of the narrator's ancestors.[59] Who are they, where did they come from, and what does Kingston want us to know about them? What can we learn from these stories?

I begin class with a study of the narrator's father, BaBa, who, from a Western perspective, is best understood within the context of narratives of exploration and discovery in the spirit of rugged individualism and the making of America, as exercise 32 illustrates. This theme is initially raised in the first interchapter, "On Discovery," which symbolizes early Chinese immigration to America in search of the Gold Mountain, and then reinforced again in "The Ghostmate." In this light, BaBa, both protagonist and antagonist in *China Men*, is a Gold Mountain sojourner, willing to risk it all in search of the American Dream. Like many others, BaBa is lured to America by the stories of the Gold Mountain, retold and relished in China: "'On the Gold Mountain, a man eats enough meat at one meal to feed a family for a month,' said Great Grandfather. 'Yes, slabs of meat.' The hungrier the family got, the bigger the stories, the more real the meat and the gold.… 'America—a peaceful county, a free country.' America. The Gold Mountain. The Beautiful Nation" (42). In many ways a prototypical immigrant, BaBa buys into the ideals of America and what it means to live the American Dream, claiming the land as his own. He is lured by America-as-opportunity, the American spirit of rugged individualism through the exploration and the mastery of uncharted territory. Making it to (and in) America takes wit, endurance, and the will to survive, as his immigration stories attest.

Forced by BaBa's silence (partially out of fear of deportation) about his immigration, the narrator constructs his story, imagining legal and illegal versions of the journey. She begins by recounting her father's experiences growing up in China, developing into a scholar, and then, seduced by tales of the Gold Mountain, immigrating to America. In the illegal version, the narrator's father is smuggled to America in a crate, and she underscores his will to survive as he hides from the white demons and "rode on, coming to claim the Gold Mountain, his own country" (52). In the legal version, BaBa goes to San Francisco and is detained, and through marvelous deception and the strength of his endurance, he withstands the frequent interrogations and passes the examinations: "he had won America" (60).

To further emphasize *China Men*'s intertextual connections to rugged individualism and the claiming of America, I include Western and

American traditions in the classroom. One such example is Daniel Defoe's *Robinson Crusoe*, since it is widely familiar to students (even if only in its popular retellings). The story has itself become more known than read, encapsulating American ideals of wisdom, prudence, industry, and faith, and in popular retellings of the story, some of the details have been lost, such as that Crusoe was a slave trader. Sharon Meagher notes that popularized versions of the story focus on Crusoe's stay on the island, resulting in a romantic individualism (150-51). Walter Cummins argues similarly, stating that in this "folklore incarnation apart from Defoe's text," Robinson Crusoe "is celebrated as an explorer who overcame solitude to civilize an untamed island"; in Defoe's text, however, Robinson Crusoe "emerges as a troubled man" influenced by capitalist greed (137).

Exercise 33 brings this crossroads text to students. Referencing *Robinson Crusoe* in the story of Lo Bun Sun, Kingston speaks to the strength of the Chinese immigrant who survives the isolation and obstacles impeding his success. Like Robinson Crusoe, whose hard work and inner resources helped him survive for twenty-four years on a small, uninhabited island, in *China Men*, "Lo Bun Sun worked. He was never idle, never lazy. He farmed the island.... Lo Bun Sun was a mule and toiling man, naked and toiling body, alone, son and grandson, himself all the generations" (Kingston 226). "Himself all the generations," Lo Bun Sun represents the collective labor and toil of Chinese men in the making of America. Kingston sketches the biographies of the men in her family—her father, grandfather, great-grandfather, uncles, and brother—to record their contributions to the history of the United States and to record the history of discrimination against them, in effect enacting a reclamation at both the individual and collective level.

Western readings of the narratives of exploration and discovery in *China Men* compel revisionist analyses as well. As Cummins suggests, Kingston raises two fundamental questions: What happens to those who search for freedom and prosperity but fail, and does political and economic freedom for some necessitate the exploitation and dehumanization of others (141-42)? Cummins argues that in "The Adventures of Lo Bun Sun," Kingston deliberately emphasizes Sing Kay Ng's reunion with his father, whereas this was ancillary in Defoe's version. Perhaps the reunion is meant to be an antidote to Lo Bun Sun's rejection of his family and tradition, but Cummins argues otherwise, claiming that not only is Sing Kay Ng a cannibal, but also that family love does not necessarily resolve the limitations of self-contained individualism, given the "hostile environment of the wider world" (144). Unlike Crusoe (and Benjamin Franklin, whom he sees as the American version of Crusoe, despite their differences), the Chinese men in *China Men* cannot sever their ties to home and to their families; Kingston's book is populated by the ghosts of those living and dead. Alex Wang observes that the theme of returning home from an attractive place recurs in all twelve intertexts, reflecting Chinese Americans' internal debate (204-05).

Thus in exercise 34 I ask students to consider the critique of individualism in "The Adventures of Lo Bun Sun" and the experiences of BaBa and Kingston's other ancestors. We also spend time with Kingston's catalogue of anti-Chinese "exclusion laws" from 1868-1978, which serve to foreground the importance of language in racial discrimination and exploitation, emphasizing the need for a counter-discourse, which is Kingston's story. Historically, only men from China were allowed into the United States for work, until the Immigration and Nationality Act in 1952 allowed Chinese women to immigrate under the same conditions as men. Moreover, any American woman who married a Chinese man would lose her citizenship. As David Li argues, "The Laws" section of *China Men* is particularly distant from fictional conventions, but Kingston includes these little-known legal documents to reveal "the oppressive power that they used to carry and the power of the contemporary writer who can transform them into a counter-language" ("*China Men*" 492). In so doing, she transforms the epic and celebrated stories of American discovery and expansion to reveal them as racist and exploitative.

Moreover, the American Dream is undercut by the racist exploitation Chinese and Chinese American men endure in America. For the grandfather and great-grandfather, at least, the Gold Mountain remains a place of unrealized desires. Kingston lauds the work of her male ancestors but simultaneously situates them as victims rather than victors, for they are consistently abused and exploited: "In their hunger [for gold] the men forgot that the gold streets had not been there when they'd gone to look for themselves" (41). Kingston uses the experiences of Bak Goong and Ah Goong to attest that the U.S. was built on the sweat and labor of Chinese men. By placing Ah Goong's trek in the wider context of labor exploitation and xenophobic violence, Kingston shows how his experiences travelling through the Northwest and toward San Francisco, filled with mass abuse, contradict the American Dream of the West:

> Good at hiding, disappearing—decades unaccounted for—he was not working in a mine when forty thousand chinamen were Driven Out of mining. He was not killed or kidnapped in the Los Angeles Massacre, though he gave money toward ransoming those whose toes and fingers, a digit per week, and ears grotesquely rotting

> or pickled, and scalped queues, were displayed in Chinatowns.... He was lucky not to be in Colorado when the Denver demons burned all chinamen homes and businesses, nor in Rock Springs, Wyoming, when the miner demons killed twenty-eight or fifty chinamen. (148)

Finally, as exercise 35 illustrates, students examine the extent to which Kingston's male ancestors obtain the American Dream, and what the implications are for Kingston. Certainly, when BaBa is cheated by his three friends out of his share of the laundry, we might agree with Qun Wang that their "cultural metamorphosis" is complete (88), having betrayed Chinese customs of fairness and equality for the "anything's fair" in competitive capitalist ideology. But despite Kingston's critique of racism and discrimination, she also documents her father's success in attaining the American Dream when he reemerges from his lethargy and opens his own laundry: "So my father at last owned his house and his business in America" (255). Shirley Geok-lin Lim asserts that "The American Father" ends with a "paean to the father's success as an immigrant in the United States" ("Twelve" 247).

The class can further interrogate the question of BaBa's American identity in "The Brother in Vietnam," for the Americanized brother in this story is in many ways uncomfortable with his identity. The family's Americanness is "certif[ied]" (299) when the government awards the brother security clearance, but he turns down the job because it would force him to interrogate prisoners of war or become a spy. Thus his American identity is problematized.

As we continue to examine the identity of Kingston's male ancestors, I move the analysis away from Western and American contexts, beginning with the Asian American literary enterprise to unravel and counter stereotypes of the emasculated Chinese American male and create an alternate view of Chinese American masculinity. Significantly, Chinese American manhood is also intricately interwoven with Chinese American literary history and the efforts by Chinese American male writers and critics to revise images of the feminized Chinese American man.

To bring this context into the classroom, I use the prefaces and/or introductions to Frank Chin's, Jeffery Paul Chan's, Lawson Fusao Inada's, and Shawn Wong's *Aiiieeeee! An Anthology of Asian American Writers* (1974) as crossroads texts. *Aiiieeeee!*'s publication was a monumental event in Asian American literary history, the first published collection of literature by Asian Americans, and a concerted effort to assert Asian American "manhood." The anger of these editors is unmistakable as they excoriate white America for demeaning and stereotyping Asian American males:

> America's dishonesty—its racist white supremacy passed off as love and acceptance—has kept seven generations of Asian American voices off the air, off the streets, and praised us for being Asiatically no-show. A lot is lost forever. But from the few decades of writing we have recovered from seven generations, it is clear that we have a lot of elegant, angry, and bitter life to show.... If the reader is shocked, it is due to his own ignorance of Asian America. (Preface xxii).

According to the editors, Asian Americans have been "cast into the role of the good guy" to make other ethnic groups "look bad" (Introduction 4); they retain their status as the "model minority" as long as they are silent and invisible, assimilating rather than challenging dominant ideologies (8-10). As such, Chin, et al. write, "the white stereotype of the acceptable and unacceptable Asian is utterly without manhood. Good or bad, the stereotypical Asian is nothing as a man. At worst, the Asian American is contemptible because he is womanly, effeminate, devoid of all the traditionally masculine qualities of originality, daring, physical courage, and creativity" (14-15). The tradition of Asian American literature, as constructed by and evidenced in *Aiiieeeee!*, focuses on the attempt to reconstruct masculinity and heroism in the face of an emasculating American culture.

From here, I turn to stereotypes of Asian American men as portrayed in American culture, from Bruce Lee to contemporary video games. Kingston herself refers to *Blackhawk* comic books that depicted Chop-Chop, a Chinese man, as a caricature, arguing that these offensive images were popular in American media, and I have used the unofficial website to bring Chop-Chop to life.[60] The *Blackhawk* comic books were introduced in a 1941 issue of *Military Comics*. The Blackhawks, a band of volunteers who fought the Nazis, were made up of characters stereotyped by nationality. However, only Chop-Chop was drawn in caricature (Zimmerman).

As exercise 36 indicates, from these stereotypes we move to "The Father From China," which documents how BaBa has been feminized and marginalized in the Chinese "bachelor" communities in New York City. From their home lives to their jobs at the laundry, BaBa (who has Americanized his name to Ed) and his friends—Woodrow, Roosevelt, and Worldster—are domesticated:

> Ed scraped the dishes onto the tablecloth, which was layers of newspapers. Then he rolled up the top layer; the

> table was instantly clean and already covered for the next meal. He sudsed the dishes with laundry soap and put them in a drainer. From the whistling tea kettle, he poured boiling water on them; the water was so hot, the dishes dried before his eyes. It was a method he remembered the slaves in China using. Dishwashing just took common sense; women had made such a to-do about it. The Gold Mountain was indeed free: no manners, no traditions, no wives. (61)

Kingston's reference to "slaves" in China is no coincidence; in fact she deliberately associates Ed's and the others' domestic roles with slavery and racist exploitation. Moreover, while Ed seems to relish his life without his Chinese wife, his rejection by the Anglo dancers underscores his emasculation by racism as well as his loneliness and isolation: "You like come home with me? Please?' 'No, honey,' she said. 'No'" (66).

"The Ghostmate," depicting a scholar's exile to a fantastical land where he lives with a beautiful ghost, pairs up with "The Father from China," which explores the personal emasculation and marginalization of BaBa.[61] According to Shu-mei Shih, "ghost" is often used by Chinese people to mean "foreigner" (thus the parallel with "The Father from China"). On another level, "The Ghostmate" belongs to a specific Chinese genre, *ch'uan-ch'i* tales, which are tales of desire (69). The consummation of the scholar's desire in the story is contrasted with the inability of BaBa to realize his desires, both as a scholar in China and as a Chinese man in America, whose literacy is turned into illiteracy and who cannot exercise his manhood (70).

In *China Men*, Kingston counteracts stereotypes by giving her father and other Chinese American men a voice, not only telling their history but creating their identity by counteracting Western stereotypes of the quiet, "inscrutable" Asian. As such, she writes within the Asian American literary tradition, as represented by *Aiiieeeee!*.

In the classroom, I use various crossroads texts to explore the male-centeredness of the Chinese American literary tradition, including Jeffery Chan's short stories, "Auntie Tsia Lays Dying" (1972), "Jackrabbit" (1974), and "The Chinese in Haifa" (1974). Exercise 37 refers to "The Chinese in Haifa" and includes questions to encourage students to make intertextual connections by considering the portrayal of Asian American manhood through Bill Wong, the story's protagonist. From his negative rantings about his ex-wife, the children's Chinese education, Chinatown as "The Chickencoop," and his affair with his attractive Jewish neighbor (during which he betrays a friendship), Bill Wong is more American than Chinese.

The class considers the extent to which Chan rebukes or approves of Bill Wong, since many critics insist he represents Chan's new definition of Chinese American manhood and since the *Aiiieeeee!* editors included the story in their collection.

For BaBa in *China Men*, Chinese manhood is constructed through Americanization and denial of the Chinese past. Like Wong, BaBa rejects his heritage:

> You say with the few words and the silences: No stories. No past. No China.... You only look and talk Chinese. There are no photographs of you in Chinese clothes nor against Chinese landscapes. Did you cut your pigtail to show your support for the Republic? Or have you always been American? Do you mean to give us a chance at being real Americans by forgetting the Chinese past? (14)

When BaBa begins his life in New York with an Americanized name, Ed, he attempts to transform himself into an American, from his clothing to his haircut to the photographs he sends his wife in China. Ed and his partners "looked all the same Americans" (64):

> In the spring, Ed sent his wife a picture of the four partners with their arms around one another's shoulders, laughing next to a Keep Off the Grass sign. He was wearing another two-hundred-dollar suit, a navy blue one, and a shirt with French cuffs, which closed with gold cuff links. For a winter picture, he sat on a rock in Central Park in his new gray greatcoat and jaunty hat and leather gloves lined with rabbit fur. (67)

Yet, the images of glamour Ed intentionally constructs in the staged photographs and in the mirror, looking like Fred Astaire, are juxtaposed and undercut by the song the men sing of their lives as launderers:

> *The laundry business is low, you say,*
> *Washing out blood that stinks like brass—*
> *Only a Chinaman can debase himself so.*
> *But who else wants to do it? Do you want it?*
> *Ask for the Chinaman. Ask the Chinaman.*(63)

Kingston problematizes her father's efforts to Americanize, thereby asserting a conception of Chinese American masculinity which can account for Baba's Chinese past. The intertextual references to Chinese legendary figures such as Tang Ao and Ch'Yuan reunite the father with this Chinese past, his identity thus intricately woven with both Chinese and American history. From this perspective, "The Ghostmate" critiques her father's suppression of his heritage, for the male protagonist of this interchapter succumbs to the lure of the "Ghostmate" while betraying his wife and family back home while "The *Li Sao*: An Elegy" juxtaposes the legendary poet Ch'Yuan's enduring influence with Baba's severing of his cultural past.

In class, we continue by examining Asian American writers' and critics' efforts to counteract the stereotypes of the emasculated Asian American male through aggressive, physical, and sexual portrayals. However, we also examine the ways in which these portrayals frequently include violence against women. Here again, "The Chinese in Haifa" serves an important purpose at the crossroads, and exercise 38 illustrates how I frame this context in a group assignment.[62] While Bill Wong is seemingly passive as his wife takes all their belongings, leaving him little more than a spoiled frozen dinner, his imagination is particularly violent toward his wife. This is most apparent during his fishing expedition when he imagines his wife as the fish caught on his line, and he is resexualized: "He shortened his grip and with both hands set the hook with a quick jerk, and he had her, he had this fish passing for his wife. He felt a violent current of energy running the length of the fishing pole.... Now the violence was real for him" (81). Chan describes the fish in graphic violent detail: "The hook must have passed through the roof of her mouth. Blood flooded the white of one bulging eyeball" (81).

This resexualization of Chinese American men in *China Men* is most apparent in the story of Kingston's grandfather Ah Goong, who, along with other Chinese men made major contributions to the building of the transcontinental railroad. Kingston presents these men with dignity and physical prowess, and highlights the strength they exhibited in the demanding physical work of cutting through the granite mountains. Denied women, Ah Goong explodes with pent-up sexual energy and masturbates into the valley below: "He grew a habit: whenever he was lowered in the basket, his blood rushed to his penis, and he fucked the world" (133).

However, because mainstream feminist criticism problematizes what Cheung calls the "rhetoric of conquest" in the story of Ah Goong (*Articulate* 109), I bring this context to students' readings of Kingston's male ancestors. In the wake of Annette Kolodny's landmark work "The Land-as-Woman: Literary Convention and Latent Psychological Content," feminist critics have long argued that settlers of the New World depicted the continent as a woman, sometimes an Indian maiden, arms generously open, offering the riches of the new land to prospective immigrants. In fact much of the language associated with the conquest myth suggests an equation between women's reproductive roles and the founding of the nation, imagining the New World as "fertile," the land as "virgin," and the creation of the new nation as a "birth." But many of these associations of the "dual maternal and sexual aspect[s]" of the land are misogynistic and violent (Kolodny, "Land" 169).

To initiate this analysis, I use various crossroads texts, including excerpts from Kolodny, J. Hector St. John de Crèvecoeur's "What is an American Farmer" from *Letters from an American Farmer*, and John Hammond's "Leah and Rachel, Or, The Two Faithful Sisters Virginia and Maryland."[63] St. John de Crèvecoeur's famous letter, as Kolodny observes, makes the very clear connection between political prosperity for men and the land as Mother, "wholly beneficent and maternally abundant" (Kolodny, "Land" 173). Hammond's text, however, makes the link between the land and violence, for he "looked upon Virginia and Maryland as upon a mistress raped and a mother plundered and widowed" (Kolodny 173).

As exercise 39 demonstrates, from these important historical and literary contexts, students return to the chapters on Bak Goong and Ah Goong, which both involve the making of America through the land: "How could they not go to the Gold Mountain again, which belonged to them, which they had invented and discovered?" (Kingston 43). However, Kingston is arguably leveling a feminist critique at male conquest and their destruction of the land for economic purposes. As Rachel Lee observes, Kingston's "contradictory impulses" are thus, on the one hand, "to show a Chinese American first-endeavor in cultivating the land (and thus first right to proprietary claims)" and, on the other hand, "a disapproving attitude toward the violence involved in harnessing the earth to trade interests" (149). Upon his arrival in Hawaii, Bak Goong realizes he is there to "hack a farm out of the wilderness" (Kingston 98). Although the Hawaiians "quit rather than help pull the boulders out of the earth" (103), Bak Goong and the remaining Chinese men "plowed around groups of big rocks in the middle of the fields. They were the first human beings to dig into this part of the island and see the meat and bones of the red earth. After rain, the mud ran like blood. The maze tree and woodrose sprouted behind the plows" (103). To clear the rugged land for laying the railroad takes tremendous work, and Kingston describes this work in aggressive, even violent language, as when the felled redwood "at last stopped its fighting" and "sap ran from its cuts like crying blind eyes" (128). Hanging over open space in a basket, Ah Goong ejaculates into "the world's vagina": he "fucked the world" (133) and, as Kolodny would argue, rapes the land.

But feminist analysis alone is insufficient, for the intersection of race on gendered lives compels readings through an Asian American feminist lens. Kingston's critique may be leveled against the white man and the paradox of what historian Perry Miller calls "nature's nation," the cultural mythos that America sprung from the very ground of nature itself.[64] For minorities and the poor, however, "nature's nation" is actually experienced as nature's burden. Rachel Stein asserts that cultural historians "have yet to examine fully the complex interconnections between the settlers' imperative to subdue the wild terrain and their contemporaneous subordination of those peoples such as women, Native Americans, and African Americans, whom they associated in differing ways with wild nature" (1-2). Stein's work thus extends Kolodny's feminist interrogations of nature and begins to account for race as well as gender.

Therefore, as exercise 40 illustrates, I have students circle back to the stories of Bak Goong and Ah Goong with Stein's ideas. As an "antidote" (Kingston 105) to his work "like a savage" (104) in the cane, Bak Goong plants a garden near the huts, acknowledging nature's beauty rather than only its utilitarian value: "he even grew flowers, for which there was no edible use whatsoever" (105). Ah Goong and his fellow workers are used as "labor of building a new country" (128), but, as David Li argues, Ah Goong "has no political nor economic mastery over the land that he helped to tame" ("*China Men*" 491). The Chinese men in *China Men* are exploited as part of white America's settlement and destruction of the land. When whites develop dynamite, Chinese men are used as guinea pigs. As effective as dynamite is in blasting through the granite, its cost in human lives is also great: "The dynamite added more accidents and ways of dying, but if it were not used, the railroad would take fifty more years to finish" (Kingston 136).

The exploitation of Chinese men and their simultaneous exploitation of the land raise issues relevant to an Asian American feminist perspective, for *China Men* "at once employs feminist strategies and inverts certain feminist preconceptions" (Cheung, *Articulate* 102). Specifically, while silence is a theme in feminist literature and criticism, it takes on a different nature in *China Men*, as a crucial strategy by which Kingston emphasizes the parallels between the plight of Chinese men in America and Chinese women throughout history.

The white bosses, who do not allow the Chinese workers in the cane fields to speak, impose silence on Bak Goong. In "The Great Grandfather of the Sandalwood Mountains," the narrator stands at the edge of the sugarcane fields on the island of Chinaman's Hat, listening for the voices of her forefathers, and hears the "voice" of the land itself (90): "I have heard the land sing. I have seen the bright blue streaks of spirits whisking through the air. I again search for my American ancestors by listening in the cane" (90). Forced into silence by their white bosses (Bak Goong is whipped when "one day—he could not help it—he sang about the black mountains reddening and how mighty was the sun that shone on him in this enchanted forest and on his family in China" [100]), Bak Goong and the other Chinese men bury their voices in the land for the wind to carry: "They had dug an ear into the world, and were telling the earth their secrets" (117). By retelling the story, the narrative voice "redeem[s] the offensive name of the island" (Linton 44); Kingston calls it a "tribute to the pioneers" (90). She recaptures their laborious and profound contributions to the making of America, from the sugarcane fields of Hawaii to the transcontinental railroad.

In exercise 41, I demonstrate how I bring Shih's notion of "double commentary" (65), a simultaneous critique of white racism and Chinese sexism, to students. BaBa, too, becomes silent, largely as a result of his humiliation at the hands of a racist white society, but his silence, along with his misogynistic rantings, were destructive to the women in his family: "Worse than the swearing and the nightly screams were your silences when you punished us by not talking. You rendered us invisible, gone" (Kingston 14). Kingston's double commentary attempts to explain BaBa as both emasculated victim and abuser, a practitioner of a patriarchal code subjugating women: "But usually you did not play. You were angry. You scared us. Every day we listened to you swear, 'Dog vomit. Your mother's cunt. Your mother's smelly cunt.'... I made a wish that you only meant gypsies and not women in general" (12). Kingston recounts a frightening memory of her sister being chased and abused by her father, writing, "I watched him kick the door; the round mirror fell off the door and crashed. The door broke open, and he beat her" (253), but creates a measure of doubt as to its authenticity by remarking that her sister remembers the episode differently.

In the classroom, we further examine Chinese American feminist double commentary through circling back to earlier textual features, such as BaBa's legal journey to America. Students' studies of the journey from an Asian American feminist perspective will reveal that the immigration to the U.S involved many of the same indignities women in Old China faced upon marrying: changing one's parentage, changing one's name, and the feelings of entrapment and fear of a fate beyond one's control. Moreover, the men on the ship are housed on a floor below the women, which they perceive as deliberate humiliation by their white captors: "'The women are up there,' the father was told. Diabolical, inauspicious beginning—to be trodden over by women. 'Living under women's legs,' said the superstitious old-fashioned men from the backward villages. 'Climbed over by women.' It was bad luck even to walk under women's pants on clotheslines. No doubt the demons had deliberately planned this humiliation" (55). However, as Goellnicht asserts, Kingston mocks the men's feelings of superiority over the women (200).

Students revisit "The Great Grandfather of the Sandalwood Mountains" through a Chinese American feminist lens by focusing on "On Mortality," the interchapter which follows the chapter about Kingston's great-grandfather. As King-kok Cheung explains, "On Mortality" is Kingston's version of a Chinese *ch'uan-ch'I* tale, popular in the T'ang and Sung Dynasties in China (*Articulate* 111-12). In "On Mortality," a Taoist monk bestows riches upon Tu Tzu-ch'un. In return, the monk requires Tu to swallow pills which cause him to experience illusions. The monk forbids Tu from speaking and screaming while experiencing these illusions, enabling the monk to create a formula for immortality. During the experiences with his illusions, Tu remains silent, even through his wife's torturing; however, when he is reborn a woman, Tu screams at the sight of her husband bashing their son against the rocks. As a result of Tu's screams, the monk's magical elixir is ruined, and humans are subject to mortality. "On Mortality" thus reinforces the message of "The Great Grandfather of the Sandalwood Mountains," in which Bak Goong and his fellow Chinese American workers undermine white-imposed silence, a symbol of their oppression. But Kingston simultaneously critiques patriarchal values that silence women. In the Chinese fable, Tu-as-woman cannot resist the temption to scream, and thus she is seen to be weaker than men, ostensibly perpetuating this stereotype. But as Cheung asserts, screaming at the injuring of her child exhibits the strength in maternal love (112). However, in Kingston's fable, Tu's scream comes too late, and her silence leads to her son's death. Kingston thus critiques Chinese patriarchy, exposing the deadliness of silence imposed on women.[65]

Finally, the class circles back to examine "On Discovery" through a Chinese American feminist lens. In "On Discovery," Tang Ao, the male explorer, is captured by female inhabitants in The Land of Women and feminized, locked in a "canopied apartment equipped with pots of makeup, mirrors, and a woman's clothes" (Kingston 3). "On Discovery" thus alludes to how the Chinese man was feminized in America. Shih explains the relationship between "On Discovery" and *Flowers in the Mirror*, the classic eighteenth-century Chinese novel upon which this interchapter is based (66-69). In *Flowers,* Tang Ao rescues his friend, Lin Chih-yang, and neither are forced into servitude. Unlike the text upon which it is based, in Kingston's version, Tang Ao has no means for escape, symbolizing the ways in which Chinese men in America were exploited and feminized in their quest for the Gold Mountain, forced into "womanly" professions such as launderers and restaurant workers. Yet

Kingston's critique of sexism in the Chinese context cannot be ignored, since Tang Ao's physical tortures (such as foot binding) were traditionally suffered by Chinese women to enhance their beauty and ensure their servitude. By reversing gender roles and subjecting a man to the tortures and humiliations women are forced to bear, Kingston exposes the inhumanity of such practices.[66]

For their final exercise on *China Men* (exercise 42), I ask students to consider Cheung's assertion that "On Listening," the final chapter of *China Men*, attests to Kingston's desire for "connection across difference" (*Articulate* 124): "To translate from different languages, to listen without insisting on a single story line is also to reach beyond one's workaday horizon, to see with other eyes, to open oneself to a variety of experiences, and to spin an intersubjective network" (125). By teaching at the crossroads of identity in *China Men* and exposing students to a variety of cultural and historical perspectives to supplement their understanding of Kingston's vision, we are realizing Kingston's desire for "connection across difference."

6 CONCLUSION

At the Crossroads and Beyond: Literature by Women of Color and the Future of Multicultural Literary Studies

Between the masks we've internalized, one on top of another, are our interfaces. The masks are already steeped with self-hatred and other internalized oppressions. However, it is the place—the interface—between the masks that provides the space from which we can thrust out and crack the masks.

—*Gloria Anzaldúa,* "Haciendo caras, una entrada"

At the Crossroads of Multiculturalism and Literary Studies

I have been using the term "crossroads" to signify a place where cultures and critical perspectives meet and to suggest a conceptual framework for how to approach multicultural women's literature in the classroom. But "crossroads" has another meaning: *a crucial point or place.* I believe multicultural literary studies is at a crossroads—a crucial point—due to sustained attacks on multiculturalism from the Right, as most readers of this book are probably aware, as well as from the Left, mainly from inside the academy itself. In this concluding chapter, I hope to convey how we can effectively counter these loud and potentially destructive voices as we work to carry on the multicultural mission of breaking down social, political, and economic heirarchies and nurturing a new world vision commensurate with the complexities of a multicultural world.

Canon debates, multiculturalism, political correctness, and cultural literacy have placed literary studies at the center of the culture wars in the public arena and in the academy. Both the purpose and scope of literary studies have been questioned, and rightly so, given the dramatic changes that multiculturalism has brought. But the attacks have become so exaggerated and relentless that it has become difficult for students to take multiculturalism seriously and for instructors to sustain its goals. In the popular press, most of what gets published is anti-academic, uncompromising in its attacks on professors, scholars, syllabi, and classrooms.[67] Opponents of multiculturalism on the Right ascribe cynical motives and consequences to the academy's multicultural mission. They see multiculturalism as the beginning of America's balkanization and downfall, its emphasis on cultural difference and diversity undermining any hope of fostering the unity they see as necessary for the creation of a harmonious nation of Americans.

Multiculturalism's embrace of cultural pluralism has led to the Right's unfounded accusations of an "anything goes" moral and cultural relativism and suggestions that what instructors do in their classrooms will obliterate all sense of shared moral principles and destroy the moral fabric of American society. Many of the most vocal opponents of multicultural education reduce the intellectual work going on in multicultural classrooms to enforced political correctness. They believe multiculturalists regard all aspects of Western culture as evil and, worse yet, try to steer our students into such a view. Clifford Orwin, for example, argues that the appeal of multiculturalism is not its theoretical consistency but its politics. Although Orwin says it is beneficial to expand the range of fields represented in university curricula (such as Russian studies, etc.), he does not believe this is what multiculturalism is about. Rather, he sees it more sinisterly, as a "repudiation of existing practice" so that "so-called multiculturalism has less to do with [teachers] exposing Western students to the serious study of other cultures" than with teachers indoctrinating students with "their critique of the West" (5). Another opponent of multiculturalism, Joseph Wagner, argues that the "theme of exclusion is central to the multiculturalist critique" because it centers on how the curriculum "is allegedly filtered through male, homophobic spectacles" (409).

Debating cultural and moral relativism at any great length is beyond the scope of this study.[68] However, it is enough to say that I believe that multiculturalism can and should differentiate between cultural pluralism and cultural relativism. That is, unlike cultural relativism, which eschews compartmentalizing evaluations and thus seems to value everything equally, cultural pluralism recognizes a wide variety of cultural practices and beliefs, but it does not necessarily validate them all, and it is incumbent upon instructors to foster critical judgment in students. Moreover, multicultural commitments—fighting inequities based on race, class, gender, and sexuality—indeed invoke shared moral principles. Clearly, then, multicultural literary study can address and redress—through the study of literary texts—the social, political, and economic injustices in American society.

Some of the attacks on multiculturalism from the academic Left raise significant questions which must be addressed. These critics argue that multiculturalism does not go far enough; it is merely a revised form of white hegemony, benign and uncritical, even as diversity is celebrated (a multiculturalism in which difference becomes sameness). Some critical multiculturalists also accuse white multiculturalists of appropriation and a benign superiority.[69] In this view, the liberal multicultural agenda superficially addresses inequities by producing what seems like a happy harmony of difference and tolerance but does not produce social, political, or economic change. Multiculturalism, they argue, turns difference into sameness, even as it seeks to celebrate diversity by lumping all nonwhite cultures together under the rubric of "difference." As such, multiculturalism fails to bring about sustantive changes in power relations.

However, other potentially detrimental conflicts have troubled multicultural literary studies and threaten its integrity. Debates over theory evidence English studies' vibrancy and indeed constitute the basis for the framework for theorizing literature by women of color at the center of this book. When these debates are racialized, however, they are divisive rather than productive, as is now the case now within multicultural studies. European-derived theories currently dominating English studies are seen by many—both white and nonwhite—as reserved for white European American intellectuals. Like questions over literary value and canonical status, the debate over theory involves questions of authority, of what is authorized—and by whom—as "theoretical enough," and whether only one kind of theory is acceptable. Many practitioners of non-Eurocentric theory believe they are devalued not only by colleagues in literary studies but by the realities of the rewards system in higher education.[70]

Yet some of these same scholars decry white scholars and instructors for practicing and teaching ethnic literature. Thus "identity politics," which Katherine Mayberry defines as the "negotiation of and for power derived from minority group affiliation" (2), comes down to who can appropriately interpret, evaluate, and teach multicultural literature, and it poses a substantial threat to multicultural literary studies. As Arnold Krupat observes, the "critical world today" is "very much a place of 'us' and 'them'" (*Turn* 2). The call for greater attention to theoretical issues in an effort to resist appropriation by the literary establishment, particularly in terms of multiculturalism's tendency to fall in line with and reinforce dominant assumptions, would be more forceful if it were not steeped in divisive rhetoric. An "us versus them" mentality is unproductive and antithetical to the larger purpose of teaching multicultural literature. Moreover, it adds fuel to conservative claims that multiculturalism in education will lead to balkanization and further hostility among the racial and ethnic groups that comprise the U.S. As Obioma Nnaemeka claims, identity politics as an end in itself rather than as a means to an end may hinder rather than promote social change: "the security that identity politics can offer may insulate us from forming the alliances necessary for political action" (302). It is time to move away from divisive rhetoric and toward fruitful debate and dialogue. Conflict can be productive if it leads to intellectual debate and change rather than irreparable division. MELUS President TuSmith's reflections on the heated exchanges over identity politics at the 2001 MELUS Conference likewise encourage open dialogue that confronts rather than skirts these explosive issues: "To tell someone what we really think, even if it's not the polite thing to say, requires caring enough to make the effort. The point is, the interchange demonstrated that we can survive such disagreements with our integrity intact. Open engagement isn't lethal" ("Message").

The identity politics argument is simply untenable, for it would be utterly counterproductive to limit one's teaching to texts representative of one's culture(s). It is important for young people of color to see themselves in the texts they read in school. But it is also important to include diverse literatures in classes largely comprised of white students, for literature by writers of multicultural backgrounds has a particular power to effect multicultural understanding. These texts allow students to experiences worlds which might be new or unfamiliar to them. The answer is not to dictate who can (and cannot) teach what, but to teach unfamiliar texts in the most meaningful, informed ways. Linda Alcoff provides a basic guide for determining when one might appropriately speak for/about others, acknowledging the potential dangers of keeping silent about multicultural issues in one's classrooms when she asks: "will it enable the empowerment of oppressed peoples?" (116). Nancy Peterson, in the context of a discussion of identity politics, argues that "white professors who are willing to examine and question their own standpoint of privileged whiteness…can help engage white students in similar kinds of critical analyses as well as demonstrate to black students that allies can be found to fight the war against racism" (35). I believe that Peterson's argument can be applied to teachers of subject matter by all nonwhite ethnic groups. The reticence of white instructors to discuss their own privilege negates much of the work that multiculturalists have struggled long to achieve.

In the introduction to *Making Face, Making Soul/Haciendo Caras*, Anzaldúa calls for "*mestizaje* theories":

> Theorists-of-color are in the process of trying to formulate "marginal" theories that are partially outside and partially inside the Western frame of reference (if that is possible), theories that overlap many "worlds." We are articulating new positions in these "in-between," Borderland worlds of ethnic communities and academies, feminist and job worlds. In our literature, social issues such as race, class and sexual difference are intertwined with the narrative and poetic elements of a text, elements in which theory is embedded. In our *mestizaje* theories we create new categories for those of us left out or pushed out of the existing ones. We recover and examine non-Western aesthetics while critiquing Western aesthetics; recover and examine non-rational modes and "blanked-out" realities while critiquing rational, consensual reality; recover and examine indigenous languages while critiquing the "languages" of the dominant culture. And we simultaneously combat the tokenization and appropriation of our literatures and our writers/artists. (xxvi)

The space instructors create for students at the crossroads of texts by women of color can accomplish such work, regardless of the instructor's color, race, ethnicity, gender, or sexual orientation. The crossroads model "transform[s]" the "theorizing space"(xxv) in such a way that knowledges intersect and enrich; as a result, this pedagogy provides intellectual challenges and experiences as well as empathic ones, and it is empathy, Anzaldúa claims, that may lead to understanding (xxi).

Anna Louise Keating claims that by breaking down the Self/Other binary by "naming the other(s) in herself, and herself in the other(s)" (39), Anzaldúa invites all of us, "whatever color, class, ethnicity, or sex 'we' are," into new spaces "where transcultural/sexual/gender/class identifications—*mestizaje* connections—can occur" (40), thereby transforming identity politics. Anzaldúa echoes this inclusivity in an interview with Ann Reuman, stating that it was "risk[y]" to "open up the concept of *mestizaje*, of the new *mestiza* and hybridity, to be non-exclusive, to be inclusive of white people and people from other communities" (6). In the same interview, she speaks of her work as a "support beam" (7) for others' theories and envisions her audience as broader than Chicana, lesbian, and working-class people (9), and she seems eager to share her work in this manner so long as these theorists resist appropriation.

We—that is, all teachers interested in fostering a diverse curriculum for a diverse student body—can fight back and counter the broad attacks on multicultural education in literary studies by creating responsible, sound, and cohesive pedagogy. Controversies come with the academic territory, but if we allow the conflicts to overwhelm the objectives of our teaching, we pave the way for multiculturalism to be merely a passing fad rather than a permanent foundation for a liberal education. We need to get beyond internal "us" versus "them" rhetorics of division and mistrust to have any hope for our students to get beyond these mentalities in the world beyond our classrooms. Constance Coiner argues, like Henry Louis Gates, Jr., that we cannot respond uncritically to the backlash against multiculturalism but must instead "turn our skepticism inward" and be "as rigorously critical of the new pluralism as we were of the exclusively white male canon and curricula" (211). I agree. Through sound pedagogy we can make headway in countering the critics of multiculturalism in the popular press and in the academy. We must carefully scrutinize and articulate our goals both inside and outside the classroom.

Teaching at the Crossroads: Ethical Multiculturalism

Finally, then, I want to clearly articulate my vision of multicultural education in literary studies. The framework I have articulated throughout this book is a step toward realizing this vision as we include texts by women of color in our classrooms. In its embrace of the pluralities in the lives of women writers of color, teaching at the crossroads fosters the values of a *multicultural democracy*, a term I use to emphasize the congruence of cultural difference and diversity with democratic values. Like Catharine Stimpson, I understand multiculturalism as "both a historical truth and a possible good, a value that promises to invigorate our culture, society, and curricula" (6). Multiculturalism attempts to understand cultural difference, especially for minority and disadvantaged groups, but it also seeks the connections among us. Cultural differences and diversity are not synonymous with disunity and separatism; these connections predispose us to work against the forces of hate, bigotry, and injustice that surround us. By invoking both shared principles and differences, multiculturalism can counteract societal practices that undermine equality and justice.

Among my goals is a critical examination of Western civilization in the context of the many and diverse cultures that comprise it. Influences and interactions are multidirectional. Multicultural education acknowledges that the history and cultures of the many ethnic groups that comprise the U.S. have been generally neglected and devalued. Multicultural education strives to bring about new and expanded understanding about cultural differences at the individual and societal levels as it simultaneously enacts a critique of the power relations that have historically worked to disenfranchise people of color in this nation, and which continue to undermine efforts at equality. I approach the rhetoric of diversity skeptically and pay careful attention to its potential to mask the fear of differences that can underlie it. Likewise, I am aware of the danger in embracing the notion of a common culture that respects and celebrates difference, the fear that it will result in the pernicious grand narratives of what one must look and be like to be "American."

Literary studies has an important role to play in multicultural education. In response to those opponents of multicultural literary study who devalue our work as scholars and teachers, I suggest that the pedagogical work with respect to texts by women of color is among the most ethically and intellectually compelling work we can do. As Liza Fiol-Matta asserts, "inclusion of the scholarship on women of color is not only working against ignorance and apathy; it is also overtly antiracist, anticlassist, antisexist work" (7). Simply put, teaching a diverse canon furthers democratic values.

James Marshall claims that perhaps literary specialists' "greatest uncertainty" is the reason for teaching literature (240). I believe, however, that there is a consensus, and that it is time to articulate it loudly and clearly. It is time to acknowledge the tacit, shared desire to influence our students' social, political, and ethical development, even though newer understandings of a text's multiple meanings, in conjunction with process-oriented approaches to literary study, have radically altered the idea that we can impart to students a text's fixed meaning. No doubt, these ideals embrace an inclusive notion of what it means to be an American in a multicultural democracy. Multicultural educators share a commitment to fairness, justice, and equality. Our literature courses teach students about cultural diversity, and representations and ideas to counter the disparaging stereotypes of popular culture. We ask students to reflect critically on what it means to live as a contributing member of a multicultural democracy. As Wayne Booth asserts, the issue is one of character development (as it has always been with the study of literature), "the construction of a certain kind of person" ("Ethics" 42), despite the anti-foundational turn in English studies. Booth points to the ethical quality of treating the "other" justly and humanely as one of the virtues we seek in our students (42). Like Lauter, I believe that one crucial reason for reading and teaching such texts is "that they *teach us* how to view experience through the prisms of gender, race, nationality, and other forms of marginalization"

("Canon Theory" 135).

Barbara Herrnstein Smith's landmark article (and a tremendous amount of scholarship following in her footsteps) on the contingency of value has completely altered our understanding of how aesthetics and politics are inextricably intertwined. Nevertheless, we cannot ignore the particular power that imaginative literature has on our lives. I have chosen the four books in my study partially because they provide important lessons about cultural diversity and because their messages of power and oppressions, hope and survival, are impossible to ignore. But I have also chosen them because they are aesthetically compelling. In the end, literature is about language, the ways in which writers use their gift of language to invigorate the thinking of their readers.

Clearly, literature alone does not have the potential to effect sweeping social and political change. No matter what we do in the literature classroom, we will not resolve the pressing issues of poverty and racism; but it is a place to start. How and what we teach to our students in literary studies surely goes beyond concerns of the English department.[71] Literature may not effect full-fledged ideological transformations in students, but it can plant the seed for students' social consciousness, and I am content to begin here. I hope students will continue to develop these values as they progress through their college and professional careers. And this is not unique to women's literary study, for as Gregory asserts, no education is ever about "once-and-for-all doneness" but about "put[ting] students on the path of developing powers that they will continue to use—and continue to develop—throughout their lives" (75).

Teaching at the crossroads is a model for productive dialogue rather than divisive conflict. Like the texts themselves, this classroom praxis enacts a dynamic interplay of cultural debate. Teaching at the crossroads "does not erase difference but also does not allow difference to be unbridgeable" (Peterson 33). I am not suggesting we ignore Palumbo-Liu's concerns about a "liberal" rather than "critical" multiculturalism, where the former simply pretends that because differences are celebrated rather than denigrated, all is equal and harmonious (Introduction 5-14). A multicultural approach to education must foster real social change, or it ceases to have value. It must be a transformative politics rather than an abstract, ineffectual ideology. But I believe in the power of language—particularly creative literature—to (re)shape beliefs. I am, therefore, suggesting that our approaches to multicultural women's literature must, like Sherley Williams asserts is true of literature itself, promote dialogue and community: "theories or ways of reading ought actively to promote the enlargement of both" (520). Rather than impose specific readings on texts by women of color or try to assimilate them to what is familiar to us as readers (and thus reduce difference to sameness), we need to open up the dialogue within. These texts have the power to transform us, as Cherríe Moraga asserts in the foreword to the second edition of Moraga's and Anzaldúa's *This Bridge Called My Back*: "The political writer…is the ultimate optimist, believing people are capable of change and using words as one way to try and penetrate the privatism of our lives" (Moraga, "Refugees").[72] Women of color write for many audiences and purposes, as Moraga claims, chief among them "to anyone who will listen with their ears open (even if only a crack) to the currents of change around them ("Refugees"). By listening to what the texts say, by hearing the conflicts and cultures within, we closely emulate in our literary critical approach the values of a committed multiculturism.

Notes

Chapter 1

1. See, for example, Bridget Murphy and Roberta Trooien; Constance Ruzich; and Jody Swilky.

2. As Patricia Bizzell asserts, "both the whats and the hows of teaching literature have been challenged on similar grounds: the literary canon because it supposedly privileges work by white middle- and upper-class men and the lecture-and-test format because it supposedly institutionalizes patriarchal power in the teacher" ("Politics" 4).

3. Some scholars believe New Critical approaches still dominate today in our classrooms (see Alberti, Introduction; Steven Lynn).

4. Of course, we know that all readings are intertwined with politics, so even New Critical approaches were never apolitical.

5. The most significant projects include Lil Brannon and Brenda Greene's *Rethinking American Literature* (1997), John Maitino and David Peck's *Teaching American Ethnic Literatures* (1996), Bonnie TuSmith and Gerald Bergevin's *Colorizing Literary Theory*, a special issue of *Modern Language Studies* (1996), John Alberti's *The Canon in the Classroom: The Pedagogical Implications of Canon Revision in American Literature* (1995), Bruce Goebel and James Hall's *Teaching a "New Canon"? Students, Teachers, and Texts in the College Literature Classroom* (1995), David Palumbo-Liu's *The Ethnic Canon: Histories, Institutions, and Interventions* (1995), and Abdul JanMohamed and David Lloyd's *The Nature and Context of Minority Discourse* (1990). Significantly, each of these texts is an edited collection, and the editors tend to draw conclusions and connections about multicultural pedagogy from the varied and diverse articles within their collections.

6. William Cain says, "the more closely one inspects debates between those who espouse theory and those who do not, the more these debates turn out to concern just what the proper procedures *are* for literary study, and thus they pivot on theoretical choices, assumptions, preferences" (4).

7. Here, my objective is to reference my use of the term "multicultural literature." In my concluding chapter, I will discuss the many forms of multiculturalism more broadly in relationship to the pedagogical framework I am advocating.

8. The following scholars also use the term "multicultural literature" to refer to the diverse literature of previously-marginalized groups: Alberti, "Teaching" (Alberti's article

underscores the notion of race, including whiteness, as a social construction); Bizzell, "Negotiating Difference"; Patrick Bjork; Goebel and Hall; Jay, "End"; Nancy Peterson; Ronald Primeau; and Joseph Trimmer.

9. At Penn State University, where I teach, English 135 is called "Alternative Voices in American Literature," and is described in the course catalog as "U.S. writers from diverse backgrounds offering varying responses to issues such as race, class, gender, and ethnicity."

10. However, Anzaldúa calls "multiculturalism" a "euphemism for the imperializing and now defunct 'melting pot'" ("Haciendo" xxii).

Chapter 2

11. Phillipa Kafka puts it this way: This "'dominant ideology' monster" too easily "subsume[s], then digest[s] and eliminate[s]," noncanonical texts ("Another" 33). Louis Owens likewise calls it a "discourse of dominance" or "critical imperialism" (53).

12. Stephen Souris combines cultural information with his analysis of this text as a multiple narrator novel.

13. Reed Dasenbrock suggests that students will never fully or genuinely understand another culture if they "translat[e] it into [their] own terms" ("Intelligibility" 18).

14. See Maitino and Peck, Introduction 12; Rico and Mano 105; Elder 6; and TuSmith, "Cultural Translator" 20.

15. Gates asserts that feminist studies has greatly impacted African American studies: "black studies and women's studies have met on the common terrain of black women's studies, ensuring a larger audience for black women authors than ever before" ("African" 304).

16. Ann duCille, however, argues that black women writers have become "politically correct, intellectually popular, and commercially precious sites of literary and historical inquiry" (24), resulting in unprecedented attention to previously neglected and ignored writing and the "quasi-canonical" status of Hurston, Morrison, and Walker (24). DuCille thus remains wary of the co-opting of black feminist criticism and black women's writing by black males, white males, and white feminists.

17. As I have argued elsewhere, despite feminist criticism's focus on the white, middle-class woman, its history does allow for the voices of women of color. Gilbert and Gubar also point to the diversity in a women's tradition, asserting the existence of "a number of traditions within [women's literary] history—the black, the regional, the lesbian, the working-class, and the native-American traditions" (Preface xxx). Thus, in this pioneering feminist work, Gilbert and Gubar already include ethnic women writers within a larger female literary tradition and as part of alternate traditions.

18. The race, class, and gender triad is still being considered. As Fox-Genovese asserts, "the most pressing issues remain economic" (238), even and especially for poor women of color. Moreover, continued gains by middle-class women may indeed be made at the expense of poor women (238).

19. This discussion emerges not only from classroom practice but also from theorizing about the strengths and weaknesses of that practice.

20. The Ford Foundation's Mainstreaming Minority Women's Program, an experiment in higher education curricular transformation, addressed the void of women of color in higher education curricula. The breadth and scope of this project, which involved hundreds of thousands of dollars and a variety of intensive conferences, seminars, colloquia, and workshops, indicates how demanding curricular reform can be.

21. Sandoval calls these interstices in which women of color exist a "third gender category," dismantling the male/female binary with which white feminist hegemony is concerned (5).

22. I have found that Shirley Geok-lin Lim's *Approaches to Teaching Kingston's* The Woman Warrior is an enormously useful book for pointing out the myriad critical and cultural approaches to *The Woman Warrior*. One way of understanding the crossroads model is to use the various contributions in Lim's collection interspersed in the same classroom, rather than as separate approaches from which an instructor chooses one over another in a given semester.

23. VanSpanckeren's article "The Asian Literary Background of *The Woman Warrior*" led me to Lady Mu's warrior song, which can be found in *Selections*.

24. Anzaldúa says she now prefers the term *nepantla* to borderlands because it emphasizes the inner, spiritual dimension (Speech, Lehigh University).

Chapter 3

25. Three recent important projects addressing these profound changes and accompanying uncertainties—Eugene Goodheart's *Does Literary Studies Have a Future?* (1999), Carl Woodring's *Literature: An Embattled Profession* (1999), and Michael Bérubé's *The Employment of English: Theory, Jobs, and the Future of Literary Studies* (1998)—evidence the tentative state of the discipline.

26. I do not want to dismiss Ruland's critique, for many of his points are instructive, raising issues that remain largely unresolved. Interested readers should consult Ruland's critique ("Art"), Lauter's response ("On the Implications"), and Ruland's response ("A Reply").

27. MELUS' website, at http://www.marshall.edu/melus/, describes the society as follows: "Founded in 1973, MELUS endeavors to expand the definition of American literature through the study and teaching of Latino American, Native American, African American, Asian and Pacific American, and ethnically specific Euro-American literary works, their authors, and their cultural contexts." The 2001 MELUS Conference focused on what the Call for Proposals called the "second wave" of the struggle to broaden American literature: "assessing the value of the uncovered and recovered texts and sharing judgments" (see Rodier).

28. While there is a good deal of debate over whether or not we should be thinking of canonizing previously-excluded texts, there can be little doubt that such canonizing does occur.

29. In particular, Berg argues that Naylor uses Whitman's controversial "Whoever You Are Holding Me Now in Hand" to inform both the relationship of two of her characters in *Linden Hills*, Winston and David, as well as to form a bridge between multicultural literature and the canonical tradition ("Giving Sound" 99).

30. Cervantes' "Visions of Mexico While at a Writing Symposium in Port Townsend, Washington" is less frequently anthologized than "Heritage."

31. Jude Todd's bibliography led me to find this folktale in Boas, *Keresan Texts Part 1*; see also Lummis for relevant Native American folktales.

32. I agree with Bizzell and Olson that thematic groupings too easily fall into the trap of universalizing experience without confronting difference, although I also think it is important for text selections to do more than just present intractable cultural differences.

33. The pedagogical model Lanier describes, designed around students' explorations of interpretive strategies, makes no mention of its applicability to ethnic or ethnic women's texts. While some would argue that the four critical approaches in this model—formalist, historical, psychoanalytic, and feminist—could be appropriately applied to ethnic women's texts, I suggest these approaches would be arbitrarily chosen rather than as emanating from the specific concerns of texts by women of color.

34. See also Dasenbrock, "Why Read," for a critique of representation as a criterion for choosing texts.

35. I think it's clear that we can never truly cover any text in a semester-long class, even if we were to spend an entire semester on it. The difference in the crossroads approach, however, is the choice to focus on one particular textual element, acknowledging at the outset that a great deal of the text's other features and meanings may not be addressed.

36. For example, Penn State University, Berks-Lehigh Valley College, where I teach, has made a strong commitment to excellent teaching as well as to the teaching-research connection.

37. These methodologies represent the paradigm shift from "instruction-centered" to "learning-centered" pedagogical practices occurring across universities and particularly in English studies (Barr and Tagg).

38. Suggested readings include Thomas Sowell's "Multicultural Education is Harmful," Lauter's "Preface to the First Edition" of *The Heath Anthology of American Literature*, Barbara Pace's "The Textbook Canon: Genre, Gender, and Race in U.S. Literature Anthologies," and Sandra Stotsky's "Academic Guidelines for Selecting Multiethnic and Multicultural Literature."

39. I will discuss the thorny issue of identity politics in greater detail in chapter 6.

40. For example, Alex Wang informs his readers that the Chinese custom of nomenclature is the reason Kingston doesn't use the given names of her grandfather and great-grandfather (203). She isn't necessarily trying to make them "universal" or represen-

tative of all Chinese or Chinese American men, as some critics have argued. Indeed, in a class where my students read both Rivera's *...y no se lo tragó la tierra*, where the unnamed narrator is likely meant to represent the collective Chicano experience, and *China Men*, it was particularly confusing.

41. Of course, this is true for many works in the canon as well, as any readers/scholars/instructors of T.S. Eliot's *The Wasteland* or Ezra Pound's *Cantos* can attest. The difference is that we cannot always find accompanying reading guides to lead us through the unfamiliar and obscure allusions in texts by women of multicultural backgrounds.

42. The phrase "cautionary tale" comes from the title of Trimmer's article.

Chapter 4

43. However, most recent feminist studies of the contemporary female *Bildungsroman* view it as emancipatory, reflecting women's progress. But others point to the ways in which class and other social, in addition to psychological, determinants problematize personal liberation, as well as the inherent contradictions in the individualist orientation of the *Bildungsroman* and the communal concerns of feminism (see Felski; Midalia).

44. However, John Akers' analysis of the use of fragmentation in Chicano literature as a "consciously chosen path" to seek integration and meaning (124) links Chicanas with their male counterparts.

45. Krupat combines Bakhtin's dialogism with Native American cultural values. David Moore uses theories of Foucault, Derrida, and other Western theorists to argue that Silko challenges modernist and postmodernist conceptions of subjectivity, thus "multiply[ing] the available positions of postcolonial subjects" (371). At the crossroads of identity, *Storyteller*'s place in the tradition of postmodern literature is apparent.

46. A number of resources can be used to bring Native American visual art into the classroom, and I am indebted to Hertha Wong's bibliography for many of these sources. For example, see Gary Witherspoon's *Language and Art in the Navajo Universe;* Frederick J. Dockstader's *Indian Art in America*; and Le Roy H. Appleton's *Indian Art of the Americas*. Originally, I included specific website addresses in this manuscript. However, I have since found that these sites come and go, so I believe it is a better idea to simply encourage instructors and students to search the Web.

47. Both Apess' and Copway's autobiographical texts are excerpted in a number of anthologies, including *The Heath Anthology of American Literature, Vol. 1*.

48. Allen's "Teaching American Indian Women's Literature" has an extensive bibliography of Keres texts. Franz Boas' *Keresan Texts Part 1* and *Keresan Texts, Vol. 1 & 2* are also excellent sources. Anthony Purley's "Keres Pueblo Concepts of Deity" includes short excerpts from a portion of the Keres Thought Woman story and a Keres origin story.

49. Allen's "Teaching American Indian Women's Literature" is an excellent source for crossroads texts.

50. This poem can be found in Jerome Beaty and J. Paul Hunter's *New Worlds of Literature*. However, it should be noted that neither the poem's headnote or accompanying study questions in *New Worlds* mention Spider Woman. The headnote states, "the speaker of this poem acknowledges the debt of life and of tradition to 'grandmother' and pays the debt by following some of the old ways, remembering and preserving them" (264). Thus the headnote does link the contemporary poem to tribal ways in a general sense, but in its mention of "grandmother," it may obscure the cultural contexts for a more universal notion of grandmother.

51. I am indebted to Susan J. Scarberry for helping me find works on and about Spider Woman.

52. Although early studies of women's autobiography tended to focus primarily on gendered differences between male and female versions of the genre, "second stage" theorizing collapsed this binary by including multiple influences on women's autobiographical writing (see Smith and Watson 10-13).

Chapter 5

53. Postmodern theories provide a number of additional entry points into the text, including explanations of the character Beloved. Rebecca Ferguson asserts that Beloved may appear to be postmodern because she "brings the whole traumatic experience of slavery with her" and "contains the *effects* that slavery had, its profound fragmentation of the self and of the connections the self might have with others .... her confusion is profound; she is dislocated within herself as well as dislocated in time, full of grief and need, love and resentment"(114).

54. A number of texts about literary criticism and theory are written specifically for students in ways that untangle the difficulties of postmodernism, poststructuralism, and deconstruction. For example, see Thomas Fink; Steven Lynn; and Lois Tyson.

55. Another Western-based approach to the infanticide is a comparison with Euripides' *Medea*. Kristina Chew argues that *Beloved* and *Medea* have remarkable thematic connections we cannot ignore, but that Morrison provides a greater sense of compassion for the mother who killed her children (67).

56. Ridley points out that Pan-African lore and analyses of its idiom, values, and aesthetics are accessible from many college and university libraries. I have used John Roberts' *From Trickster to Badman: The Black Folk Hero in Slavery and Freedom*, which Ridley cites in his article, to further educate myself on some of these traditions. Other sources include H.C. Brearley's "Ba-ad Nigger," which is a short but thorough analysis.

57. See Vanessa E. Jones; Joan Morgan; and Robin Roberts for discussions of black women, feminism, and rap music.

58. *China Men* is the companion book to *The Woman Warrior* (1977). Though I

would recommend reading both books, I absolutely believe *China Men* can stand on its own and does not need to be read in conjunction with *The Woman Warrior*.

59. Arguably, *China Men* is equally or more concerned with Kingston's desire to understand herself, a personal story to reconstruct family history. Kingston says in an interview that "In *The Woman Warrior* 'I' begin the quest for self by understanding the archetypal mother. In *China Men*, 'I' become more whole because of the ability to appreciate the other gender" (qtd. in Cheung, *Articulate* 101). Yet because her past, especially her father and the role of Chinese men in the U.S., plays such a critical role in the narrator's understanding of self, the book has both a personal and a collective purpose.

60. As of this writing, the unofficial *Blackhawk* website can be found at http://www.geocities.com/Area51/Labyrinth/1693/blk_main.html. The website has excerpts from the comics, as well as pictures of the characters, including Chop-Chop. It also leads readers to an article called "From Chop-Chop to Wu Cheng: The Evolution of the Chinese Character in *Blackhawk* Comic Books," by Carla Zimmerman. Zimmerman traces Chop-Chop's evolution throughout the years of *Blackhawk*'s existence, from faithful and subservient cook/assistant (1941-55) to a nondescript quasi-Caucasian (1956-66), to a master in the martial arts (1967-69; 1976), to the only non-Caucasian member in a multinational team (1982-84). She argues that this evolution reflects the country's increasing sensitivity to ethnic stereotyping. (Interestingly, Zimmerman calls him Blackhawk's "Man Friday," an obvious reference to *Robinson Crusoe*.) Chop-Chop's next stage as a nondescript culture-less being occurred as a result of America's involvement with Korea against Communist China. By the late 1960s, Chop-Chop was reinvented as Dr. Hand, a martial arts expert, which Zimmerman calls a step forward, even if in retrospect another stereotype. In 1983 (the comic book was out of print for a number of years), after seeking public response, Chop-Chop was finally addressed by his real name, Wu Cheng, and given an official black leather uniform.

61. Alex Wang asserts that "The Ghostmate" is modeled after Pu Songling's ghost stories, which were an integral part of the childhood of Chinese children (206). Wang uses one of these ghost stories, "The Painted Skin," in his class to consider how and why Kingston would want to rewrite it.

62. Frank Chin's poem, "SONG OF THE MONOGRAM WARNER BROS. CHINK: News to Raise the Dead," also works in this context, although I have not used it because I find the poem too disturbing and misogynistic. As Elaine Kim argues, the "first step in reclaiming the manhood of the Chinese American [through "SONG"] is to gang-rape Joy, who represents the indifferent white majority" (*Asian* 181-82).

63. In my experiences, without these texts in the classroom, students are quite skeptical about feminist readings of the conquest myth.

64. The phrase "nature's nation" comes from the title of Miller's renowned work.

65. Goellnicht argues similarly that "muteness/silence is held up by patriarchy as an ideal of womanhood," evidenced by Tu's parents' comments about her silence as an example to other women (195). Kingston, however, reinscribes maternal love as superior to immortality, simultaneously playing on the Edenic myth and Eve's disobedience (196).

66. Pin-chia Feng observes that Kingston also refers in "On Discovery" to Empress Wu, the "only woman in Chinese history who founded a dynasty by herself and the only one who appropriated the male royal title by making herself an 'Emperor'" (145). However, she has been downplayed and dismissed as a "wily fox spirit" in Chinese history (145). By referring to Wu, Kingston comments on the parallelism of Chinese "official" history and its erasure of women's voices to the U.S. erasure of Chinese immigrants from American history (145).

Chapter 6

67. Jay points out that these attacks are often "cast in the exaggerated and sensational language of scandal and cynicism that now constitutes the tone of American journalism" (*American* 3).

68. Interested readers can consult, among others, David Annis; Reed Way Dasenbrock, "Why Read"; Judith Wagner DeCew; and Phyllis Mentzell Ryder.

69. For example, Palumbo-Liu suggests that the "assumptions and elisions of the liberal argument for multiculturalism" appropriate both the scholarship and literature ("Introduction" 10), essentially accusing whites of self-serving goals in their commitment to reading, interpreting, and teaching multicultural literature.

70. TuSmith feels it necessary to defend her own work as theoretical, because it has been attacked and demeaned by those she claims subscribe to "the Big-T" ("Opening" 60), a "narrowly specialized discourse" that she attacks as "unintelligible" (60) and "overspecialized, elitist, and mostly irrelevant" (64).

71. Again, I quote Lauter: "What is at stake, after all…is what a society sees as important from its past to the construction of its future, who decides that, and on what basis" (Lauter, "Canon Theory" 143).

72. Moraga's foreword to the second edition of *This Bridge Called My Back* is not numbered. This quote, as well as the one that follows, appear on the third page of the foreword.

Appendix A: Classroom Exercises

The following series of exercises offers an example of classroom assignments and activities derived from the specific crossroads approaches to *The House on Mango Street*, *Storyteller*, *Beloved*, and *China Men* described in chapters 4 and 5. These exercises also demonstrate the ways that the crossroads model can be used to teach any text. Most of these exercises encourage students to do two things: to examine particular features of a crossroads text, and to make connections between the crossroads texts and the primary text under study. In my classroom I have used most of these exercises as discussion questions in various forms. For example, sometimes I give students questions as homework assignments to prepare them for class discussions, while other times I use the same set of questions (perhaps modified in minor ways) to stimulate small group discussions in class.

I have also included four culminating writing assignments for *The House on Mango Street*, *Storyteller*, *Beloved*, and *China Men*, respectively. At the end of crossroads study of a particular text, I almost always use a writing assignment as a way for students to reflect on and bring together the numerous perspectives they have studied. Often, these writing assignments lead us to rich class discussions.

This appendix begins with a two-part exercise that launches crossroads study by bringing students' attention to the issues of multiculturalism, canonization, and literary value. Part two of that exercise describes a group project requiring students to study and evaluate the literature curricula of local high schools through a multicultural lens. This project has been enormously successful; one group's report was recently published in *The Oswald Review*, a national undergraduate English research journal (see McFeaters, et al.). Finally, I have included a few sample research projects designed to provide students with a context for understanding the crossroads of texts and cultures which may be unfamiliar to many of them.

I hope that these exercises serve as examples of the kinds of assignments relevant to the crossroads model. In particular, I believe such assignments should bring cultural and critical perspectives to bear on the primary texts by making connections between and among crossroads texts and the primary text. The assignments will necessarily be modified in accordance with the type and level of the class as well as the instructor's goals for crossroads study.

1 Part One

Teaching at the crossroads necessitates that instructors find ways for students to understand and enter the cultural and critical debates of multicultural and feminist literary study, including canonization and literary value. I often bring the crucial conflicts of multicultural and feminist literary study into the classroom through a variety of readings and active and collaborative learning assignments, before or simultaneous with the primary texts. Parts 1 and 2 are sample assignments which raise these issues.

During the first class, I ask students to respond to the following questions in writing:

1) Why do students study literature? That is, what is the purpose(s) of studying literature?
2) How did you study literature in high school? What aspects of a literary text did your teacher focus on, and why?

Their homework assignment continues this inquiry. I ask students to make a detailed list of the readings from their high school English/literature classes. I require that they have both titles and authors of the works, which often necessitates some research. During the next class, I put students in groups and ask them to respond to the following prompts:

1) Share your lists of high school readings. Where do the lists overlap (if at all)?
2) Think about and discuss why the books/stories/poems on your lists are frequently taught in high school.
3) Which of these books/stories/poems do the group consider to be "great literature"?
4) What criteria did your group use to define "great literature"?

Part Two

In the group project described below, students evaluate the literature curricula in local high schools in the context of the debates within multicultural literary studies by conducting primary research, examining the school district's required texts, and interviewing teachers and principals. This project brings to life the notion that scholars make canons, as students are able to put human faces on canon-makers. The project fosters a more critical understanding of the profound significance of decisions about literary merit on schoolchildren nationwide.

Group Project: Multiculturalism, The Canon, and Berks County High Schools

Description: For this assignment, assume you have been asked by the School Board to submit an evaluation with recommendations of the high school literature curriculum of one public high school in the Berks County School District.

Your written work will include the following:

1. **Table of contents**
2. **1-2 page introduction** in which you discuss the background information/context for your study (i.e., what are the major issues facing literary studies today)
3. **5-7 page "Evaluation Report of the High School Literature Curriculum."** Your report should include the following sections:

    A. Description of the existing high school literature curriculum (you will modify and add to this as your fieldwork dictates)

    - What works of literature are included in this high school's literature curriculum?
    - How often do these works change? When was the last time the curriculum changed, what changes were made, and why?
    - Who is in charge of the high school literature curriculum?
    - Do teachers have choices about what works of literature to include, or is the curriculum prescribed for them? How much flexibility do they have?
    - What rationale is there (according to administrators and/or teachers) for their curricular choices in

literature?

- To what extent are those making curricular decisions aware of and concerned with multiculturalism in education?
- Is there disagreement among any administrators, teachers, or even the school board about the curricular choices in literature?
- Have there been any recent public debates over literary choices at the high school?
- Does the current curriculum include literary works by women and by men of color?

B. Evaluation of the literature curriculum

When you evaluate, you make a judgment. Therefore, it is your job to judge the quality of the literature curriculum based on issues of the canon and multiculturalism. Since it is unlikely that everyone in your group will agree on these issues, you may need to seek some kind of compromise.

As you evaluate, consider the following:

- How "traditional" is the literature curriculum in this high school? That is, to what extent does the curriculum include works by women and men of color?
- Define your group's position vis-à-vis multiculturalism and the canon. Are you traditionalists or revisionists?
- Does this curriculum meet your group's standards in terms of multiculturalism and the canon?

C. Recommendations

Based on your evaluation, what recommendations do you have for this high school's literature curriculum?

Research: You will need to conduct library research for this assignment. Your library research will be an important part of the introduction as well as Part B of your Evaluation Report. Web sources are also permitted, provided you establish the source's credibility (we will work on the research process in class). Of course, you can also cite any of the articles from our class packet.

Purpose: We've spent a great deal of time reading about and discussing multiculturalism, the canon, and literary studies throughout the semester thus far. Now you will explore real-life practices in relation to these issues.

This project will enable you to continue to learn to work on collaborative projects, which will be an ongoing part of your college education. Moreover, you will be introduced to the research process and MLA style for documenting sources in academic writing.

Procedure: Your group must decide which Berks County public high school you will evaluate, and you must let me know immediately (no later than the next class). The first group to "claim" a high school will get it (so be sure to have a back-up plan).

In addition to library research, this project includes "field" research, which means that you must go out into the field to gather your information. You will need to conduct interviews (in person and/or by phone) and/or use questionnaires. Your first contact must be the high school principal.

Of course, you can go out into the field "virtually" (via email) if your group should decide this would work best and if the principal and others at the school agree.

Note: I encourage you to get started on your field research immediately. It will be a few class periods before I introduce you to the library research process, so you can hold off on your library research for about a week.

2 *The following discussion questions encourage students to consider* Mango Street *at the crossroads of* Bildungsroman *traditions through its relationship to Faulkner's "Barn Burning." The questions below address comparisons and contrasts between* Mango Street *and "Barn Burning" as well as more general issues of the* Bildungsroman *genre.*

1) To what extent does "Barn Burning" fulfill *Bildungsroman* characteristics? Is this text a good representation of the tradition, based on the information I gave you in class? Does Faulkner critique the ideologies inherent in the *Bildungsroman* tradition?

2) To what extent does *The House on Mango Street* conform to and/or challenge the American *Bildungsroman* tradition represented by "Barn Burning"? You may also take into account the list of *Bildungsroman* char-

acteristics we discussed in class. For example, you might think about the classic *Bildungsroman* hero's rejection of family as he breaks free from societal constraints. Does Esperanza repeat this pattern or not? Note also that "conform" implies acceptance and "challenge" implies rejection.

3) What is Cisneros' purpose(s) in reinforcing, modifying, or rejecting specific *Bildungsroman* characteristics?

4) To what extent do Faulkner and Cisneros adhere to or reject the American concept of individualism? Refer to our discussions of Stewart's and Bennett's analyses of American individualism and self-reliance as you consider this question.

3 *I usually begin discussions of Rivera's …*y no se lo tragó la tierra *(…And the Earth Did Not Devour Him) with group work focusing on the multiple interpretations of the text's structure and narration, using the assignment below:*

A great deal of controversy surrounds the fragmented structure of *…y no se lo tragó la tierra (…And the Earth Did Not Devour Him.)* This text lacks traditional "narrative guideposts" such as a set narrator, a logical progression of events and character development, and a readily identifiable "denouement" (i.e., there's some kind of identifiable resolution: the action or intrigue ends in success or failure for the protagonist, the mystery is solved, or the misunderstanding cleared away). Thus, how are we to interpret the meaning of this fragmentation, this lack of traditional narrative guideposts?

I will assign each group one of the interpretations below. Please use your text as well as the information you've learned about Chicano history and culture as you formulate your responses.

1) Ultimately, the structure is not fragmented, but is unified by the final chapter, which ties together the novel's segments. Rivera thus aims for a cyclical format that in turn evokes the futility of the migrants' existence: a never-ending cycle of backbreaking work, forced exodus, and disillusionment.

2) The chaotic structure serves to represent the chaos of the characters' lives. Since life is a series of adjustments to new and different challenges, and since Chicanos face constant struggles in a culture that oppresses them, chaotic representations make sense.

3) The fragmented structure serves to challenge the traditional *Bildungsroman* and the values it embodies.

4) The fragmented structure is intended to represent the lives of all Chicanos, not just the individual boy, and to create a Chicano cultural identity. It serves to gather together the pieces of Chicano history. Thus, this book has a social and political purpose rather than a purely aesthetic (artistic) one.

5) The fragmented structure captures the sense of oral literature, an important part of the Chicano literary tradition.

Once we have discussed ...y no se lo tragó la tierra, *we move to its intertextuality with both* Mango Street *and "Barn Burning." The following topics are useful for individual writing and group discussion*:

1) To what extent does *Mango Street* reinforce and/or challenge the values inherent in *...y no se lo tragó la tierra*? Remember that the book, written in 1971, is considered the classic Chicano *Bildungsroman*, and it is likely that fifteen years later, when Cisneros wrote *Mango Street*, she was familiar with it. Note also that "conform" implies acceptance and "challenge" implies rejection, so be sure to consider Cisneros' purpose(s). You should also bring in your knowledge of Chicano and/or Chicana history and literature where relevant.

2) To what extent does *...y no se lo tragó la tierra* conform to and/or challenge the original, white male *Bildungsroman* tradition? Note that "conform" implies acceptance and "challenge" implies rejection, so be sure to consider Rivera's purpose(s). You should also bring in your knowledge of Chicano history and literature where relevant.

3) To what extent do you see intertextual connections between "Barn Burning" and *...y no se lo tragó la tierra*?

4 *I begin our examination of* Mango Street *and the female* Bildungsroman *by giving students information on the women's* Bildungsroman *tradition. After we discuss some of its most salient characteristics, we turn to Chopin's* The Awakening. *I use the following questions to stimulate class discussion on this text:*

1) What does the title suggest? Has Edna "awakened," and, if so, to what?

2) What images in the text suggest oppression?

3) Many women's *Bildungsroman* texts end in death or madness. What does Edna's suicide suggest? What led her to suicide? Was it her abandonment by Robert Lebrun? Was it motherhood? Was it something else?

4) How do you feel about Edna's suicide? Do you have compassion for her, or not?

5) Does *The Awakening* suggest that there is something more important for women than motherhood? Do you agree?

6) Does this text reinforce American individualism, as we have considered it thus far?

Then, we turn to the intertextual relationships between The Awakening *and* Mango Street, *an inquiry which is rich with possibilities.*

1) What images of confinement exist in *Mango Street?*

2) To what extent do these images likewise suggest the possibilities of escape and freedom?

3) Both *The Awakening* and *Mango Street* possess circular structures. Given what you know about linear structures, circular structures, and the *Bildungsroman* tradition, what is each text's structure suggesting?

4) How might we argue that Esperanza transcends her circumstances, even if Edna cannot?

5) Think about the different times and cultures in which both authors were writing. What specific constraints does each protagonist face? What prescriptions on women's sexuality existed in nineteenth-century America? What prescriptions on defining womanhood exist in contemporary Chicano culture?

5 *After discussing Madonna Kolbenschlag's critique of "Cinderella," I use group work to have students analyze, through a feminist lens, the vignettes in which Cisneros uses fairy tales: "Family of Little Feet," "There Was An Old Woman," "Linoleum Roses," "Beautiful and Cruel," "Rafaela Who Drinks Coconut & Papaya Juice on Tuesdays," "Chanclas," and "Marin." Then, I use some of the following topics as writing or discussion assignments:*

1) In what ways does Cisneros use fairy tales in her story? What is her main point in using these fairy tales? Would she be likely to agree with Kolbenschlag about fairy tales' influence on women's socialization?

2) Adrienne Rich writes that "Re-vision—the act of looking back, of seeing with fresh eyes, of entering an old text from a new critical direction—is for us more than a chapter in cultural history: it is an act of survival" (1037). Use Rich's article and the ideas and issues about feminist criticism discussed in class to address Cisneros' use of fairy tales as an act of re-vision.

3) View the recent Disney version of *Cinderella* starring Brandy as Cinderella or the Drew Barrymore film *Ever After* (available on reserve at the library). Does the film version you choose address and revise any of the issues Kolbenschlag raises in her feminist analysis? What kind of values does this version of the Cinderella story represent?

4) Choose any well-known fairy tale other than "Cinderella," read it carefully, and apply a feminist analysis to it (this does not mean that ultimately you'd have to agree with a feminist perspective on the tale). That is, does this tale have negative or positive messages about girls' socialization and gender identity? Is it a harmless tale, or one that inculcates girls with a specific set of values? Are these positive and/or negative values?

5) Is the "Cinderella Syndrome"—from classic fairy tales to television, films, advertisements, beauty competitions, comics, and newspapers—endemic in our popular culture? Is it destructive or beneficial?

6 *When the class returns to Rivera's* ...y no se lo tragó la tierra/...And the Earth Did Not Devour Him, *we focus on Rivera's portrayal of women as well as the text's ending, specifically the question of the protagonist's passivity. Some questions for group or individual work include the following:*

1) How does Rivera portray women in this text? Can you make a general characterization of the women, or are you unable to draw such larger conclusions?

2) Are there differences between how he portrays the women and men in the text?

3) To what extent is Rivera's protagonist passive by the book's end? What has he "discovered," if anything? What does the text's circular structure suggest?

From here, we move back to an examination of Mango Street *from a Chicana feminist perspective*:

Read and think about the following excerpt from Chicana feminist critic Yvonne Yarbro-Bejarano (from "Chicana Literature from a Chicana Feminist Perspective"). Then, consider the extent to which you can identify a Chicana feminist perspective in *Mango Street*. What are the prescribed gender roles within Chicano culture, according to *Mango Street*? To what extent does Cisneros critique them?

> The term 'Chicana feminist perspective' also implies certain similarities with and differences from either an exclusively 'feminist' or 'Chicano' perspective. While sharing with the feminist perspective an analysis of questions of gender and sexuality, there are important differences between a Chicana perspective and the mainstream feminist one with regard to issues of race, culture and class. The Chicano perspective, while incorporating these important facets of race, culture and class, has traditionally neglected issues of gender and sexuality. The Chicana feminist is confronted with a dilemma, caught between two perspectives which appeal strongly to different aspects of her experience.... While recognizing her Chicana cultural identity and affirming her solidarity with all Chicanos and other Third World men and women to combat racial and economic oppression, the Chicana feminist also spearheads a critique of the destructive aspects of her culture's definition of gender roles. (139-40)

7 *As we embark on the* corrido *tradition in Chicano literature, I sometimes assign an extra credit project, so that one or two students can present the class with their research on the* corrido *and, specifically,* "El Corrido de Gregorio Cortez." *I usually assign* "El Corrido" *as well as excerpts from Américo Paredes'* With His Pistol in His Hand: A Border Ballad and Its Hero *(1958) (excerpts from this book are included in Gordon Hutner's* American Literature, American Culture *[1999]). These questions may be used for discussion, group work, and/or individual writing assignments.*

"El Corrido de Gregorio Cortez"

1) What characteristics does the hero, Gregorio Cortez, possess?
2) Why do you think Cortez has been elevated to heroic status?
3) How are whites portrayed in "*El Corrido*"? Why?
4) How might "*El Corrido*" be critiqued from a feminist perspective?

Then we move to Lorna Dee Cervantes' poem, "Visions of Mexico," and how it critiques, resists, and subverts "El Corrido."

"Visions of Mexico"

1) What are the "old words" in line 1?
2) Does the speaker use her "own words" to merge with the Mexico she's heard of and read about?
3) In lines 1-20, does the speaker enter into the visions or stay outside them?
4) In lines 20-34, what evidence is there that the speaker has been left out of Mexican American history?
5) Why is the speaker angry?
6) What is meant by line 34, "and the poet within us bays"?
7) Why does Part 2 shift to the north, in Washington?
8) How are women portrayed in the bar scene?
9) What is the speaker's response to what occurs in the bar (lines 55-67)?
10) How does the speaker's resistance differ from Cortez's?

Finally, we move from these poems back to Mango Street, *specifically to interrogate how Cisneros, like Cervantes, combines feminist re-visioning strategies with Chicano/a contexts to appropriate and subvert* "El Corrido" *and cultural images. Many of these questions focus on Esperanza's (and Cisneros') belief in the power of writing as a political act.*

Making Connections

1) What intersections do you see between "Visions of Mexico" and *Mango Street?* How does the bar scene in "Visions" remind you of some of the scenes on Mango Street?
2) What intersections do you see between "*El Corrido de Gregorio Cortez*" and *Mango Street?*

3) What characteristics does Esperanza possess that are similar to those of Cortez? Different from Cortez?

4) What evidence is there that Esperanza, like the speaker in "Visions of Mexico," will use writing to resist and transform her world?

8 *After I introduce the story of La Malinche (sometimes I do this through a student presentation), we discuss Chicano nationalism, particularly in terms of how it is embodied in Rodolfo Gonzáles'* I Am Joaquín/Yo Soy Joaquín. *Then we move to Tafolla's "La Malinche" and finally back to* Mango Street. *(Instructors can find information about La Malinche in Elba Birmingham Pokorny's "La Malinche: A Feminist Perspective on Otherness in Mexican and Chicano Literature," Sandra Messinger Cypess'* La Malinche in Mexican Literature from History to Myth, *and Ann McBride Limaye's "Metamorphoses of La Malinche and Mexican Cultural Identity.") The following questions can be used in class discussion, group work, and/or individual writing assignments.*

I Am Joaquín/Yo Soy Joaquín

1) How does *I Am Joaquín /Yo Soy Joaquín* embody Chicano nationalism?

2) What characteristics does Joaquín embody?

3) Does Joaquín remind you of Gregorio Cortez? Why or why not?

4) What evidence, if any, is there in this poem that Chicano nationalism excluded and/or demeaned women?

"La Malinche"

1) In Tafolla's "La Malinche," what does the first line signify? Is it deliberately intertextual with *I Am Joaquín/Yo Soy Joaquín*, in your opinion?

2) What kind of identity does the speaker of "La Malinche" appropriate?

3) How is this poem "re-visionary" in the feminist sense of the word (think back to the essay you read by Adrienne Rich, "When We Dead Awaken: Writing As Re-Vision")?

Making Connections

1) In what ways does *Mango Street* intersect with "La Malinche"? Consider the characteristics of Esperanza (as she matures) and La Malinche of Tafolla's poem.

2) Even though Cisneros never refers specifically to La Malinche, do you believe she is drawing on this legendary figure? Explain. What characteristics do Esperanza and La Malinche share?

9 *Because talking about stereotypes is often difficult for individual students in large groups, I usually do this assignment as group work.*

1) Think about stereotypes and what they mean. Have people in your work group been stereotyped?

2) Are you at all familiar with stereotypes of Chicanos? What are some of these stereotypes? You might want to think about how Chicanos are portrayed in popular culture.

3) We've already discussed a Chicana feminist approach to *Mango Street* when we read excerpts from Yvonne Yarbro-Bejarano's "Chicana Literature from a Chicana Feminist Perspective." But do you believe that Cisneros also tries to dispel stereotypes of Chicanos? That is, does she sympathize with her male counterparts in addition to her critique of them? Point to specific passages in the book to support your views.

10 *To culminate our study of* Mango Street, *I present Gloria Anzaldúa's notion of a crossroads, and how this metaphor might be pertinent to their experience with* Mango Street. *This final writing assignment culminates our study of* Mango Street *at the crossroads.*

In *Borderlands*, Gloria Anzaldúa, a Chicana feminist theorist who has greatly influenced how I teach texts by women of color, writes about what it's like to live at the crossroads of cultures. On the one hand, it is a scary place to be:

> Alienated from her mother culture, "alien" in the dominant culture, the woman of color does not feel safe within the inner life of her Self. Petrified, she can't respond, her

> face caught between *los intersticios*, the spaces between the different worlds she inhabits (42).

On the other hand, the crossroads allows her a space from which to overcome the alienating forces of the borderlands, sites where multiple cultures collide: "To survive the Borderlands/you must live *sin fronteras*/be a crossroads" (217).

In your essay, reflect on what it means to live and learn at the crossroads. How might these negative and positive experiences apply to how we read the various genres of *Mango Street?* Think about the many perspectives we brought to our reading.

11 *I like to begin discussions of* Storyteller *in the American autobiographical tradition by having students talk in groups about the various autobiographies they've read and what their expectations are from this genre. Then I move to our examination of Franklin's* Autobiography. *The following questions will vary depending on how much of the text I have assigned.*

1) In what ways does Franklin's *Autobiography* fulfill your expectations for autobiography? In what ways does it contrast with your expectations?

2) Most literary scholars and historians recognize Franklin's *Autobiography* for its contribution to the creation of a national identity. What quintessential "American" values do you see in this text? Explain.

3) Do you believe that *Autobiography* is all fact and no fiction? Explain.

4) What rhetorical strategies does Franklin use to convince you of the "truth" of his story (think about the narrative voice, dramatic scenes, letters, and quotes in the text)? Are you convinced? Why or why not?

12 Storyteller *is a challenging and difficult text for many students. I begin our examination of* Storyteller *with an in-class writing assignment and discussion that addresses students' reading experiences before we move to analysis of the text vis à vis autobiography:*

Describe your experience reading *Storyteller*. What "worked" for you with this text? What was challenging, difficult, or just plain different about reading *Storyteller*?

Then we move to group work or class discussion about Storyteller *as autobiography. These questions center on the problematized autobiographical subject in the text of* Storyteller:

1) Who is the autobiographical subject in *Storyteller*?
2) How does the narration in *Storyteller* lend itself to the questions typically posed in autobiography? Look at the first selection in the text. What is the significance of Silko beginning with third person narration? At what point does she acknowledge herself as the writer?
3) Find evidence of the autobiographical subject throughout the book, passages pertaining to the narrator's personal and familial life. Where, how, and why does the narrator insert herself into the text? Be specific.

13 *I begin this exercise by asking students questions about the structures of both Franklin's* Autobiography *and* Storyteller *and their relationship to "meaning." At the crossroads of* Storyteller *and* Autobiography, *students consider the ways in which* Storyteller's *nonlinear, fragmented structure challenges Western autobiography, which tends to be linear and unified in the autobiographical subject's movement toward self-discovery. The questions below ask students to consider the structural development of* Storyteller *and the autobiographical subject in relation to* Autobiography.

1) In keeping with the traditional genre of autobiography, Franklin's *Autobiography* has a linear structure. Please describe what you think is meant by this statement, referring specifically to the text.
2) How does the structure of Franklin's *Autobiography* enhance the text's message(s) or meaning(s)? Explain.
3) What kind of structure, if any, do you see in *Storyteller*? Is it linear? Is it more complicated than this?
4) What does this suggest, in your opinion?

From here, I point students to the chapters on Silko's life and ask them to trace the development of the autobiographical subject.

Let's look specifically at those sections directly dealing with the narrator. Are you able to trace any narrative growth (emotional, spiritual, vocational, physical)? At what points, if any, do you see signs of recognition?

14 *The class continues its study of the autobiographical subject in* Storyteller *through a tribal perspective. The following series of questions examine* Storyteller's *intersections with an essay and two poems by Simon Ortiz. The questions can be addressed through group work and/or class discussions.*

Today, we'll examine the autobiographical subject in *Storyteller* from the perspective of tribal culture. Specifically, we'll examine the role of stories in tribal life using Simon Ortiz's essay and poems.

"My Father's Song"

1) Who is speaking? Are there two different speakers?
2) Whose song is it? Is it clear?
3) Do the father and son merge? Explain. What does the son gain by remembering his father?
4) Why does the image of sand recur throughout the poem?

"Poems I Have Lost"

1) How does this poem differ from "My Father's Song" in terms of its tone and events?
2) What kind of vision of America does this poem describe?
3) How does the image of falling work in the poem?
4) Can the speaker reconcile his losses? How?

"Language We Know"

1) How does Ortiz describe his childhood?
2) How did he learn English? What was school like for him? Why was he sent to boarding school? How does he feel about the experience?
3) How do English and Acoma influence his writing?
4) Why is knowledge important to him?
5) What did the stories teach him?
6) What role did his grandfather play in his life?
7) What happens to Ortiz when his family moves to Skull Valley?

8) What was the "unspoken vow" (191)?

9) What does Ortiz write about? What function does writing play in his life?

Finally, how do Ortiz's works enrich your understanding of Silko's autobiographical stance?

15 *Because there is such a wide variety of preliterate art forms, I believe this assignment works best as a group research project. If students have difficulty finding material I have an extensive bibliography to help them, and I give them enough time to order sources through the university's Interlibrary Loan.*

Each group will be assigned a different form of preliterate Native American autobiography to research: coup story, naming rituals, tipis, shields, blankets, dance, or ceremony. You will make a brief (5-10 minute) presentation to the class about what you find. You may conduct both Web and library research. Please see me if you need help finding sources. In your presentations, please include the following:

1) representative examples of the preliterate autobiographical form you have been assigned

2) discussion of the intracultural collaborative nature of this form

3) discussion of how your research sheds light on *Storyteller*

16 *Below I provide general questions on Apess' and Copway's autobiographies that can be used in group work or individual writing assignments. Questions can, of course, be tailored to specifically address particular excerpts, depending upon what the instructor uses in class.*

William Apess' *A Son of the Forest*

1) Who is Apess' audience, and what strategies does he use to appeal to them?

2) Why does Apess rely so heavily on Christianity and passages from the Bible?

3) What picture of himself does Apess portray?

4) What "picture" is Apess presenting of Native Americans?
5) What is Apess' ultimate purpose(s) in his autobiographical writing?

George Copway's *The Life, Letters, and Speeches*

1) Who is Copway's audience, and what strategies does he use to appeal to them?
2) Why does Copway rely so heavily on Christianity and passages from the Bible?
3) What picture of himself does Copway portray?
4) What "picture" is Copway presenting of Native Americans?
5) For what purpose does Copway use oral traditions in his writing?
6) What is Copway's ultimate purpose(s) in his autobiographical writing?

Making Connections

1) What similarities do you see between the nineteenth-century Native American autobiographers Copway and Apess and Silko?
2) What differences do you see?
3) How can you account for those differences?

17 *The following questions, useful for individual and/or group assignments, examine two contemporary Native American autobiographies, Jim Barnes' "On Native Ground" and Joy Harjo's "Ordinary Spirit," in relationship to one another and to* Storyteller. *The questions focus on the extent to which these writers trace back materials from the past in an effort to heal the pain of loss, both personally and culturally.*

Jim Barnes' "On Native Ground"

1) Does this essay seem more like autobiography to you than *Storyteller?* Why or why not? What is the narration like? What about the structure?
2) What meaning does the narrator's story of his brother bring to the essay?
3) What happens when the writer returns to the "gnarled clump of trees" of his childhood (89)?
4) How does the narrator describe Fourche Maline, then and now?
5) In many ways, this essay is a catalogue of loss. What is lost, accord-

ing to Barnes?

6) Does the writer also convey a sense of recovery or hope? Why or why not?

7) How does the narrator feel about the "literary establishment"? What does he object to?

8) Are his concerns about writing as a Native American in contemporary culture similar to Silko's?

9) How well does the narrator merge the Native American and white worlds?

10) Is this an individual's autobiography? A collectivist one? Both?

Joy Harjo's "Ordinary Spirit"

1) In what ways is this essay autobiographical? What is Harjo writing about? In what ways is it similar to and different from Barnes? Silko? What is the narration like? What about the structure?

2) What are Harjo's most important themes? Is she also writing about loss? Does she achieve a sense of recovery or hope?

3) Why is there such a self-consciousness about her writing of poetry? What messages does she wish to impart in her poetry?

4) Look at the last paragraphs of the essay. How might these paragraphs reinforce the notion of collectivism rather than individualism as an important feature of tribal life?

18 *I begin class work by reminding students of our earlier examination of the nonlinear and fragmentary nature of* Storyteller *in terms of the subject's developing sense of identity as compared with Franklin's* Autobiography. *I explain that Linda Danielson's assertions about* Storyteller's *feminist stance will bring a new perspective to the text's structure. At the same time, we examine the text in light of an excerpt from Stein's* The Autobiography of Alice B. Toklas, *a representative text from the women's autobiographical tradition.*

1) Describe *Storyteller*'s structure. Is it fragmented and discontinuous? Explain.

2) In an article entitled "Storyteller: 'Grandmother Spider's Web,'" Linda Danielson argues that Silko engages in the kind of re-visioning of the white literary establishment's notion of literature and the canon that pervades feminist criticism, appropriating canonical conventions and forms for her own purposes:

> in effacing her own authorship, crediting the community, mixing once-sacrosanct genres, and abjuring linear structure—in short, by denying the standards and customs of white male-dominated literary criticism—Silko reclaims the making of books from the white male critical establishment. (330)

Explain how Danielson would interpret *Storyteller*'s structure. If it is revisionist, what is Silko re-visioning, and why? (Think back to Franklin's text.)

3) Describe the narrative structure of Stein's "Gertrude Stein Before She Came to Paris."

4) Is there evidence in Stein's text about her distaste for the white male literary establishment?

5) Is *Storyteller*'s structure similar to or different from that in the excerpt from Stein?

19 *Linda Danielson claims that* Storyteller's *structure is like a spiderweb, a "coherent work about how tribal people survive" ("Storytellers in* Storyteller" *21), for Silko connects the last story to the first to emphasize "the ongoing life of the people" ("Grandmother Spider's Web" 351). Radiating strands of the spiderweb-like structure cluster around specific themes, and these themes are connected to one another through the lateral threads that focus on storytellers and storytelling. The following exercises ask students to examine* Storyteller *in light of Danielson's assertions and then explore the spiderweb theme in contemporary poems by Native American writers James Welch and Paula Gunn Allen. I ask students (in group work) to first do two tasks:*

1) Draw a spiderweb.

2) Support Danielson's assertion that *Storyteller*'s structure fits the pattern as you drew it.

Then we turn to the spiderweb theme in contemporary poems by Welch and Allen.

Welch's "Snow Country Weavers"

1) To whom is the speaker of the poem addressing?

2) What messages about nature does the poem convey, especially

through the images of the birds and the wolves?

3) What function does the spiderweb play in the poem?

4) Why are the webs filled with words?

5) From what source does the poet get his artistic inspiration?

Allen's "Grandmother"

1) What is the relationship between the speaker and her grandmother?

2) How is the grandmother characterized?

3) In the last stanza, the speaker mends the blanket her grandmother created. Explain the significance of this action.

4) To what extent does the spiderweb image exist in this poem, even if it is not directly stated?

20 *I begin our discussions of women's roles in Native cultures by having students prepare a short research presentation to the class on gynocracy and tribal cultures.*

In this short research project, I'd like you to research *gynocracy*—specifically, how it is relevant to many tribal cultures. Each group will make a short presentation to the class. Please focus on the following questions in your research and presentation.

1) What is a gynocracy?

2) What values does it embody?

3) What roles do men and women play in such a societal organization?

4) To what extent are some tribal cultures still gynocratic? Has contact with white culture changed gynocratic ways and values? Explain.

Then we turn back to Storyteller *and consider the extent to which gynocratic values exist in the work.*

1) What role do women play?

2) How vital are they to communal life? To survival? To creativity?

Finally, we read Linda Hogan's poem, "The Women Speaking." I center class discussion around the following questions:

1) To whom are the women speaking, and why?
2) About what are the women speaking?
3) Who are these women? That is, are they only Native American women?
4) What is happening in the poem?
5) What does Hogan suggest about women and their roles?

21 *In this exercise, students examine* Storyteller *in light of Kathleen Sands' assertions about Native women's autobiography as well as Janet St. Clair's and Patricia Riley's claims about mixed-blood women and their role as cultural mediators. While numerous Native American feminist critics and writers point to convergences between Native American and feminist cultures and writing, this exercise attempts to highlight the differences as well. Specifically, Sands argues that* Storyteller, *like other Native American women's autobiographies, extends beyond the personal to the cultural life of the community and resists any claims to truth (283-84). Both St. Clair and Riley underscore the role of the mixed-blood writer as cultural mediator, a stance Silko arguably assumes in* Storyteller.

1) Sands calls *Storyteller* "a new kind of autobiographical text" in its use of both personal and cultural stories. To what extent do you agree? Explain.
2) Does Harjo's essay "Ordinary Spirit" use a similar strategy? That is, does Harjo also intersperse cultural and personal stories?
3) Both Harjo and Silko are "mixed-bloods." How do they each see their role as mixed-bloods? Is it disadvantageous? Advantageous? Are they mediators between cultures?

22 *The final writing project for the study of the crossroads of* Storyteller *asks students to bring together the various perspectives we've studied through crossroads texts by considering and applying Paula Gunn Allen's notion of* confluence *(the linking together of cultures, of present and past, and of land and borders) to their study of* Storyteller.

In an autobiographical essay entitled "The Autobiography of a Confluence," Paula Gunn Allen describes the Southwest where she grew up as "the confluence of cultures" (145). Later in the same essay, she uses the term "confluence" to describe her own life, an image of overlapping cultures and communities.

Use this metaphor of "confluence" to reflect upon your reading of *Storyteller* at the crossroads (or confluence) of cultures.

23 *In preparation for this exercise, I introduce students to postmodernist and deconstructionist ideas, using a variety of readings and/or a handout which summarizes a number of accessible explanations (for example, excerpts from Ray Linn's* A Teacher's Introduction to Postmodernism, *Brenda Marshall's* Teaching the Postmodern, *and Steve Lynn's "A Passage into Critical Theory"), as well as class lectures. I then ask students to apply these concepts to* Beloved.

Using your class notes, handouts, and readings on postmodernism and deconstructionism, apply these ideas to *Beloved*. Find passages from *Beloved* that deal with the notion of language, naming, and defining with respect to the following:

1) Sethe's sense of humanity
2) Paul D's sense of manhood
3) naming: Sweet Home, Baby Suggs, Stamp Paid
4) the morality of the infanticide

24 *I begin our class discussion of Sethe's infanticide by having students read James Rachels' "The Challenge of Cultural Relativism" (chapter 2 of* The Elements of Moral Philosophy). *Because cultural relativism is a difficult concept, I use the following group exercise to help students as they closely analyze the chapter.*

Rachels breaks down his chapter on cultural relativism into seven sections. To gain a thorough grasp on his thesis and argument, each group will be assigned one of the sections. The groups will answer the questions below and then report your findings to the class on the board. Use specific examples, as well as your interpretation of them, to back up your findings.

1) What is the main point of the section?
2) What are the major supporting points of the section?
3) How does the section fit in with the larger argument of the chapter (how does it work toward supporting the thesis)?

Example:

1) What is the main point of the section?
In section 2.1, Rachels states that anthropologists have long believed that different cultures have different moral codes.
2) What are the major supporting points of the section?
Rachels uses three examples to show why anthropologists believe that different cultures have different moral codes:
   - *Ancient Greeks cremated dead bodies, while Callatians ate the dead bodies of their fathers.*
   - *There are differences within Eskimo culture in marriage and sexual practices.*
   - *Infanticide is common in Eskimo societies, while in other cultures it is not.*
3) How does the section fit in with the larger argument of the chapter (how does it work toward supporting the thesis)?
Rachels introduces the concept of differing moral codes among cultures to set us up for determining whether varying practices actually mean different moral codes.

After considering Rachels' arguments, the class applies some of these concepts of moral relativism to their analysis of the moral issues in Beloved.

1) Make an argument about the morality of Sethe's act of infanticide in *Beloved.* That is, do you find her actions to be morally justified or not? If you believe you cannot make a judgement about Sethe's actions, your essay should explain your reasoning for this position. Are you advocating cultural relativism, universalism, or something in between? Explain and be very specific.

2) Think about the various moral issues in *Beloved* in addition to the infanticide. For example, consider these questions:
   - Can Mr. Garner and/or Mrs. Garner be considered

"good" people, even if they owned slaves?

- Was it a moral act for Stamp to tell Paul D about Sethe's act of infanticide? Was he justified?
- Was Paul D morally justified in sleeping with Beloved? Was he morally justified in leaving Sethe after he finds out about the infanticide?
- Did the community act morally when they failed to warn Sethe and her family about the slave catcher? Were they justified in their ostracism of Sethe, either before or after the infanticide?
- To what extent does being a slave mitigate otherwise immoral behavior, according to Morrison?

25 *By the time students get to this assignment, we have already discussed the ways in which the institution of slavery devastated slave families. In group work, I ask students to consider Sethe's sense of identity in accordance with definitions of motherhood and family:*

1) Using what you've learned about the treatment of slave families, find evidence in the novel that families were separated for economic gain.
2) What was Sethe's relationship with her mother?
3) What external circumstances influenced and shaped their relationship?
4) What kind of effect did this relationship have on Sethe's sense of personhood? What about her sense of herself as a mother?
5) What do we learn about Sethe's mother and her other babies? Why is this important to how we might judge Sethe's behavior?
6) What happens to Sethe in the latter part of the novel? Why does she devote all her energies to Beloved?
7) What kind of mother is Sethe to her children?

26 *When teaching Douglass'* Narrative *I use either "How I Learned to Read and Write" or "Resurrection," both frequently anthologized excerpts. "How I Learned to Read and Write" is especially relevant to how slaves used reading and writing "to writ[e] themselves into being" (Young 369) and portray themselves as human; "Resurrection" presents the incident* *that allowed Douglass to become human, to see himself as different than the construction of "slave" that had been imposed on him.*

"How I Learned to Read and Write"

1) Why does Douglass place so much importance on learning to read?
2) Why did whites want slaves to be illiterate?
3) What influence did Douglass' reading of "The Columbian Orator" and Sheridan's speeches on emancipation have on him?
4) Before he escapes, Douglass learns to write. Why did he make this decision?
5) In what ways does Douglass present himself as human and deserving of rights?
6) Who is Douglass' audience? What is his purpose in writing?
7) Do you think he's an effective writer, given his audience and purpose?
8) Does Douglass challenge conventional notions of slaves as illiterate? Why is this important to his narrative?

"Resurrection"

1) What does Douglass mean when he states, "You have seen how a man was made slave; you shall see how a slave was made man" (107)?
2) What occurred in this episode to transform him from slave to man?
3) Why does Douglass describe this episode in such detail? What does he want his readers to *see?*
4) Is there any way to see Sethe's killing her child in a similar vein, as an act of fighting back?
5) How does Douglass underscore the illogic of the slave system?
6) Is it possible that Sethe experienced a resurrection similar to Douglass'?

27 *After I have introduced the contexts of the black vernacular and African folk legends through Ridley's or Brearley's articles, I use this assignment to have students apply those contexts to a reading of Sethe's sense of identity, especially in light of her act of infanticide.*

Use what you learned about tales of "badness" to analyze and interpret Sethe's sense of identity, her "claiming ownership of that freed self" (Morrision 95), and her act of infanticide. Moreover, think about Paul D's and the community's response to Sethe and her actions.

I will assign each group a scene from the novel. Read through the assigned pages and try to interpret the situation in light of the characteristics associated with "badness": claiming, violence, autonomy, status, power, and self-sufficiency. Remember that the community both admires and fears the "bad" slave and responds with self-protection.

1) Baby Suggs' story of Sethe's arrival at 124 Bluestone and her own arrival years earlier
2) the infanticide
3) Stamp Paid reflects on telling Paul D about the infanticide
4) Stamp and Paul D talk about the infanticide
5) the community learns about Beloved and begins their exorcism

28 *I use the following exercise to apply a feminist critique to Sethe's sense of identity:*

Kashinath Ranveer writes, "In most of Morrison's novels, the black man is depicted as a weak man who is incapable of living with dignity and respect" (44). Many scholars of African American literature—especially males—agree with Ranveer. In fact, Morrison has been vilified by many male scholars of African American literature who claim that her portrayal of black men undermines their efforts to combat racism and dispel stereotypes.

These are serious accusations, and it is important to consider Sethe's sense of self in the context of the men that surround her. Is Ranveer's assessment accurate with respect to *Beloved?* Let's examine Morrison's portrayal of men in this novel.

1) How is Halle portrayed? What happened that caused him to abandon Sethe as they were planning their escape? Do you believe he is a weak man, one incapable of living with dignity?
2) How does Morrison present him?
3) How do you feel about Stamp Paid? What kind of man is he? What characteristics does he possess?
4) Paul D is someone we should examine carefully. What kinds of behavior does he engage in that would seem to fulfill Baby Suggs'

assertion that "A man ain't nothing but a man" (23)?

5) What do we know about Paul D that might allow us to excuse, forgive, or understand his behavior? Do you think Morrison wants us to forgive him?

6) What positive changes can Paul D bring to Sethe's life?

7) Do you think Sethe is better off with Paul D or without him? What does Morrison think?

29 *I typically use excerpts from scholarly work by Kashinath Ranveer or/and Hazel Carby to move from general feminist and African American issues to African American feminist issues. In the exercise that follows, I have students apply material from lectures and readings to further interrogate Sethe's sense of identity and the act of infanticide at the novel's core.*

Ranveer describes African American feminist consciousness as "an awakening that one is oppressed not because one is ignorant, not because one is lazy, not because one is stupid, but just because one is African-American and female. African-American feminist consciousness is the consciousness of victimization. It is an apprehension that one is a victim because one is African-American, female and poor" (35).

In your groups, reflect on our earlier discussions of African American feminist consciousness, especially in terms of how African American women have been demeaned and stereotyped with a particular emphasis on sexual stereotyping. Then, please respond to the following questions:

1) What happened in Sethe's life that has stripped her of a sense of her own humanity, what Ranveer refers to as the "true erosion of her very black female self" (43)?

2) To what extent are black female slaves seen as economic commodities?

3) What examples are there from *Beloved* that black female sexuality is exploited as a commodity?

4) What do you think Ranveer means when she states that when Sethe kills her own child, she "retains her dignity as a human being" (43)? Do you agree or disagree?

5) How might Sethe's attack on Bodwin pertain to the question of whether Sethe achieves a sense of African American feminist consciousness and of her worth as a human being?

30 *My approach to Jacobs'* Incidents *varies, according to how much of the text I have assigned, as well as my presentation of Morgan's article "Gender-Related Difference in the Slave Narratives of Harriet Jacobs and Frederick Douglass." I've listed a number of general discussion questions which can be used in this exercise.*

1) Describe and analyze the various relationships in Jacobs' life: with her grandmother, parents, children, brother, uncles, aunts, slave owners (the Flints), employers, and the larger slave community.

2) Morgan claims that Jacobs' narrative, unlike Douglass', emphasizes Jacobs' dependence on this network of others. Do you agree or disagree?

3) How does Morrison depict Sethe's relationship to others? That is, to what extent is her healing dependent upon acceptance by others?

4) Compare and contrast Jacobs' and Sethe's relationships with their children.

5) How does Jacobs' narrative address the issue of black women's sexuality, as we discussed it earlier? How does she address the stereotype of a "fallen woman," and why do you think she takes this stance?

6) How does Douglass define freedom? Jacobs? Sethe?

7) Is literacy important to Jacobs? Sethe?

31 *I hope to have students reflect on their experiences with* Beloved *at the crossroads of perspectives by using a final writing assignment, which can be used to stimulate class discussion:*

In *Beloved*, Morrison writes, "Perhaps a conversation, they thought, an exchange of views or something would help" (4). What kind of conversations have you been involved in over the past few weeks as you've interpreted Sethe's identity development from diverse perspectives?

32 *This group exercise begins study of* China Men *through a Western/American perspective by focusing on narratives of exploration and discovery in the spirit of rugged individualism and the making of America. Students examine the character BaBa as an immigrant in search of the American Dream, circling back to his successes and failures by studying the final chapter, "The Father from China," through three of the text's interchapters, "On Discovery," "The Ghostmate," and "On Fathers."*

Today, we will examine *China Men* from the Western/American perspective by thinking about it in relation to a narrative of exploration and discovery. In your groups, please respond to the first and second questions. After our class discussion on these questions, you will return to your groups and work on the final three questions.

1) How is the American Dream defined in *China Men*?
2) To what extent does BaBa achieve the American Dream?
3) How does "On Discovery" relate to "The Father from China?"
4) How does "On Fathers" relate to "The Father from China?"
5) How does "The Ghostmate" relate to "The Father from China?"

33 *Due to the length of* Robinson Crusoe, *I do not use Defoe's text in its entirety. Rather, because many students are somewhat familiar with popular retellings of the story, I use an abridged version by DK Publishing (Eyewitness Classics, 1998). In the context of* China Men, *my focus is to have students consider how Kingston's text intersects with certain aspects of* Robinson Crusoe. *Discussion questions can center around the following issues:*

1) What characteristics does Robinson Crusoe possess?
2) Do the men in Kingston's book remind you in any ways of Robinson Crusoe?
3) How do Kingston's men differ from Robinson Crusoe?
4) Compare and contrast Crusoe and Lo Bun Sun.
5) Why does Kingston emphasize Sing Kay Ng's reunion with his father?
6) How is Friday presented? How does Friday compare with Sing Kay Ng?
7) What is the relationship between Friday and Crusoe? Between Lo Bun Sun and Sing Kay Ng?
8) Why does Kingston rewrite the Robinson Crusoe story?

34 *In this exercise, I ask students to examine the critique of the American Dream and American exploitation and discrimination against male Chinese immigrants in Kingston's novel through the following discussion questions:*

1) What evidence exists in "The Father from China" and "The American Father" to suggest that Kingston critiques the American Dream?
2) Is her critique leveled at the dream itself and/or at the obstacles preventing the achievement of the dream?
3) How does "The Adventures of Lo Bun Sun," in its "re-visions" of *Robinson Crusoe*, continue this critique?
4) What does "The Laws" section add to the text?
5) What kinds of discrimination do the great-grandfather and grandfather endure?

35 *Still interrogating the concept of the American Dream in* China Men, *the class turns to the chapters "The American Father" and "The Brother in Vietnam" to consider Kingston's male ancestors' success as Americans through the following discussion questions:*

1) What happens to Kingston's father in "The American Father"? How does the chapter end?
2) What does the title of the chapter suggest? What is the narrator's attitude toward her father?
3) To what extent does her father achieve the American Dream, as he defines it? As you define it?
4) What new themes were introduced in "The Brother in Vietnam"?
5) To what extent is the brother "Americanized"?
6) What happens when the brother looks for his relatives?
7) What does the family's "security clearance" represent, at least in their minds?
8) To what extent does the brother's story suggest the idea that this family has "made it" as Americans?
9) To what extent does the brother's story undercut the American Dream for Chinese immigrants in America?

36 *I often use student group presentations to bring stereotypes of Asian American men to the class' attention. After our discussion of these stereotypes, we move to the following questions about BaBa:*

1) In "The Father from China," how does Kingston portray the stereotype of the feminized Chinese man? Look carefully at the lives of BaBa and his friends.
2) What is their home life like?
3) What does their vocation as launderers suggest?
4) What is their relationship to women?
5) How does "The Ghostmate" serve to reinforce these stereotypes?

37 *The following discussion questions are designed to convey how Chan's "The Chinese in Haifa" presented a new identity for Chinese men in America, and to interrogate BaBa's identity in light of this context.*

1) What is the identity of the Chinese American man, as represented by Bill Wong? What specific examples can you use to support your answer?
2) Does Jeffery Paul Chan admire Bill Wong? How can you tell? What evidence can you give for your answer?
3) What are your feelings and thoughts about Bill Wong?
4) How are the women portrayed in this story?
5) In what ways is Bill Wong similar to and different from BaBa?
6) In what ways does BaBa counteract the stereotypes of the feminized Chinese man?
7) In what ways does Kingston reject Americanization as an antidote to these stereotypes?
8) Reconsider "The Ghostmate" as you respond to this question.
9) Would Maxine Hong Kingston admire Bill Wong? Explain.

38 *In our discussion of Bill Wong's Americanization, many of my students have observed that Bill Wong seems to be "just like any man" by having an affair. Such observations have led us to a further examination of the literary construction of Asian American manhood in "The Chinese in Haifa" and* China Men.

1) In your groups, please consider the extent to which Chan's definition of manhood, as represented by Bill Wong, includes sexualization and even violence. Please turn your attention to Wong's affair (and the events leading to it) as well as the fishing episode. What kind of portrayal of manhood does Chan project?

2) Continue to examine this notion of resexualization and aggression by reconsidering the story of Ah Goong, the narrator's grandfather in *China Men*. Go back to "The Grandfather of the Sierra Nevada Mountains" and search for evidence that Kingston presents Ah Goong in this manner.

39 *This exercise considers Kolodny's feminist critique of the conquest myth in "The Land-as-Woman: Literary Convention and Latent Psychological Content" using J. Hector St. John de Crevecoeur's "What is an American Farmer" from* Letters from an American Farmer *and John Hammond's "Leah and Rachel, Or, The Two Faithful Sisters Virginia and Maryland." Then we apply this critique to* China Men, *specifically in terms of Ah Goong and Bak Goong and their efforts to build America. I ask students to consider both Crevecoeur's and Hammond's texts before we move on to* China Men.

1) Crevecour describes and interprets the natural landscape around him. That is, he finds meaning in it. What are his views of nature? How do they relate to his notions of democracy, citizenship, and rights? To what extent do his views include or exclude women? Can you find evidence of Kolodny's claims in Crevecoeur's writings?

2) In what ways are Hammond's views of nature similar to and/or different from Crevecoeur's? How does Hammond describe Maryland and Virginia? Why does he describe them as sisters? To what extent do you see Kolodny's claims as relevant to Hammond's text?

3) Given Kolodny's critique of the conquest myth as well as your readings of Crevecoeur and Hammond, to what extent might Kingston participate in such a critique? Specifically, what evidence is there in the chapters on Bak Goong and Ah Goong that Kingston is critiquing their violence and sexuality toward the land?

40 *In this exercise, I complicate Kolodny's mainstream feminist analysis of the conquest myth by bringing issues of race into the picture. To what extent, I ask students, does the conquest of land simultaneously involve the exploitation of ethnic minorities? After having discussed Rachel Stein's work in relationship to the expropriation of Native American lands and the exploitation of labor in the institution of slavery, we turn to Kingston's* China Men. *Does Kingston attempt to include her Chinese male ancestors in this history of exploitation?*

Going back to the chapters on Bak Goong and Ah Goong, find evidence for the assertion that the U.S. was built, at least partially, on the labor and exploitation of Chinese men. Here are some suggestions:

1) How is nature represented in this chapter? Is it only there for utilitarian purposes, or do Bak Goong and Ah Goong find it a source of comfort as well?
2) What happens when dynamite is developed?
3) How do Bak Goong and Ah Goong get involved in using dynamite?
4) What happens to them when using dynamite?

41 *In this exercise, we continue to examine the identity of the male characters in* China Men *from an Asian American feminist perspective. After discussing Shu-mei Shih's article "Exile and Intertextuality in Maxine Hong Kingston's* China Men," *we circle back to parts of the text we've already covered, looking for evidence of "double commentary."*

Each group will be assigned one of the following themes from *China Men*. Use close reading and careful analysis to find evidence of what Shu-mei Shih refers to as *double commentary* in your assigned theme.

1) BaBa's treatment of his family
2) BaBa's "legal" journey to America
3) the silencing of the great-grandfather in the Sandalwood Mountains
4) the interchapters "The Ghostmate," "On Discovery," and "On Mortality"

42 *In the final writing assignment at the crossroads of* China Men, *I use the following quote by Cheung to stimulate students' reflections on their experiences at the crossroads of* China Men.

In her book *Articulate Silences*, King-kok Cheung, a prolific and respected Asian American feminist scholar, writes: "To translate from different languages, to listen without insisting on a single story line is also to reach beyond one's workaday horizon, to see with other eyes, to open oneself to a variety of experiences, and to spin an intersubjective network" (125).

As you think back on and discuss your experiences with various critical and cultural perspectives while reading *China Men*, consider whether your vision and knowledge of Chinese and Chinese American history have indeed broadened.

Appendix B: Critical Bibliographies

As I began to study the scholarship relevant to teaching texts by women of color, particularly the four texts in my study, I was initially struck by the similarities among many of the critical communities. At first glance, it seemed that African American, Asian American, Chicano/a, and Native American scholars had forged similar paths and were grappling with similar issues. After recovering and uncovering previously excluded texts, scholars in each of these critical communities worked to identify literary tradition(s), recurring themes, tropes, styles, and languages. They also wrestled with theoretical methods, critical categories and tools, issues of canonization, identity politics, and issues of essentialism (particularly in Native American and Asian American critical communities). Equally striking, African American, Asian American, Chicana, and Native American feminist critical discourse also seemed to have emerged in similar ways. Each grew out of the problems or gaps that feminist scholars of color had identified in their larger (male) critical communities. Thus began the process of uncovering, recovering, reevaluating and, ultimately, the identifying of a literary tradition(s). Finally, these critical communities seemed to grapple with similar issues: their relationship to mainstream feminist criticism, their relationship to one another, and their relationship to their male counterparts.

But as I continued to read the voluminous scholarship in conjunction with the literary texts, the similarities I had originally thought were so strong began to reconfigure themselves merely as broad outlines. What began to interest me more were the nuances, the intricacies, the differences. What is distinct, for example, about African American feminist consciousness from Chicana feminist consciousness? How was I to understand the Chinese contexts so important to *China Men?* How do Cisneros' and Silko's uses of legendary female figures, real and imagined, differ from each other? Obviously, answering these and the many other questions I could use as examples would take another book (or more). Instead, I am including in this appendix critical bibliographies for African American, Asian American, Chicano/a, and Native American literature to provide a beginning point from which instructors who are new to these traditions might initiate their research into them. It is, indeed, the nuances that inform teaching at the crossroads. I hope you find the journey as intellectually stimulating as I did.

African American Literary Criticism

Awkward, Michael. *Inspiriting Influences: Tradition, Revision, and Afro-American Women's Novels*. New York: Columbia UP, 1989.

—. "Race, Gender, and the Politics of Reading." *Black American Literature Forum* 22.1 (1988): 5-27.

Baker, Houston A, Jr. *Blues, Ideology, and Afro-American Literature: A Vernacular Theory*. Chicago: U of Chicago P, 1984.

Baker, Houston A., Jr. and Patricia Redmond, eds. *Afro-American Literary Study in the 1990s*. Chicago: U of Chicago P, 1989.

Carby, Hazel V. *Reconstructing Womanhood: The Emergence of the Afro-American Woman Novelist*. New York: Oxford UP, 1987.

—. "White Woman Listen! Black Feminism and the Boundaries of Sisterhood." *Materialist Feminism: A Reader in Class, Difference, and Women's Lives*. Ed. Rosemary Hennessy and Chrys Ingraham. New York: Routledge, 1997. 110-28.

Christian, Barbara. "But What Do We Think We're Doing Anyway: The State of Black Feminist Criticism(s) or My Version of a Little Bit of History." *Changing Our Own Words: Essays on Criticism, Theory, and Writing by Black Women*. Ed. Cheryl A. Wall. New Brunswick: Rutgers UP, 1989. Rpt. in *Within the Circle: An Anthology of African American Literary Criticism*. Ed. Angelyn Mitchell. Durham: Duke UP, 1994. 499-514.

—. "The Highs and Lows of Black Feminist Criticism." *Feminisms: An Anthology of Literary Theory and Criticism*. Ed. Robin R. Warhol and Diane Price Herndl. New Brunswick: Rutgers UP, 1997. 51-56.

Gates, Henry Louis, Jr. "African American Criticism." *Redrawing the Boundaries: The Transformation of English and American Literary Studies*. Ed. Stephen Greenblatt and Giles Gunn. New York: MLA, 1992. 303-19.

—. "Canon-Formation, Literary History, and the Afro-American Tradition: From the Seen to the Told." *Afro-American Literary Study in the 1990's*. Ed. Houston A. Baker, Jr. and Patricia Redmond. Chicago: U of Chicago P, 1989. 14-39.

—. " 'Ethnic and Minority' Studies." *Introduction to Scholarship in Modern Languages and Literatures*. 2nd ed. Ed. Joseph Gibaldi. New York: MLA, 1992. 288-302.

—. *Loose Canons: Notes on the Culture Wars*. New York: Oxford UP, 1992.

—. "The Master's Pieces: On Canon Formation and the Afro-American Tradition." *Conversations: Contemporary Critical Theory and the Teaching of Literature*. Ed. Charles Moran and Elizabeth F. Penfield. Urbana: NCTE, 1990. 55-75.

—. *The Signifying Monkey: A Theory of African American Literary Criticism*. New York: Oxford UP, 1988.

—, ed. *Black Literature and Literary Theory*. New York: Methuen, 1984.

Joyce, Joyce A. *Warriors, Conjurers and Priests: Defining African-Centered Criticism*. Chicago: Third World, 1994.

Kraft, Marion. *The African Continuum and Contemporary African American Women Writers*. Frankfurt am Main: Peter Lang, 1995.

Martin, Reginald. "Current African American Literary Theory: Review and Projections." *Understanding Others: Cultural and Cross-Cultural Studies and the Teaching of Literature*. Ed. Joseph Trimmer and Tilly Warnock. Urbana: NCTE, 1992. 107-114.

McDowell, Deborah E. *"The Changing Same": Black Women's Literature, Criticism, and Theory*. Bloomington: Indiana UP, 1995.

—. "New Directions for Black Feminist Criticism." *Black American Literature Forum* 14 (1980): 153-59. Rpt. in *The Critical Tradition. Classic Texts and Contemporary Trends*. Ed. David H. Richter. New York: St. Martin's P, 1989. 1137-46.

—. "Race, Gender, and the Practice of Theory." *Studies in Historical Change*. Ed. Ralph Cohen. Charlottesville: UP of Virginia, 1992. Rpt. in *Feminisms: An Anthology of Literary Theory and Criticism*. Ed. Robin R. Warhol and Diane Price Herndl. New Brunswick: Rutgers UP, 1997. 234-47.

—. "Transferences: Black Feminist Discourse: The 'Practice' of 'Theory.' " *Feminism Beside Itself*. Ed. Diane Elam and Robyn Wiegman. New York: Routledge, 1995. 93-118.

McKay, Nellie. "Reflections on Black Women Writers: Revising the Literary Canon." *The Impact of Feminist Research in the Academy*. Ed. Christie Farnham. Bloomington: Indiana UP, 1987. Rpt. in

Feminisms: An Anthology of Literary Theory and Criticism. Ed. Robin R. Warhol and Diane Price Herndl. New Brunswick: Rutgers UP, 1997.151-63.

Mitchell, Angelyn. "Introduction: Voices Within the Circle: A Historical Overview of African American Literary Criticism." *Within the Circle: An Anthology of African American Literary Criticism*." Ed. Angelyn Mitchell. Durham: Duke UP, 1994. 1-18.

—, ed. *Within the Circle: An Anthology of African American Literary Criticism*." Durham: Duke UP, 1994.

Savery, Pancho. "The Third Plane at the Change of the Century: The Shape of African-American Literature To Come." *Left Politics and the Literary Profession*. Ed. Lennard J. Davis and M. Bella Mirabella. New York: Columbia UP, 1990. 236-53.

—. " 'Who Was That Masked Man?' Literary Criticism and the Teaching of African American Literature in Introductory Classes." *Practicing Theory in Introductory College Literature Courses*. Ed. James. M. Calahan and David B. Downing. Urbana: NCTE, 1991. 189-98.

Smith, Barbara. "Toward a Black Feminist Criticism." *Within the Circle: An Anthology of African American Literary Criticism from the Harlem Renaissance to the Present*. Ed. Angelyn Mitchell. Durham: Duke UP, 1994. 410-27.

—, ed. *Home Girls: A Black Feminist Anthology*. New Brunswick: Rutgers UP, 2000.

Stepto, Robert B. "Afro-American Literature." *Columbia Literary History of the United States*. Ed. Emory Elliott. New York: Columbia UP, 1988. 785-99.

—. *From Behind the Veil: A Study of Afro-American Narrative*. 2nd ed. Urbana: U of Illinois P, 1991.

Walker, Alice. *In Search of Our Mothers' Gardens*. 1967. San Diego: Harcourt Brace Jovanovich, 1983.

Wall, Cheryl A., ed. *Changing Our Own Words: Essays on Criticism, Theory, and Writing by Black Women*. New Brunswick: Rutgers UP, 1989.

Washington, Mary Helen. "Teaching Black-Eyed Susans: An Approach to the Study of Black Women Writers." *Black American Literature Forum* 11 (1977): 20-24.

Waxman, Barbara Frey. "Canonicity and Black American Literature: A Feminist View." *MELUS* 14.2 (1987): 87-93.

Young, Reggie. "On Stepping into Footprints Which Feel Like Your Own: Literacy, Empowerment, and the African-American Literary Tradition." *Literary Influence and African-American Writers: Collected Essays*. Ed. Tracy Mishkin. New York: Garland, 1996. 359-85.

Asian American Literary Criticism

Cheung, King-kok. *Articulate Silences: Hisaye Yamamoto, Maxine Hong Kingston, Joy Kogawa*. Ithaca: Cornell UP, 1993.

—. "Of Men and Men: Reconstructing Chinese American Masculinity." *Other Sisterhoods: Literary Theory and U.S. Women of Color*. Urbana: U of Illinois P, 1998. 173-99.

—. "Re-Viewing Asian American Literary Studies." *An Interethnic Companion to Asian American Literature*. Ed. King-kok Cheung. New York: Cambridge UP, 1997. 1-36.

—. "*The Woman Warrior* versus *The Chinaman Pacific:* Must a Chinese American Critic Choose between Feminism and Heroism?" *Conflicts in Feminism*. Ed. Marianne Hirsch and Evelyn Fox Keller. New York: Routledge, 1990. 234-51.

—, ed. *An Interethnic Companion to Asian American Literature*. New York: Cambridge UP, 1997.

Chin, Frank, Jeffery Paul Chan, Lawson Fusao Inada, and Shawn Wong. "An Introduction to Chinese and Japanese American Literature." *Aiiieeeee! An Anthology of Asian American Writers*. Ed Frank Chin, Jeffery Paul Chan, Lawson Fusao Inada, and Shawn Wong 1974. New York: Mentor, 1991. 3-38.

—. Preface. *Aiiieeeee! An Anthology of Asian American Writers*. Ed. Frank Chin, Jeffery Paul Chan, Lawson Fusao Inada, and Shawn Wong. 1974. New York: Mentor, 1991. xi-xxii.

—. "Preface to the Mentor Edition." *Aiiieeeee! An Anthology of Asian American Writers*. Ed. Frank Chin, Jeffery Paul Chan, Lawson Fusao Inada, and Shawn Wong. 1974. New York: Mentor, 1991. xxiii-xli.

Goellnicht, Donald C. "Blurring Boundaries: Asian American Literature as Theory." *An Interethnic Companion to Asian American Literature*. Ed. King-kok Cheung. New York: Cambridge UP, 1997. 338-65.

Kim, Elaine H. "Asian American Literature." *Columbia Literary History of the United States*. Ed. Emory Elliott. New York: Columbia UP, 1988. 811-21.

—. *Asian American Literature: An Introduction to the Writings and Their Social Context*. Philadelphia: Temple UP, 1982.

—. " 'Such Opposite Creatures': Men and Women in Asian American Literature." *Michigan Quarterly Review* 29.1 (1990): 68-93.

Koshy, Susan. "The Fiction of Asian American Literature." *The Yale Journal of Criticism* 9.2 (1996): 315-46.

Li, David Leiwei. "Filiative and Affiliative Textualization in Chinese American Literature." *Understanding Others: Cultural and Cross-Cultural Studies and the Teaching of Literature*. Ed. Joseph Trimmer and Tilly Warnock. Urbana: NCTE, 1992. 177-200.

—. "The Formation of Frank Chin and Formations of Chinese American Literature." *Asian Americans: Comparative and Global Perspectives*. Ed. Shirley Hume, Hyung-chan Kim, Stephen S. Fugita, and Amy Ling. Pullman: Washington State UP, 1991. 211-23.

Lim, Shirley Geok-lin. "Feminist and Ethnic Literary Theories in Asian American Literature." *Feminist Studies* 19.3 (1993): 571-95.

Lim, Shirley Geok-lin, and Amy Ling, eds. *Reading the Literatures of Asian America*. Philadelphia: Temple UP, 1992.

Ling, Amy. "Chinese American Women Writers: The Tradition Behind Maxine Hong Kingston." *Redefining American Literary History*. Ed. A. Lavonne Brown Ruoff. New York: MLA, 219-36.

—. " 'Emerging Canons' of Asian American Literature and Arts." *Asian Americans: Comparative and Global Perspectives*. Ed. Shirley Hume, Hyung-chan Kim, Stephen S. Fugita, and Amy Ling. Pullman: Washington State UP, 1991. 191-97.

—. "I'm Here: An Asian American Woman's Response." *Feminisms: An Anthology of Literary Theory and Criticism*. Ed. Robyn R. Warhol and Diane Price Herndl. New Brunswick: Rutgers UP, 1997. 776-83.

—. "Maxine Hong Kingston and the Dialogic Dilemma of Asian American Writers." *The Bucknell Review: A Scholarly Journal of Letters, Arts, and Sciences*. 39.1 (1995): 151-66.

—. "Twelve Asian American Writers: In Search of Self-Definition." *Redefining American Literary History*. Ed. A. Lavonne Brown Ruoff. New York: MLA, 1990. 237-50.

Slapsys, Richard. "Asian-American Literature: Reviews and Criticism of Works by American Writers of Asian Descent." *Reference and User Services Quarterly* 38.3 (1999): 297-98.

Wong, Sau-ling Cynthia. "Chinese American Literature." *An Interethnic Companion to Asian American Literature.* Ed. King-kok Cheung. New York: Cambridge UP, 1997. 39-61.

Chicano/a Literary Criticism

Alarcón, David Cooper. *The Aztec Palimpset: Mexico in the Modern Imagination.* Tucson: U of Arizona P, 1997.

Anzaldúa, Gloria. *Borderlands/*La Frontera. 2nd ed. San Francisco: Aunt Lute Books, 1999.

Arteaga, Alfred. *Chicano Poetics: Heterotexts and Hybridities.* New York: Cambridge UP, 1997.

Bruce-Novoa, Juan. "Chicano Literary Space: Cultural Criticism/Cultural Production. *Retrospace: Collected Essays on Chicano Literature.* Houston: Arte Público, 1990. 157-75.

—, ed. *Retrospace: Collected Essays on Chicano Literature.* Houston: Arte Público, 1990.

Calderón, Héctor. "At the Crossroads of History, on the Borders of Change: Chicano Literary Studies Past, Present, and Future." *Left Politics and the Literary Profession.* Ed. Lennard J. Davis and M. Bella Mirabella. New York: Columbia UP, 1990. 211-35.

Calderón, Héctor, and José David Saldívar. "Editors' Introduction: Criticism in the Borderlands." *Criticism in the Borderlands: Studies in Chicano Literature, Culture, and Ideology*. Ed. Héctor Calderón and José David Saldívar. Durham: Duke UP, 1991. 1-7.

—, eds. *Criticism in the Borderlands: Studies in Chicano Literature, Culture, and Ideology.* Durham: Duke UP, 1991.

Chabram, Angie. "Chicano Critical Discourse: An Emerging Critical Practice." *Aztlán* 18.2 (1989): 45-90.

Franco, Dean. "Ethnic Writing/Writing Ethnicity: The Critical Conceptualization of Chicano Identity." *Post-Identity* 2.1 (1999): 104-22.

González, María. "Love and Conflict: Mexican American Women Writers as Daughters." *Women of Color: Mother-Daughter Relationships in Twentieth Century Literature*. Ed. Elizabeth Brown-Guillory. Austin: U of Texas P, 1996. 153-71.

Herrera-Sobek, María. Introduction. *Chicana Creativity and Criticism: Charting New Frontiers in American Literature.* Ed. María Herrera-Sobek and Helena María Viramontes. Houston: Arte Público, 1988. 9-39.

Herrera-Sobek, María, and Helena María Viramontes, eds. *Chicana Creativity and Criticism: Charting New Frontiers in American Literature.* Houston: Arte Público, 1988.

Hurtado, Aída. "Sitios y Lenguas: Chicanas Theorize Feminisms." *Hypatia* 13.2 (1998): 134-61. Online. ProQuest. 24 May 1999.

Limón, José. *Mexican Ballads, Chicano Poems: History and Influence in Mexican-American Social Poetry*. Berkeley: U of California P, 1992.

McCracken, Ellen. "Latina Narrative and Politics of Signification: Articulation, Antagonism, and Populist Rupture." *Critica: A Journal of Critical Essays* 2.2 (1990): 202-07.

Paredes, Raymund A. "Contemporary Mexican-American Literature, 1960-Present." *A Literary History of the American West*. Ed. Thomas J. Lyon. Fort Worth: Texas Christian UP, 1987. 1101-18.

Pérez-Torres, Rafael. "Chicano Studies at the Millennium." *Contemporary Literature* 39.4 (1998): 675-86.

Rebolledo, Tey Diana. "The Politics of Poetics: Or, What Am I, a Critic, Doing in This Text Anyhow?" *Chicana Creativity and Criticism: Charting New Frontiers in American Literature.* Houston: Arte Público, 1988. 129-38.

Rebolledo, Tey Diana, and Eliana S. Rivero. "Foremothers." *Infinite Divisions: An Anthology of Chicana* Literature. Ed. Tey Diana Rebolledo and Eliana S. Rivero. Tucson: U of Arizona P, 1993. 35-39.

—. Introduction. *Infinite Divisions: An Anthology of Chicana Literature.* Ed. Tey Diana Rebolledo and Eliana S. Rivero. Tucson: U of Arizona P, 1993. 1-33.

Rivero, Eliana S. "Hispanic Literature in the United States: Self-Image and Conflict." *International Studies in Honor of Tomás Rivera*. Ed. Julian Olivares. Houston: Arte Público, 1986. 173-91.

Saldívar, José David. *Border Matters: Remapping American Cultural Studies*. Berkeley: U of California P, 1997.

Saldívar, Ramón. *Chicano Narrative: The Dialectics of Difference*. Madison: U of Wisconsin P, 1990.

Sánchez, Rosaura. "Discourses of Gender, Ethnicity and Class in Chicano Literature." *Las Americas* Review 10.2 (1992): 72-88. Rpt in *Feminisms: An Anthology of Literary Theory and Criticism*. Ed. Robin R. Warhol and Diane Price Herndl. New Brunswick: Rutgers UP, 1997. 1009-22.

Native American Literary Criticism

Allen, Paula Gunn. *The Sacred Hoop: Recovering the Feminine in American Indian Traditions*. Boston: Beacon, 1986.

—, ed. *Spider Woman's Granddaughters*. Boston: Beacon, 1989.

—. *Studies in American Indian Literature*. New York: MLA, 1983.

Brant, Beth. "The Good Red Road: Journeys of Homecoming in Native Women's Writing." *American Indian Culture and Research Journal* 21.1 (1997): 193-206.

Donovan, Kathleen M. *Feminist Readings of Native American Literature: Coming to Voice*.Tucson: U of Arizona P, 1998.

Fleck, Richard F., ed. *Critical Perspectives on Native American Fiction*. 2nd ed. Pueblo, CO: Passeggiata Press, 1997.

Hanson, Elizabeth I. *Forever There: Race and Gender in Contemporary Native American Fiction*. New York: Peter Lang, 1989.

Jaskoski, Helen, ed. *Early Native American Writing: New Critical Essays*. New York: Cambridge UP, 1996.

Krupat, Arnold. *For Those Who Come After: A Study of Native American Autobiography*. Berkeley: U of California P, 1985.

—. Introduction. *New Voices in Native American Literary Criticism*. Ed. Arnold Krupat. Washington: Smithsonian Institution Press, 1993. xvii-xxv.

—. "Native American Autobiography and the Synedochic Self." *American Autobiography: Retrospect and Prospect*. Ed. Paul John Eakin. Madison: U of Wisconsin P, 1991. 171-94.

—. *The Turn to the Native: Studies in Criticism and Culture*. Lincoln: U of Nebraska P, 1996.

—. *The Voice in the Margin: Native American Literature and the Canon*. Berkeley: U of California P, 1989.

Ruoff, A. Lavonne Brown. *American Indian Literatures: An Introduction, Bibliographic Review, and Selected Bibliography*. New York: MLA, 1990.

Schweninger, Lee. "Writing Nature: Silko and Native Americans as Nature Writers." *MELUS* 18.2 (Summer 1992): 47-60.

Vizenor, Gerald, ed. *Narrative Chance: Postmodern Discourse on Native American Indian*. Albuquerque: U of New Mexico P, 1989. 55-68.

Wiget, Andrew. "The Study of Native American Literature: An Introduction." *Critical Essays on Native American Literature*. Boston: G.K. Hall, 1985. 1-20.

—, ed. *Critical Essays on Native American Literature*. Boston: G.K. Hall, 1985.

Works Cited

Achebe, Chinua. *Things Fall Apart.* 1958. New York: Knopf, 1992.

Ahokas, Pirjo. "Maxine Hong Kingston's *The Woman Warrior:* Constructing a Female Chinese-American American Subjectivity." *Nordic Journal of Women's Studies* 4.1 (1993): 3-15.

Akers, John C. "Fragmentation in the Chicano Novel: Literary Technique and Cultural Identity." *International Studies in Honor of Tomás Rivera.* Ed. Julián Olivares. Houston: Arte Público, 1985. 121-35.

Alberti, John, ed. *The Canon in the Classroom: The Pedagogical Implications of Canon Revision in American Literature.* New York: Garland, 1995.

—. "Introduction: Reconstructing the Pedagogical Canon." Alberti, *The Canon in the Classroom* xi-xxx.

—. "Teaching the Rhetoric of Race: A Rhetorical Approach to Multicultural Pedagogy." Brannon and Greene, *Rethinking American Literature* 203-15.

Alcoff, Linda Martín. "The Problem of Speaking for Others." *Who Can Speak? Authority and Critical Identity.* Ed. Judith Roof and Robyn Wiegman. Urbana: U of Illinois P, 1995. 97-119.

Alighieri, Dante. *Inferno.* Trans. Robert Hollander and Jean Hollander. New York: Doubleday, 2000.

Allen, Paula Gunn. "The Autobiography of a Confluence." Swann and Krupat, *I Tell You Now* 143-54.

—. " 'Border Studies': The Intersection of Gender and Color." Gibaldi *Introduction to Scholarship* 303-19.

—. "Grandmother." 1978. Beaty and Hunter, *New Worlds* 264-65.

—. "Grandmother of the Sun: Ritual Gynocracy in Native America." *The Sacred Hoop: Recovering the Feminine in American Indian Traditions.* Boston: Beacon, 1986. 13-29.

—. Introduction. *The Sacred Hoop: Recovering the Feminine in American Indian Traditions.* By Allen. Boston: Beacon, 1986. 1-7.

—. Introduction. *Spider Woman's Granddaughters.* Ed. Paula Gunn Allen. Boston: Beacon, 1989. 1-21.

—. "Kochinnenako in Academe: Three Approaches to Interpreting a Keres Indian Tale." *The Sacred Hoop: Recovering the Feminine in American Indian Traditions.* Paula Gunn Allen. Boston: Beacon, 1986. 222-44.

—. "Teaching American Indian Women's Literature." Allen, *Studies in American* 134-44.

—. *Studies in American Indian Literature.* New York: MLA, 1983.

Anderson, Karen. *Changing Woman: A History of Racial Ethnic Women in Modern America*. New York: Oxford UP, 1996.

Andrews, Larry R. "Black Sisterhood in Gloria Naylor's Novels." *CLA Journal* XXXIII.1 (1989): 1-25.

Annis, David. "The Relativity of Values and the Implications for Multicultural and Values Education." *Thresholds in Education* 22.3-4 (Aug/Nov 1995): 15-20.

Anzaldúa, Gloria. *Borderlands/*La Frontera. 2nd ed. San Francisco: Aunt Lute Books, 1999.

—. "Haciendo caras, una entrada." *Making Face, Making Soul/Haciendo Caras*. Ed. Gloria Anzaldúa. San Francisco: Aunt Lute Books, 1990. xv- xxviii.

—. "*La conciencia de la mestiza*." Anzaldúa, *Borderlands* 99-120.

—. "La Prieta." Moraga and Anzaldúa, *This Bridge Called My Back* 198-209.

—. "Preface to the First Edition." Anzaldúa *Borderlands* 19-20.

—. "Speaking In Tongues: A Letter to Third World Women Writers." Moraga and Anzaldúa. *This Bridge Called My Back* 165-74.

—. Speech. Humanities Center Lecture Series on Space/Place. Lehigh University, Bethlehem, PA. 26 Apr. 2001.

—. "To live in the Borderlands means you." *Borderlands* 216-17.

Apess, William. *A Son of the Forest: The Experience of William Apess, a Native of the Forest*. 1829. A Son of the Forest *and Other Writings*. Ed. Barry O'Connell. Amherst: U of Massachusetts P, 1997. 1-56.

Asante, Molefi Kete. *The Afrocentric Idea*. Philadelphia: Temple UP, 1987.

Bacon, Jacqueline Lee. "Impasse or Tension? Pedagogy and the Canon Controversy." *College English* 55.5 (1993): 501-14.

Bakhtin, M.M. *The Dialogic Imagination*. Trans. C. Emerson and M. Holquist. Ed. M. Holquist. Austin: U of Texas P, 1981.

Bambara, Toni Cade. "The Lesson." *Gorilla, My Love*. 1972. New York: Vintage, 1992. 85-96.

—. "Sweet Town." *Gorilla, My Love*. 1972. New York: Vintage, 1992. 119-25.

Barnes, Jim. "On Native Ground." Swann and Krupat, *I Tell You Now* 85-97.

Barr, Robert B., and John Tagg. "From Teaching to Learning—A New Paradigm for Undergraduate Education." *Change* 27.6 (1995): 12-27.

Barth, John. "Lost in the Funhouse." 1967. Lauter, et al., *The Heath Anthology* 2nd ed. 3005-20.

Beaty, Jerome, and J. Paul Hunter, eds. *New Worlds of Literature*. New York: Norton, 1989.

Benstock, Shari. "Women's Literary History: To Be Continued." *Tulsa Studies in Women's Literature* 5.2 (1983): 165-83.

Berg, Christine G. " 'Giving Sound To the Bruised Places in Their Hearts': Gloria Naylor and Walt Whitman." *The Critical Response to Gloria Naylor*. Ed. Sharon Felton and

Michelle C. Loris. Westport: Greenwood, 1997. 98-111.

—. "Methods of Intertextuality in Gloria Naylor's *Linden Hills*." Diss. Lehigh U. 1997.

Berthoff, Ann. "Reclaiming the Active Mind." *College English* 61.6 (1999): 671-80.

Bérubé, Michael. *The Employment of English: Theory, Jobs, and the Future of Literary Studies.* New York: New York UP, 1998.

Bevis, William. "Native American Novels: Homing In." Fleck, *Critical Perspectives* 15-45.

Bhabha, Homi. *The Location of Culture.* New York: Routledge, 1994.

Birmingham Pokorny, Elba D. "La Malinche: A Feminist Perspective on Otherness in Mexican and Chicana Literature." *Confluencia: Revista Hispanica de Cultura y Literatura* 11.2 (1996): 120-36.

Bizzell, Patricia. " 'Contact Zones' and the Structure of English Studies." *College English* 56.2 (1994): 163-69.

—. "Negotiating Difference: Teaching Multicultural Literature." Brannon and Greene, *Rethinking American Literature* 163-74.

—. "The Politics of Teaching Virtue." *ADE Bulletin* 103 (Winter 1992): 4-7.

Bjork, Patrick Bryce. "Teaching Toward a Multicultural Perspective in the Land That Time Forgot." Goebel and Hall, *Teaching a "New Canon"?* 81-95.

Bloom, Allan. "Music." 1987. *Common Culture.* Ed. Michael Petracca and Madeleine Sorapure. 2nd ed. Upper Saddle River, NJ: Prentice Hall, 1998. 253-65.

Boas, Franz. *Keresan Texts.* 2 vols. New York: AMS, 1974.

—. *Keresan Texts Part 1.* New York: Memoirs of the American Ethnological Society, 928.

Bonnycastle, Stephen. *In Search of Authority: An Introductory Guide to Literary Theory.* 2nd ed. Peterborough, ON: Broadview, 1998.

Booth, Wayne C. "The Ethics of Teaching Literature." *College English* 61.1 (1998): 41-55.

—. *The Rhetoric of Fiction.* 2nd ed. Chicago: U of Chicago P, 1983.

Bower, Anne L. "Sharing Responsibility for American Lit: 'A Spectacular and Dangerous World of Choice.' " Alberti, *The Canon in the Classroom* 221-40.

Braendlin, Bonnie Hoover. "*Bildung* in Ethnic Women Writers." *Denver Quarterly* 17.4 (1983): 75-87.

Brannon, Lil, and Brenda M. Greene. Introduction. Brannon and Greene, *Rethinking American Literature* vii-xi.

—, eds. *Rethinking American Literature.* Urbana: NCTE, 1997.

Brearley, H.C. "Ba-ad Nigger." *Mother Wit From the Laughing Barrel: Readings in the Interpretation of Afro-American Folklore.* Ed. Alan Dundes. Englewood Cliffs: Prentice-Hall, 1973. 578-85.

Brontë, Charlotte. *Jane Eyre.* 1847. New York: Norton, 2001.

Browdy de Hernández, Jennifer. "Laughing, Crying, Surviving: The Pragmatic Politics of Leslie Marmon Silko's *Storyteller*." *Auto/biography Studies* 9.1 (1994): 18-42.

—. "Writing (for) Survival: Continuity and Change in Four Contemporary Native American Women's Autobiographies." *Wicazo Sa Review* 10.2 (1994): 40-63.

Burnham, Margaret A. "An Impossible Marriage: Slave Law and Family Law." *Law and Inequality* 5 (1987): 187-225.

Cahalan, James M., and David B. Downing. Introduction. Cahalan and Downing, *Practicing Theory* 1-16.

—, eds. *Practicing Theory, in Introductory College Literature Courses.* Urbana: NCTE, 1991.

Cain, William E. "Contemporary Theory, the Academy, and Pedagogy." Sadoff and Cain, *Teaching Contemporary Theory* 3-14.

Carbonell, Ana María. "From Llorona to Gritona: Coatlicue in Feminist Tales by Viramontes and Cisneros." *MELUS* 24.2 (1999): 53-74.

Carby, Hazel V. *Reconstructing Womanhood: The Emergence of the Afro-American Woman Novelist.* New York: Oxford UP, 1987.

Cervantes, Lorna Dee. "Beneath the Shadow of the Freeway." 1977. Lauter, et al., *The Heath Anthology* 2580-82.

—. "Heritage." *The Americas Review* (formerly *Revista Chicano-Riqueña*) 10.1-2 (1982): 48.

—. "Visions of Mexico While at a Writing Symposium in Port Townsend, Washington." *Emplumada*. Pittsburgh: U of Pittsburgh P, 1981. 45-47.

Chan, Jeffery Paul. "Auntie Tsia Lays Dying." *Asian American Authors*. Ed. Kai-yu Hsu and Helen Palubinskas. Boston: Houghton Mifflin, 1972. 77-85.

—. "The Chinese in Haifa." Chin, Chan, Inada, and Wong, *Aiiieeeee!* 71-92.

—. "Jackrabbit." *Yardbird Reader*. Ed. Frank Chin and Shawn Hsu Wong. Vol. 3. Berkeley: Yardbird, 1974. 217-38.

Chapman, David, Jeanett Harris, and Christine Hult. "Agents for Change: Undergraduate Writing Programs in Departments of English." *Rhetoric Review* 13.2 (1995): 421-34.

Cheung, King-kok. *Articulate Silences: Hisaye Yamamoto, Maxine Hong Kingston, Joy Kogawa*. Ithaca: Cornell UP, 1993.

—. "Re-Viewing Asian American Literary Studies." Cheung, *An Interethnic Companion* 1-36.

—, ed. *An Interethnic Companion to Asian American Literature.* New York: Cambridge UP, 1997.

Chew, Kristina. "What Does *E Pluribus Unum* Mean? Reading the Classics and Multicultural Literature Together." *The Classical Journal* 93.1 (1997): 55-81.

Chin, Frank. *The Chickencoop Chinaman. The Chickencoop Chinaman; and, The Year of the Dragon: Two Plays.* Seattle: U of Washington P, 1981.

—. "SONG OF THE MONOGRAM WARNER BROS. CHINK: News to Raise the Dead." *Yardbird Reader*. Ed. Ishmael Reed. Vol. 1. Berkeley: Yardbird, 1971. 131-33.

Chin, Frank, Jeffery Paul Chan, Lawson Fusao Inada, and Shawn Wong. "An Introduction to Chinese and Japanese American Literature." Chin, Chan, Inada, and Wong, *Aiiieeeee!* 3-38.

—. Preface. Chin, Chan, Inada, and Wong, *Aiiieeeee!* xi-xxii.

—, eds. *Aiiieeeee! An Anthology of Asian American Writers.* 1974. New York. Mentor, 1991.

Chopin, Kate. *The Awakening.* 1899. Ed. Margo Culley. 2nd ed. New York: Norton, 1994.

Cisneros, Sandra. *The House on Mango Street.* 1984. New York: Vintage, 1991.

—. *Woman Hollering Creek and Other Stories.* New York: Random House, 1991.

Clark, Beverly Lyon, et al. "Giving Voice to Feminist Criticism: A Conversation." Sadoff and Cain. *Teaching Contemporary Theory* 125-40.

Cofer, Judith Ortiz. *Silent Dancing: A Partial Remembrance of a Puerto Rican Childhood.* Houston: Arte Público, 1990.

Cohen, Ralph. "Genre Theory, Literary History, and Historical Change." *Theoretical Issues in Literary History.* Ed. David Perkins. Cambridge: Harvard UP, 1991. 85-115.

Coiner, Constance. "Introduction: Is Multiculturalism Enough?" *Women's Studies: An Interdisciplinary Journal* 20.3-4 (1992): 209-15.

Collins, Patricia Hill. *Black Feminist Thought.* New York: Routledge, 1991.

Conrad, Joseph. *Heart of Darkness.* 1902. New York: Knopf, 1993.

Copway, George. *Life, Letters, & Speeches.* 1847. Ed. A. LaVonne Brown Ruoff and Donald B. Smith. Lincoln: U of Nebraska P, 1997.

Crabtree, Claire. "The Confluence of Folklore, Feminism and Black Self-Determination in Zora Neale Hurston's *Their Eyes Were Watching God.*" *Southern Literary Journal* XVII.2 (Spring 1985): 54-66.

Culley, Margo, ed. *American Women's Autobiography: Fea(s)ts of Memory.* Madison: U of Wisconsin P, 1992.

Cummins, Walter. " 'They Fancied Themselves Free': Exploration and Individualism." *Weber Studies* 11.2 (1994): 137-47.

Cutter, Martha J. "If It's Monday This Must Be Melville: A Canon, Anticanon Approach to Redefining the American Literature Survey." Alberti, *The Canon in the Classroom* 119-51.

Cypess, Sandra Messinger. *La Malinche in Mexican Literature from History to Myth.* Austin: U of Texas P, 1991.

Danielson, Linda J. "Storyteller: 'Grandmother Spider's Web.' " *The Journal of the Southwest* 30.3 (1988): 325-55.

—. "The Storytellers in *Storyteller.*" *Studies in American Indian Literatures* 1.2 (1989): 21-31.

Dasenbrock, Reed Way. "Intelligibility and Meaningfulness in Multicultural Literature in English." *PMLA* 102.1 (1987): 10-19.

—. "Why Read Multicultural Literature? An Arnoldian Perspective." *College English* 61.6 (1999): 691-701.

Davenport, Doris. "Pedagogy and/of Ethnic Literature: The Agony and the Ecstasy." *MELUS* 16.2 (1989-90): 51-62.

Davis, Angela Y. *Women, Race and Class*. New York: Random House, 1981.

Davis, Lennard J., and M. Bella Mirabella, eds. *Left Politics and the Literary Profession*. New York: Columbia UP, 1990.

DeCew, Judith Wagner. "Moral Conflicts and Ethical Relativism" *Ethics* 101 (Oct 1990): 27-41.

Defoe, Daniel. *Robinson Crusoe*. 1719. New York: Norton, 1975.

—. *Robinson Crusoe*. 1719. Abr. ed. New York: DK, 1998.

Del Río, Carmen M. "Chicana Poets: Re-Visions from the Margin." *Revista Canadiense de Estudios Hispanicos* XIV.3 (1990): 431-45.

Didion, Joan. "On Going Home." *Slouching Towards Bethlehem*. 1968. New York: Washington Square, 1981. 166-69.

Dockstader, Frederick J. *Indian Art in America*. 3rd ed. Greenwich: New York Graphic Society, 1966.

Douglass, Frederick. *Narrative of the Life of Frederick Douglass, An American Slave*. 1845. New York: Penguin, 1982.

Doyle, Jacqueline. "More Room of Her Own: Sandra Cisneros' *The House on Mango Street*." *MELUS* 19.4 (1994): 5-35.

Drew, Julie. "Cultural Tourism and the Commodified Other: Reclaiming Difference in the Multicultural Classroom." *The Review of Education/Pedagogy/Cultural Studies* 19.2-3 (1997): 297-309.

duCille, Ann. "The Occult of True Black Womanhood: Critical Demeanor and Black Feminist Studies." *Female Subjects in Black and White: Race, Psychoanalysis, Feminism*. Ed. Elizabeth Abel, Barbara Christian, and Helene Moglen. Berkeley: U of California P, 1997. 21-56.

Dynnikov, Yelena. "Women are Under a Rap Attack." *Harvard Educational Review* 65.2 (1995) Start pg. 271. Online. ProQuest. 28 July 2001.

Eakin, Paul John. Introduction. Eakin, *American Autobiography* 3-22.

—, ed. *American Autobiography: Retrospect and Prospect*. Madison: U of Wisconsin P, 1991.

"El Corrido de Gregorio Cortez." Trans. Hally Wood. *With His Pistol in His Hand: A Border Ballad and Its Hero*. Ed. Américo Paredes. Austin: U of Texas P, 1958. N. pag.

Elder, Arlene A. "Criticizing From the Borderlands." *Modern Language Studies* 26.4 (1996): 5-11.

Eliot, T.S. "Tradition and the Individual Talent." *The Sacred Wood: Essays on Poetry and Criticism*. 7th ed. London: Methuen, 1970. 47-59.

—. *The Waste Land*. 1922. *The Complete Poems and Plays 1909-1950*. New York: Harcourt, Brace & World, 1952.37-55.

Erdrich, Louise. "The Red Convertible." *Love Medicine*. 1984. New York: HarperPerennial, 1993. 181-93.

Erkkilä, Betsy. "Ethnicity, Literary Theory, and the Grounds of Resistance." *American Quarterly* 47.4 (1995): 563-94.

Euripides. *Medea*. Ed. Denys L. Page. Oxford: Clarendon, 1961.

Ewell, Barbara C. "Empowering Otherness: Feminist Criticism and the Academy." *Reorientations. Critical Theories and Pedagogies*. Ed. Bruce Henricksen and Thaïs E. Morgan. Urbana: U of Illinois P, 1990. 43-62.

Faulkner, William. "Barn Burning." 1939. Lauter, et al., *The Heath Anthology* 2nd ed. Vol. 2. 1553-65.

—. "Dry September." *The Collected Stories of William Faulkner*. New York: Random House, 1950. 169-83.

Felski, Rita. "The Novel of Self-Discovery: A Necessary Fiction?" *Southern Review: Literary and Interdisciplinary Essays* 19.2 (1986): 131-48.

Feng, Pin-chia. *The Female* Bildungsroman *by Toni Morrison and Maxine Hong Kingston: A Postmodern Reading*. New York: Peter Lang, 1998.

Ferguson, Rebecca. "History, Memory and Language in Toni Morrison's *Beloved*." *Feminist Criticism: Theory and Practice*. Ed. Susan Sellers, Linda Hutcheon, and Paul Perron. Toronto: U of Toronto P, 1991. 109-27.

Fink, Thomas. "Reading Deconstructively in the Two-Year College Introductory Literature Classroom." Cahalan and Downing, *Practicing Theory* 239-47.

Fiol-Matta, Liza. Introduction. *Women of Color and the Multicultural Curriculum*. Ed. Liza Fiol-Matta and Mariam K. Chamberlain. New York: Feminist, 1994. 1-13.

Fitzgerald, F. Scott. *The Great Gatsby*. 1925. New York: Collier, 1986.

Fleck, Richard F., ed. *Critical Perspectives on Native American Fiction*. Washington, D.C.: Three Continents, 1993.

Foster, Frances Smith. "But, Is It Good Enough to Teach?" Brannon and Greene, *Rethinking American* 193-202.

Fox-Genovese, Elizabeth. "Difference, Diversity, and Divisions in an Agenda for the Women's Movement." Young and Dickerson, *Color, Class, & Country* 232-48.

Freedman, Diane P. *An Alchemy of Genres: Cross-Genre Writing by American Feminist Poet-Critics*. Charlottesville: UP of Virginia, 1992.

Gallagher, Susan VanZanten. "Contingencies and Intersections: The Formation of Pedagogical Canons." *Pedagogy: Critical Approaches to Teaching Literature, Language, Composition, and Culture* 1.1 (2001): 53-67.

Gates, Henry Louis, Jr. "African American Criticism." Greenblatt and Gunn, *Redrawing the Boundaries* 303-19.

—. " 'Ethnic and Minority' Studies." Gibaldi, *Introduction to Scholarship* 288-302.

Gibaldi, Joseph, ed. *Introduction to Scholarship in Modern Languages and Literatures.* 2nd ed. New York: MLA, 1992.

Gilbert, Sandra, and Susan Gubar. Preface. Gilbert and Gubar, *The Norton Anthology* xxvii-xxxii.

—, eds. *The Norton Anthology of Literature by Women: The Tradition in English.* New York: Norton, 1985.

Gilman, Charlotte Perkins. "The Yellow Wall-Paper." 1892. Lauter, et al., *The Heath Anthology Vol. 2.* 761-73.

Glancy, Diane. *Claiming Breath.* Lincoln: U of Nebraska P, 1992.

—. "Two Dresses." Swann and Krupat, *I Tell You Now* 167-83.

Goebel, Bruce A., and James C. Hall. Introduction. Goebel and Hall, *Teaching a "New Canon"?* xi-xv.

—. eds. *Teaching a "New Canon"? Students, Teachers, and Texts in the College Literature Classroom.* Urbana: NCTE, 1995.

Goellnicht, Donald C. "Tang Ao in America: Male Subject Positions in *China Men.*" *Reading the Literatures of Asian America.* Ed. Shirley Geok-lin Lim and Amy Ling. Philadelphia : Temple UP, 1992. 191-212.

Gonzáles, Rodolfo. *I Am Joaquín/ Yo Soy Joaquín.* 1967. Denver: El Gallo Newspaper, 1991.

Goodheart, Eugene. *Does Literary Studies Have a Future?* Madison: U of Wisconsin P, 1999.

Graff, Gerald. *Beyond the Culture Wars: How Teaching the Conflicts Can Revitalize American Education.* New York: Norton, 1992.

—. "Why Theory?" Davis and Mirabella, *Left Politics* 19-35.

Greenblatt, Stephen, and Giles Gunn. Introduction. Greenblatt and Gunn, *Redrawing the Boundaries* 1-11.

—, eds. *Redrawing the Boundaries: The Transformation of English and American Literary Studies.* New York: MLA, 1992.

Greene, Brenda M. "Remembering as Resistance in the Literature of Women of Color." Brannon and Greene, *Rethinking American* 97-114.

Gregory, Marshall. "Curriculum, Pedagogy, and Teacherly Ethos." *Pedagogy: Critical Approaches to Teaching Literature, Language, Composition, and Culture* 1.1 (2001): 69-89.

Hall, Cheryl. "Beyond the 'Literary Habit': Oral Tradition and Jazz in *Beloved.*" *MELUS* 19.1 (1994): 89-95.

Hall, James C. "Toward the 'Success' of a 'New Canon: Radical Introspection as Critical Practice.' " Goebel and Hall, *Teaching a "New Canon"?* 3-21.

Hamilton, Patricia L. "*Feng Shui*, Astrology, and the Five Elements: Traditional Chinese Belief in Amy Tan's *The Joy Luck Club.*" *MELUS* 24.2 (1999): 125-45.

Hammond, John. "Leah and Rachel, Or, The Two Faithful Sisters Virginia and Maryland." 1656. *Narratives of Early Maryland, 1633-1684*. Ed. C.C. Hall. New York: Charles Scribner's Sons, 1910. 281-308.

Harjo, Joy. "Ordinary Spirit." Swann and Krupat, *I Tell You Now* 263-70.

Hawthorne, Nathaniel. *The Scarlet Letter*. 1850. New York: Bantam, 1986.

Heller, Dana. "Reconstructing Kin: Family, History and Narrative in Toni Morrison's *Beloved*." *College Literature* 21.2 (1994): 105-117. Online. SearchBank. 18 April 1997.

Hemingway, Ernest. *In Our Time*. 1925. New York: Macmillan, 1988.

Hewitt, Nancy A. "Compounding Differences." *Feminist Studies* 18.2 (1992): 313-26.

Hogan, Linda. "The Two Lives." Swann and Krupat, *I Tell You Now* 231-49.

—. "The Women Speaking." *Daughters, I Love You*. Denver: Loretto Heights College, 1981. 15.

hooks, bell, et. al. "Symposium: The Crisis of African American Gender Relations." *Transition* 66 (1995): 91-175.

Hungry Wolf, Beverly. *The Ways of My Grandmothers*. New York: Quill, 1982.

Hurston, Zora Neale. *Their Eyes Were Watching God*. 1937. Urbana: U of Illinois P, 1991.

Hutner, Gordon, ed. *American Literature, American Culture*. New York: Oxford UP, 1999.

Jackson, Edward M. *Images of Black Men in Black Women Writers, 1950-1990*. Bristol, IN: Wyndham Hall, 1992.

Jacobs, Harriet Ann. *Incidents in the Life of a Slave Girl*. 1861. New York: Signet, 2000.

Jahner, Elaine. "Indian Literature and Critical Responsibility." *Studies in American Indian Literature* 1.1 (1977): 3-10. Rpt. in *Studies in American Indian Literature* 5.2 (1993): 7-12.

Jamieson, Sandra. "Text, Context, and Teaching Literature by African American Women." Trimmer and Warnock, *Understanding Others* 139-152.

JanMohamed, Abdul R., and David Lloyd. "Introduction: Toward a Theory of Minority Discourse: What Is To Be Done?" JanMohamed and Lloyd. *The Nature and Context* 1-16.

—. Preface. JanMohamed and Lloyd, *The Nature and Context* ix-xi.

—, eds. *The Nature and Context of Minority Discourse*. New York: Oxford UP, 1990.

Jay, Gregory S. *American Literature and the Culture Wars*. Ithaca: Cornell UP, 1997.

—. "The End of 'American' Literature: Toward a Multicultural Practice." *College English* 53.3 (1991): 42-48.

Jelínek, Estelle C. Introduction. Jelínek, *Women's Autobiography* 1-20.

—. *The Tradition of Women's Autobiography: From Antiquity to the Present*. Boston: Twayne, 1986.

—, ed. *Women's Autobiography: Essays in Criticism*. Bloomington: Indiana UP, 1980.

Johnston, Sue Ann. "Empowerment Through Mythological Imaginings in *Woman Warrior*." *Biography* 16.2 (1993): 136-46.

Jordan, Jennifer. "Feminist Fantasies: Zora Neale Hurston's *Their Eyes Were Watching God*." *Tulsa Studies in Women's Literature* 7.1 (1988): 105-17.

Joyce, James. *A Portrait of the Artist as a Young Man*. 1916. New York: Modern Library, 1996.

Kafka, Phillipa. "Another Round of Canon Fire: Feminist and Multi-Ethnic Theory in the American Literature Survey." *MELUS* 16.2 (1989-90): 31-49.

—. "A Multicultural Introduction to Literature." Cahalan and Downing, *Practicing Theory* 179-88.

Kanhai, Rosanne. " 'Sensing Designs in History's Muddles': Global Feminism and the Postcolonial Novel." *MLS* 26.4 (1996): 119-30.

Keating, Anna Louise. "(De)Centering the Margins? Identity Politics and Tactical (Re)Naming." Stanley, *Other Sisterhoods* 23-43.

Keesey, Donald. "Intertextual Criticism: Literature as Context." *Contexts for Criticism*. 2nd ed. Mountain View: Mayfield, 1994. 257-70.

Keizer, Arlene R. "*Beloved*: Ideologies in Conflict, Improvised Subjects." *African American Review* 33.1 (1999): 105-23. Online. ProQuest. 6 May 1999.

Kelley, Margot. "A Minor Revolution: Chicano/a Composite Novels and the Limits of Genre." *Ethnicity and the American Short Story*. Ed. Julie Brown. New York: Garland, 1997. 63-84.

Kim, Elaine. *Asian American Literature: An Introduction to the Writings and Their Social Context*. Philadelphia: Temple UP, 1982.

Kingston, Maxine Hong. *China Men*. 1977. New York: Vintage, 1989.

—. *The Woman Warrior: Memoirs of a Girlhood Among Ghosts*. 1975. New York: Knopf, 1976.

Kolb, Harold. "Defining the Canon." Ruoff, *Redefining American* 35-51.

Kolbenschlag, Madonna. "A Feminist's View of 'Cinderella.' " *Writing and Reading Across the Curriculum*. Ed. Laurence Behrens and Leonard J. Rosen. 6th ed. New York: Longman. 533-39.

Kolodny, Annette. "Dancing Through the Minefield: Some Observations on the Theory, Practice, and Politics of a Feminist Literary Criticism." *Feminist Studies*. 6 (1980): 1-25. Rpt. in *Falling Into Theory: Conflicting Views on Reading Literature*. Ed. David H. Richter. Boston: Bedford, 1994. 278-85.

—. "The Land-as-Woman: Literary Convention and Latent Psychological Content." *Women's Studies* 1 (1973): 167-82.

Krupat, Arnold. "The Dialogic of Silko's *Storyteller*." *Narrative Chance: Postmodern Discourse on Native American Indian Literatures*. Ed. Gerald Vizenor. Albuquerque: U of New Mexico P, 1989. 55-68.

—. Introduction. Krupat, *New Voices* xvii-xxv.

—. "Native American Autobiography and the Synecdochic Self." Eakin, *American Autobiography* 171-94.

—. *The Turn to the Native: Studies in Criticism and Culture*. Lincoln: U of Nebraska P, 1996.

—. *The Voice in the Margin: Native American Literature and the Canon*. Berkeley: U of California P, 1989.

—. ed. *New Voices in Native American Literary Criticism*. Washington: Smithsonian Institution Press, 1993.

Lanier, Douglas. "Less Is More: Coverage, Critical Diversity, and the Limits of Pluralism." Cahalan and Downing, *Practicing Theory* 199-212.

Lanser, Susan S. "The *T* Word: Theory as Trial and Transformation of the Undergraduate Classroom." Sadoff and Cain, *Teaching Contemporary Theory* 57-68.

Laughlin, James S. "Beyond *Beyond the Culture Wars*: Students Teaching Themselves the Conflicts." Brannon and Greene, *Rethinking American Literature* 231-45.

Lauter, Paul. "Canon Theory and Emergent Practice." Davis and Mirabella, *Left Politics* 128-46.

—. "On the Implications of the *Heath Anthology*: Response to Ruland." *American Literary History* 4.2 (1992): 329-33.

—. "Preface to the First Edition." Lauter, et al., *The Heath Anthology* 2nd ed. xxx-xl.

Lauter, Paul, et al., eds. *The Heath Anthology of American Literature.* 2 vols. Lexington: Heath, 1990.

—, eds. *The Heath Anthology of American Literature.* 2nd ed. 2 vols. Lexington: Heath, 1994.

Lee, Rachel. "Claiming Land, Claiming Voice, Claiming Canon: Institutionalized Challenges in Kingston's *China Men* and *The Woman Warrior*." *Reviewing Asian America: Locating Diversity*. Ed. Wendy L. Ng, Soo-Young Chin, James S. Moy, and Gary Y. Okihiro. Pullman: Washington State UP, 1995. 147-59.

Levine, George. "The Two Nations." *Pedagogy: Critical Approaches to Teaching Literature, Language, Composition, and Culture* 1.1 (2001): 7-19.

Li, David Leiwei. "*China Men*: Maxine Hong Kingston and the American Canon." *American Literary History* 2.3 (1990): 482-502.

—. "Filiative and Affiliative Textualization in Chinese American Literature." Trimmer and Warnock, *Understanding Others* 177-200.

Li, Ju-chen. *Flowers in the Mirror*. Trans. Lin Tai-yi. Singapore: Federal, 1983.

Lim, Shirley Geok-lin, ed. *Approaches to Teaching Kingston's* The Woman Warrior. New York: MLA, 1991.

—. "Twelve Asian American Writers: In Search of Self-Definition." Ruoff, *Redefining American* 237-50.

Ling, Amy. "I'm Here: An Asian American Woman's Response." Warhol and Herndl, *Feminisms* 776-83.

Linton, Patricia. " 'What Stories the Wind Would Tell': Representation and Appropriation in Maxine Hong Kingston's *China Men.*" *MELUS* 19.4 (1994): 37-48.

Lorde, Audre. *Sister Outsider*. Trumansburg, NY: Crossing, 1984.

Lummis, Charles F. *Pueblo Indian Folk Stories*. 1894. Lincoln: U of Nebraska P, 1992.

Lynn, Steven. "A Passage into Critical Theory." *Conversations: Contemporary Critical Theory and the Teaching of Literature*. Ed. Charles Moran and Elizabeth F. Penfield. Urbana: NCTE, 1990. 99-113.

Maitino, John, and David R. Peck. Introduction. Maitino and Peck, *Teaching American* 3-16.

—, eds. *Teaching American Ethnic Literatures*. Albuquerque: U of New Mexico P, 1996.

Marshall, Brenda K. *Teaching the Postmodern: Fiction and Theory*. New York: Routledge, 1992.

Marshall, James. "Getting Beyond 'Kum Ba Ya.' " Goebel and Hall, *Teaching a "New Canon"?* 237-41.

Marshall, Paule. "To Da-Duh, In Memoriam." 1967. Lauter, et al., *The Heath Anthology* Vol. 2. 1971-79.

Mason, Mary G. "The Other Voice: Autobiographies of Women Writers." *Autobiography: Essays Theoretical and Critical*. Ed. James Olney. Princeton: Princeton UP, 1980. 207-35.

Matchie, Thomas. "Literary Continuity in Sandra Cisneros's *The House on Mango Street*." *The Midwest Quarterly* 37.1 (1993): 67-80. Online. Searchbank. 18 April 1997.

Mayberry, Katherine J. "Introduction: Identity Politics in the College Classroom." Mayberry, *Teaching What You're Not* 1-19.

—, ed. *Teaching What You're Not: Identity Politics in Higher Education*. New York: New York UP, 1996.

McBride Limaye, Ann. "Metamorphoses of La Malinche and Mexican Cultural Identity." *Comparative Civilizations Review* 19 (Fall 1988): 1-28.

McDowell, Deborah E. "Race, Gender, and the Practice of Theory." *Studies in Historical Change*. Ed. Ralph Cohen. Charlottesville: UP of Virginia, 1992. Rpt. in Warhol and Herndl, *Feminisms* 234-47.

—. "Transferences: Black Feminist Discourse: The 'Practice' of 'Theory.' " *Feminism Beside Itself*. Ed. Diane Elam and Robyn Wiegman. New York: Routledge, 1995. 93-118.

McKenna, Teresa. " 'An Utterance More Pure Than Word': Gender and the Corrido Tradition in Two Contemporary Chicano Poems." *Feminist Measures: Soundings in Poetry and Theory*. Ed. Lynn Keller and Cristanne Miller. Ann Arbor: U of Michigan P, 1994.184-207.

Meagher, Sharon. "Resisting Robinson Crusoe in Dechanel's Film." *Robinson Crusoe: Myths and Metamorphoses*. Ed. Lieve Spaas and Brian Stimpson. Houndmills, England: Macmillan, 1996. 148-56.

Meese, Elizabeth A. "The Whole Truth: Frameworks for the Study of Women's Noncanonical Literature." *Teaching Women's Literature from a Regional Perspective.* New York: MLA, 1982. 15-22.

Melchior, Bonnie. "A Marginal 'I': The Autobiographical Self Deconstructed in Maxine Hong Kingston's *The Woman Warrior.*" *Biography* 17.3 (1994): 281-95.

Midalia, Susan. "The Contemporary Female *Bildungsroman*: Gender, Genre, and the Politics of Optimism." *Westerly: A Quarterly Review* 41.1 (1996): 89-104 .

Mihesuah, Devon A. "Commonalty of Difference: American Indian Women and History." *American Indian Quarterly* 20.1 (1996): 15-27.

Miller, Perry. *Nature's Nation.* Cambridge: Belknap P of Harvard UP, 1967.

Miller, Richard. "Fault Lines in the Contact Zone." *College English* 56.4 (1994): 389-408.

Mishkin, Tracy. "Theorizing Literary Influence and African American Writers." Mishkin, *Literary Influence* 3-20.

—, ed. *Literary Influence and African-American Writers: Collected Essays.* New York: Garland, 1996.

Momaday, N. Scott. *House Made of Dawn.* New York: Harper & Row, 1968.

Moore, David L. "Myth, History, and Identity in Silko and Young Bear: Postcolonial Praxis." Krupat, *New Voices* 370–95.

Moraga, Cherríe. "Refugees of a World on Fire: Foreword to the Second Edition." Moraga and Anzaldúa. *This Bridge Called My Back.* N pag.

Moraga, Cherríe, and Gloria Anzaldúa. "Between the Lines: On Culture, Class, and Homophobia." Moraga and Anzaldúa, *This Bridge Called My Back* 105-06.

—, eds. *This Bridge Called My Back: Writings by Radical Women of Color.* 2nd ed. New York: Kitchen Table: Women of Color Press, 1983.

Morgan, Janice. "Subject to Subject/Voice to Voice: Twentieth-Century Autobiographical Fiction by Women Writers." *Redefining Autobiography in Twentieth-Century Women's Fiction.* Ed. Janice Morgan and Colette T. Hall. New York: Garland, 1991. 3-19.

Morgan, Winifred. "Gender-Related Difference in the Slave Narratives of Harriet Jacobs and Frederick Douglass." *American Studies* 35.2 (1994): 73-94.

Morrison, Toni. *Beloved.* 1987. New York: Penguin, 1988.

—. *The Bluest Eye.* 1969. New York: Washington Square, 1972.

—. *Song of Solomon.* 1977. New York: Knopf, 1994.

Mullen, Harryette. " 'A Silence Between Us Like a Language': The Untranslatability of Experience in Sandra Cisneros's *Woman Hollering Creek.*" *MELUS* 21.2 (1996): 3-20.

Murphy, Bridget and Roberta Peirce Trooien. "Rumblings from the Back Row: Do We Have to Read Another Victim Story?" *Teaching English in the Two-Year College* 23 (1996): 296-303.

Murray, Heather. "Charisma and Authority in Literary Study and Theory Study." *Theory, Pedagogy, Politics: Texts for Change*. Ed. Donald Morton and Mas'ud Zevarzadeh. Urbana: U of Illinois P, 1991. 187-200.

Myers, Linda James. *Understanding an Afrocentric Worldview: Introduction to an Optimal Psychology*. Dubuque: Kendall/Hunt, 1988.

Naylor, Gloria. *Linden Hills*. 1985. New York: Penguin, 1986.

—. *The Women of Brewster Place*. 1980. New York: Penguin, 1988.

Nnaemeka, Obioma. "Bringing African Women into the Classroom: Rethinking Pedagogy and Epistemology." *Borderwork: Feminist Engagements with Comparative Literature*. Ed. Margaret R. Higonnet. Ithaca: Cornell UP, 1994. 301-18.

Olsen, Tillie. *Tell Me a Riddle*. 1956. New York: Delta Trade, 1989.

Olson, Gary. "Encountering the Other: Postcolonial Theory and Composition Scholarship." *JAC: A Journal of Composition Theory* 18.1 (1998): 45-56.

O'Neill, James M. "Liberal-Arts Educations Decline as Students Grease Career Paths." *Philadelphia Inquirer* 2 Feb. 2001: A01

Ortiz, Simon J. "The Language We Know." Swann and Krupat, *I Tell You Now* 185-94.

—. "My Father's Song." *Going for the Rain*. New York: Harper, 1976. 20.

—. "Part I: The Historical Matrix Towards a National Indian Literature: Cultural Authenticity in Nationalism." Fleck, *Critical Perspectives* 64-68.

—. "The Poems I Have Lost." *Going for the Rain*. New York: Harper, 1976. 43-45.

Orwin, Clifford. "All Quiet on the (Post) Western Front." *Public Interest* 123 (Spring 1996): 3-21. Online. Periodical Abstracts. 12 Feb. 1999.

Owens, Louis. " 'The Song Is Very Short': Native American Literature and Literary Theory." *Weber Studies* 12.3 (Fall 1995): 51-62.

Owusu, Kofi. "Rethinking Canonicity: Toni Morrison and the (Non)Canonic 'Other.' " *Rewriting the Dream. Reflections on the Changing American Literary Canon*. Ed. W. M. Verhoeven. Atlanta: Rodopi, 1992. 60-74.

Pace, Barbara. "The Textbook Canon: Genre, Gender, and Race in U.S. Literature Anthologies." *English Journal* 81.5 (1992): 33-38.

Palmer, Trudy Christine. "Changes in the Neighborhood: Integrating the Academy and Diversifying the Curriculum." *Women's Studies: An Interdisciplinary Journal* 20.3-4 (1992): 217-24.

Palumbo-Liu, David. Introduction. Palumbo-Liu, *The Ethnic Canon* 1-27.

—, ed. *The Ethnic Canon: Histories, Institutions, and Interventions*. Minneapolis: U of Minnesota P, 1995.

Paredes, Américo. *With His Pistol in His Hand: A Border Ballad and Its Hero*. Austin: U of Texas P, 1958.

Paredes, Raymund A. "Contemporary Mexican-American Literature, 1960-Present." *A Literary History of the American West*. Ed. Thomas J. Lyon. Fort Worth: Texas Christian UP, 1987. 1101-18.

Perreault, Jeanne. "New Dreaming: Joy Harjo, Wendy Rose, Leslie Marmon Silko." *Deferring a Dream: Literary Sub-Versions of the American Columbiad.* Comp. Buelens and Ernst Rudin. Boston: Birkhäuser Verlag, 1994. 120-36.

Peterson, Nancy J. "Redefining America: Literature, Multiculturalism, Pedagogy." Mayberry, *Teaching What You're Not* 23-46.

Pollock, Kimberly Joyce. "A Continuum of Pain: A Woman's Legacy in Alice Walker's *Possessing the Secret of Joy.*" *Women of Color: Mother-Daughter Relationships in Twentieth Century Literature.* Ed. Elizabeth Brown-Guillory. Austin: U of Texas P, 1996. 38-56.

Poniatowska, Elena. "Mexicanas and Chicanas." *MELUS* 21.3 (1996): 35-51.

Pound, Ezra. *Cantos.* 1917. New York: New Directions, 1971.

Pratt, Mary Louise. "Arts of the Contact Zone." *Profession 91.* New York: MLA, 1991. 33-40.

—. " 'Yo soy la Malinche': Chicana Writers and the Poetics of Ethnonationalism." *Twentieth Century Poetry: From Text to Context.* Ed. Peter Verdonk. London: Routledge, 1993. 171-87.

Primeau, Ronald. "Writing Portfolios in the Multicultural Literature Class." Goebel and Hall. *Teaching a "New Canon"?* 180-95.

Pryse, Marjorie. "Teaching American Literature as Cultural Encounter: Models for Organizing the Introductory Course." Brannon and Greene. *Rethinking American* 175-92.

Puhr, Kathleen. "Healers in Gloria Naylor's Fiction." *Twentieth Century Literature* 40 (Winter 1994): 518-27.

Purley, Anthony F. "Keres Pueblo Concepts of Deity." *American Indian Culture and Research Journal* 1.1 (1974): 29-32.

Rachels, James. *The Elements of Moral Philosophy.* 2nd ed. New York: McGraw-Hill,1993.

Ranveer, Kashinath. "African-American Feminist Consciousness in the Novels of Toni Morrison." *Indian Journal of American Studies* 23.2 (Summer 1993): 35-45.

Renza, Louis A. "Influence." *Critical Terms for Literary Study.* Ed. Frank Lentricchia and Thomas McLaughlin. Chicago: Chicago UP, 1990. 186-202.

Reuman, Ann E. "Coming Into Play: An Interview with Gloria Anzaldúa." *MELUS* 25.2 (2000): 3-45.

Rich, Adrienne. "When We Dead Awaken: Writing as Re-Vision." 1979. *The Norton Reader.* Ed. Linda H. Peterson, John C. Brereton, and Joan E. Hartman. 10th ed. New York: Norton, 2000. 1036-48.

Rico, Barbara Roche, and Sandra Mano. "New 'Themes for English B': Reimagining Contexts for Learning in Multiethnic Writing Classes." Alberti, *The Canon in the Classroom* 99-116.

Ridley, Chauncey A. "Sethe's 'Big Bad' Love." Trimmer and Warnock, *Understanding Others* 153-64.

Riley, Patricia. "The Mixed Blood Writer as Interpreter and Mythmaker." Trimmer and Warnock, *Understanding Others* 230-42.

Rivera, Tomás. *...y no se lo tragó la tierra.* 1971. Trans. Evangelina Vigil-Piñón. Houston: Arte Público, 1992.

Roberts, John W. *From Trickster to Badman: The Black Folk Hero in Slavery and Freedom.* Philadelphia: U of Pennsylvania P, 1989.

Robinson, Lillian. "Treason Our Texts." *Tulsa Studies in Women's Literature* 2 (1983): 83-98. Rpt. in Warhol and Herndl, *Feminisms* 115-28.

Rodier, Katharine. " 'Taking Stock of Multiethnic Literatures': Call for Papers." *NewsNotes, E-Publication for the Society for the Study of the Multi-Ethnic Literature of the United States.* (n.d.): n pag. Online. Internet. 4 Mar. 2001. Available http://www.marshall.edu/melus/newsnotes.

Ruland, Richard. "A Reply to Paul Lauter." *American Literary History* 4.2 (1992): 334-36.

—. "Art and a Better America." *American Literary History* 3.2 (1991): 337-59.

Ruoff, A. Lavonne Brown. "Three Nineteenth-Century American Indian Autobiographers." Ruoff, *Redefining American* 251-69.

—, ed. *Redefining American Literary History.* New York: MLA, 1990.

Ruzich, Constance M. "White Students' Resistance to Multicultural Literature: Breaking the Sullen Silence." *Teaching English in the Two-Year College* 26 (1999): 299-304.

Ryder, Phyllis Mentzell. "I'm OK, You're (Not) OK: Teaching in a World of Relativism." *JAC: Journal of Composition Theory* 15.3 (1995): 511-25.

Sadoff, Diane F., and William E. Cain, eds. *Teaching Contemporary Theory to Undergraduates.* New York: MLA, 1994.

Salinger, J.D. *The Catcher in the Rye.* 1945. Boston: Little, Brown, 1991.

Sands, Kathleen Mullen. "Indian Women's Personal Narrative: Voices Past and Present." Culley, *American Women's Autobiography* 268-94.

Sandoval, Chela. "U.S. Third World Feminism: The Theory and Method of Oppositional Consciousness in the Postmodern World." *GENDERS* 10 (Spring 1991): 1-24.

Savage, William J., Jr. "Authors, Authority, and the Graduate Student Teacher: Against Canonical Pedagogy." Alberti, *The Canon in the Classroom* 283-301.

Scarberry, Susan J. "Grandmother Spider's Lifeline." Allen, *Studies in American Indian Literature* 100-07.

Schweickart, Patrocino P. "Add Gender and Stir." *Reader* 13 (1985): 1-9.

Selden, Raman. *Practicing Theory and Reading Literature: An Introduction.* Lexington: UP of Kentucky, 1989.

Selections from The Book of Songs. Trans. Yang Xianyi, Gladys Yang, and Hu Shiguang. Beijing: China Publications, 1983.

Shih, Shu-mei. "Exile and Intertextuality in Maxine Hong Kingston's *China Men*." *The Literature of Emigration and Exile*. Ed. James Whitlark and Wendell Aycock. Lubbock: Texas Tech UP, 1992. 65-77.

Showalter, Elaine. "The Female Tradition." *The Critical Tradition: Classic Texts and Contemporary Trends*. Ed. David H. Richter. New York: St. Martin's P, 1989. 1103-18.

Silko, Leslie Marmon. *Ceremony*. New York: Viking, 1977.

—. *Storyteller*. New York: Arcade, 1981.

—. "Yellow Woman and a Beauty of the Spirit." 1996. *Essays in Context*. Ed. Sandra Fehl Tropp and Ann Pierson D'Angelo. New York: Oxford, 2001. 725-30.

Smith, Barbara Hernnstein. "Contingencies of Value." *Critical Inquiry* 10.1 (1983): 1-35.

Smith, Sidonie, and Julia Watson. "Introduction: Situating Subjectivity in Women's Autobiographical Practices." *Women, Autobiography, Theory: A Reader*. Ed. Sidonie Smith and Julia Watson. Madison: U of Wisconsin P, 1998. 3-52.

Souris, Stephen. "Multiperspectival Consensus: Alice Walker's *Possessing the Secret of Joy*, the Multiple Narrator Novel, and the Practice of 'Female Circumcision.'" *CLA Journal* XL.4 (1997): 405-31.

Soto, Gary. "Black Hair." *Black Hair*. Pittsburgh: U of Pittsburgh P, 1985. 3.

—. "Mexicans Begin Jogging." *Where Sparrows Work Hard*. Pittsburgh: U of Pittsburgh P, 1981. 24.

Sowell, Thomas. "Multicultural Education is Harmful." *Culture Wars*. Ed. Fred Whitehead. San Diego: Greenhaven, 1994. 104-08.

Spigelman, Candace. "Taboo Topics and the Rhetoric of Silence: Discussing *Lives on the Boundary* in Basic Writing." *Journal of Basic Writing* 17.1 (1998): 42-55.

Stanley, Sandra Kumamoto. Introduction. Stanley, *Other Sisterhoods* 1-19.

—, ed. *Other Sisterhoods: Literary Theory and U.S. Women of Color*. Urbana: U of Illinois P, 1998.

Stein, Gertrude. *The Autobiography of Alice B. Toklas*. 1933. New York: Vintage, 1990.

Stein, Rachel. *Shifting the Ground: American Women Writers' Revisions of Nature, Gender, and Race*. Charlottesville: UP of Virginia, 1997.

St. Clair, Janet. "Fighting for Her Life: The Mixed-Blood Woman's Insistence upon Selfhood." Fleck, *Critical Perspectives* 46-53.

Stewart, Edward and Milton Bennett. *American Cultural Patterns*. Rev. ed. Yarmouth, ME: Intercultural, 1991.

Stimpson, Catharine R. "Multiculturalism and Its Discontents." *Sacred Heart University Review* 14.1-2 (1993-94): 1-17.

St. John de Crèvecoeur, J. Hector. *Letters from an American Farmer*. 1782. Ed. Susan Manning. Oxford: Oxford UP, 1997.

Stotsky, Sandra. "Academic Guidelines for Selecting Multiethnic and Multicultural Literature." *English Journal* (1994): 27-34.

Stowe, Harriet Beecher. *Uncle Tom's Cabin.* 1852. New York: Penguin, 1966.

Swann, Brian, and Arnold Krupat. Introduction. *I Tell You Now* ix-xv.

—, eds. *I Tell You Now: Autobiographical Essays by Native American Writers.* Lincoln: U of Nebraska P, 1987.

Swilky, Jody. "Resisting Difference: Student Response to Multicultural Texts." *Writing Instructor* 13.1 (1993): 21-33.

Tafolla, Carmen. "La Malinche." *To Split a Human: Mitos, Machos y La Mujer Chicana.* San Antonio: Mexican American Cultural Center, 1985. 17-18.

Tan, Amy. *The Joy Luck Club.* New York: Ivy, 1989.

—. *The Kitchen God's Wife.* New York: Putnam, 1991.

Taylor, Ula Y. "Making Waves: The Theory and Practice of Black Feminism." *The Black Scholar* 28.2 (1998): 18-28. Online. ProQuest. 3 Aug. 2000.

Thoreau, Henry David. *Walden.* 1854. Oxford: Oxford UP, 1999.

Todd, Jude. "Knotted Bellies and Fragile Webs: Untangling and Re-Spinning in Tayo's Healing Journey." *The American Indian Quarterly* 19.2 (1995): 155-71.

Tompkins, Jane. " 'But Is It Any Good?': The Institutionalization of Literary Value." *Sensational Designs: The Cultural Work of American Fiction, 1790-1860.* Oxford: Oxford UP, 1985. 186-201.

Treichler, Paula A. "Teaching Feminist Theory." *Theory in the Classroom.* Ed. Cary Nelson. Urbana: U of Illinois P, 1986. 57-128.

Trimmer, Joseph F. "Teaching Others: A Cautionary Tale." Brannon and Greene, *Rethinking American* 249-56.

Trimmer, Joseph F., and Tilly Warnock, eds. *Understanding Others: Cultural and Cross Cultural Studies and the Teaching of Literature.* Urbana: NCTE, 1992.

Turner, James E. "Foreword: Africana Studies and Epistemology: A Discourse in the Sociology of Knowledge." *The Next Decade: Theoretical and Research Issues in Africana Studies.* Ed. James E. Turner. Ithaca: Cornell UP, 1984. v-xxv.

TuSmith, Bonnie. *All My Relatives: Community in Contemporary Ethnic American Literatures.* Ann Arbor: U of Michigan P, 1993.

—. "The Cultural Translator: Toward an Ethnic Womanist Pedagogy." *MELUS* 16.2 (1989-90): 17-29.

—. "Message from the President." *NewsNotes: E-Publication for the Society for the Study of the Multi-Ethnic Literature of the United States.* (Spring/Summer 2001): n pag. Online. Internet. 22 May 2001. Available http://www.marshall.edu/melus.

—. "Opening Up Theory." *Modern Language Studies* 26.4 (1996): 59-70.

TuSmith, Bonnie, and Gerald W. Bergevin. "Introduction: Theory and Multicultural Literature." *Modern Language Studies* 26.4 (1996): 1-3.

TuSmith, Bonnie, and Gerald W. Bergevin, eds. *Modern Language Studies* 26.4 (1996).

Twain, Mark. *The Adventures of Huckleberry Finn*. 1885. New York: Oxford UP, 1996.

Tyson, Lois. "Teaching Deconstruction: Theory and Practice in the Undergraduate Literature Classroom." Cahalan and Downing, *Practicing Theory* 227-38.

Van Leer, David. "Identity and Ownership: Gays as Other." *Women's Studies: An Interdisciplinary Journal* 20.3-4 (1992): 225-29.

VanSpanckeren, Kathryn. "The Asian Literary Background of *The Woman Warrior*." Lim, *Approaches to Teaching* 44-51.

Wagner, Joseph. "The Trouble With Multiculturalism." *Soundings* 77.3-4 (1994): 409-27.

Walker, Alice. *The Color Purple*. 1982. New York: Harcourt Brace, 1992.

—. "In Search of Our Mothers' Gardens." *In Search of Our Mothers' Gardens*. 1967. San Diego: Harcourt Brace Jovanovich, 1983. 231-43.

—. *In Search of Our Mothers' Gardens*. 1967. San Diego: Harcourt Brace Jovanovich, 1983.

—. *Possessing the Secret of Joy*. New York: Washington Square, 1992.

Walker, Nancy. "No Laughing Matter: The WASPS Climb Down." Culley, *American Women's Autobiography* 232-51.

Wang, Alex J. "Teaching *China Men* as a Chinese." Goebel and Hall, *Teaching a "New Canon"?* 199-210.

Wang, Qun. " 'Double Consciousness,' Sociological Imagination, and the Asian American Experience." *Race, Gender & Class* 4.3 (1997): 88-94.

Ward, Kathryn B. "'Lifting as We Climb': How Scholarship by and about Women of Color Has Shaped My Life as a White Feminist." Young and Dickerson, *Color, Class, & Country* 199-217.

Warhol, Robyn R., and Diane Price Herndl, eds. *Feminisms: An Anthology of Literary Theory and Criticism*. New Brunswick: Rutgers UP, 1997.

Waxman, Barbara Frey. "Feminist Theory, Literary Canons, and the Construction of Textual Meanings." Cahalan and Downing, *Practicing Theory* 149-60.

Welch, James. "Snow Country Weavers." *Riding the Earthboy 40*. 1971. New York: Harper & Row, 1976. 47

White, Deborah Gray. *Ar'n't I a Woman? Female Slaves in the Plantation South*. New York: Norton, 1985.

Whitman, Walt. "Whoever You are Holding Me Now in Hand." *Leaves of Grass: A Textual Variorum of the Printed Poems*. Eds. Sculley Bradley, Harold W. Blodgett, Arthur Golden, and William White. 3 vols. New York: New York UP, 1980.

Wilentz, Gay. "If You Surrender to the Air: Folk Legends of Flight and Resistance in African American Literature." *MELUS* 16.1 (1989-90): 21-32.

Williams, Jeffrey. "Brave New University." *College English* 61.6 (1999): 742-51.

Williams, Sherley Anne. "Some Implications of Womanist Theory." *Reading Black, Reading Feminist: A Critical Anthology*. Ed. Henry Louis Gates, Jr. New York: Meridian, 1990. Rpt. in *Within the Circle: An Anthology of African American Literary Criticism*." Ed. Angelyn Mitchell. Durham: Duke UP, 1994. 515-21.

Wilson, August. *Fences*. New York: Signet, 1986.

Witherspoon, Gary. *Language and Art in the Navajo Universe*. Ann Arbor: U of Michigan P, 1977.

Wong, Hertha D. "Pre-literate Native American Autobiography: Forms of Personal Narrative." *MELUS* 14.1 (1987): 17-32.

Wong, Jade Snow. *Fifth Chinese Daughter*. New York: Harper, 1950.

Wong, Sau-ling Cynthia. "Chinese American Literature." Cheung, *An Interethnic Companion* 39-61.

Woodring, Carl. *Literature: An Embattled Profession*. New York: Columbia UP, 1999.

Woolf, Virginia. *A Room of One's Own*. 1921. New York: Harcourt Brace Jovanovich, 1991.

Wright, Richard. "Long Black Song." *Uncle Tom's Children*. New York: Harper & Row, 1936. 103-28.

Yamamoto, Hisaye. "Seventeen Syllables." 1985. *Seventeen Syllables and Other Stories*. Latham, NY: Kitchen Table: Women of Color Press, 1988. 8-19.

Yarbro-Bejarano, Yvonne. "Chicana Literature from a Chicana Feminist Perspective." *Chicana Creativity and Criticism: Charting New Frontiers in American Literature*. Ed. María Herrera-Sobek and Helena María Viramontes. Houston: Arte Público, 1988. 139-45.

Yen, Ts'ai. *The Eighteen Laments*. Trans. Rewi Alley. Peking: New World Press, 1963.

Young, Gay, and Bette J. Dickerson, eds. *Color, Class, and Country: Experiences of Gender*. London: Zed, 1994.

Young, Reggie. "On Stepping into Footprints Which Feel Like Your Own: Literacy, Empowerment, and the African-American Literary Tradition." Mishkin, *Literary Influence* 359-85.

Zimmerman, Carla. "From Chop-Chop to Wu Cheng: The Evolution of the Chinese Character in *Blackhawk* Comic Books." *Ethnic Images in the Comics: An Exhibition in the Museum of the Balch Institute for Ethnic Studies September 15 - December 20, 1986*. Online. Internet. 1 March 2000. Available http://www.libertynet.org/balch/comics/comics.html.

Zinn, Maxine Baca, and Bonnie Thornton Dill. "Introduction: Difference and Domination." *Women of Color in U.S. Society*. Ed. Maxine Baca Zinn, and Bonnie Thornton Dill. Philadelphia: Temple UP, 1994. 3-12.

—. "Theorizing Difference from Multiracial Feminism." *Feminist Studies* 22.2 (1996): 321-31.

Index

G

H

I

J

K

L

N

O

P

W

Y

Z

Laurie Grobman is an assistant professor of English and co-coordinator of the Professional Writing degree program at Penn State University, Berks-Lehigh Valley College, where she teaches multicultural literature, women's literature, basic writing, first year composition, and rhetorical theory. Her articles on such topics as multiculturalism in writing and literary studies, basic writing, and critical pedagogy have appeared in literary journals, including *College Literature* and *MELUS,* and composition journals, including *Journal of Basic Writing* and *Journal of Business and Technical Communication.*

Aunt Lute Books is a multicultural women's press that has been committed to publishing high quality, culturally diverse literature since 1982. In 1990, the Aunt Lute Foundation was formed as a nonprofit corporation to publish and distribute books that reflect the complex truths of women's lives and the possibilities for personal and social change. We seek work that explores the specificities of the very different histories from which we come, and that examines the intersections between the borders we all inhabit.

Please write, phone or email (books@auntlute.com) us if you would like us to send you a free catalog of our books or if you wish to be on our mailing list for news of future titles. You may buy books directly from us by phone or by mailing a check with the catalog order form.

Please visit our website at www.auntlute.com.

Aunt Lute Books
P.O. Box 410687
San Francisco, CA 94141
415.826.1300

This publication of this book would not have been possible without the kind contributions of the Aunt Lute Founding Friends:

Anonymous Donor
Anonymous Donor
Rusty Barcelo
Marian Bremer
Marta Drury
Diane Goldstein
Diana Harris
Phoebe Robins Hunter
Diane Mosbacher, M.D., Ph.D.
William Preston, Jr.
Elise Rymer Turner